Britain's Long War

Also by Peter R. Neumann

IRA: LANGER WEG ZUM FRIEDEN

AL GORE: EINE BIOGRAPHIE

Britain's Long War

British Strategy in the Northern Ireland Conflict, 1969–98

Peter R. Neumann
Research Fellow in International Terrorism
King's College London

First published 2003 by
PALGRAVE MACMILLAN
Houndmills, Basingstoke, Hampshire RG21 6XS and
175 Fifth Avenue, New York, N.Y. 10010
Companies and representatives throughout the world

PALGRAVE MACMILLAN is the global academic imprint of the Palgrave Macmillan division of St. Martin's Press, LLC and of Palgrave Macmillan Ltd. Macmillan® is a registered trademark in the United States, United Kingdom and other countries. Palgrave is a registered trademark in the European Union and other countries.

ISBN 1–4039–1779–5

This book is printed on paper suitable for recycling and made from fully managed and sustained forest sources.

A catalogue record for this book is available from the British Library.

Library of Congress Cataloging-in-Publication Data
Neumann, Peter, 1974–
    Britain's long war: British strategy in the
Northern Ireland conflict, 1969–98/Peter R. Neumann.
        p. cm.
    Includes bibliographical references (P.) and index.
    ISBN 1–4039–1779–5
        1. Northern Ireland – History – 1969–1994. 2. British – Northern
Ireland – History – 20th century. 3. Northern Ireland – History, Military.
4. Northern Ireland – History – 1994– I.

DA990.U46N415 2003
941.60824—dc21   2003053644

10 9 8 7 6 5 4 3 2 1
12 11 10 09 08 07 06 05 04 03

Printed and bound in Great Britain by
Antony Rowe Ltd, Chippenham and Eastbourne

Contents

List of Figures and Tables

Figures

Tables

Foreword

In a frequently misquoted passage, the American philosopher George Santayana argued that: 'Those who cannot remember the past are condemned to repeat it.' It is often assumed that Northern Ireland's problem is exactly the opposite. Those who live there are condemned to repeat the past precisely because that past is remembered all too well. Yet, what is the past that is remembered? Do people remember it well? Or do they, rather like Bob Hope in that haunting duet, remember it well enough to get it wrong? The common sense understanding of the past, as Sir Lewis Namier once observed, assumes that the past is the realm of fact. Furthermore, it assumes that the future is the realm of imagination. From such initial assumptions a remarkable inversion takes place. Since the future is yet to be, there is a tendency to make of it what we know about the present. Since the past has already been, there is a tendency to make of it an imaginary explanation for the present. The past, in other words, has a tendency to become not only a platform on which to express moral and political opinions. It also has a tendency to become a useful narrative that justifies immediate objectives or that vindicates ideological presuppositions. The common sense view seeks to make the past coherent and harmonious but only in the sense of making it conform to a particular perspective on the world. The challenge for the historian, then, is to evoke the past coherently but only in the sense of seeking conformity with the evidence. The challenge for the *contemporary* historian is an even greater one because of the passionate intensity of recent events in Northern Ireland and because of the passionately held popular beliefs about those events. These are the things that myths are made of. Thus, the British Government 'binned' the Mitchell Report of January 1996, thereby provoking the IRA's bombing of Canary Wharf in February of that year. The Major Government's policy on Northern Ireland was determined by its reliance on Unionist votes in the House of Commons. The Belfast Agreement of 1998 represented a logical completion of the policy that informed the Anglo-Irish Agreement of 1985. None of these 'truths' happen to be true even though they are widely held to be self-evident. For the contemporary historian, real knowledge is only advanced through the proper scrutiny of sources. Writing which conveys such knowledge, Benedetto Croce argued, must rise above the level of 'historical novel' (by which he meant the imaginative past of common sense) and be solely explained in thought (by which he meant a perspective which is compelling because it is a consequence of what the evidence obliges us to believe).

Peter Neumann's new study does provide such a compelling perspective and does significantly advance our knowledge of that curiously neglected subject of political research, British Government policy in Northern Ireland. Curiously neglected, because we probably know more about the theological differences between minor republicans than we do about the policy dispositions of major British officials. Also curiously neglected, because much of what has been written on British policy has often failed to rise above the level of historical novel. Neumann's strategic analysis is valuable because it helps us to make sense of the way policy-makers tried to develop a coherent approach to the Northern Ireland question. More importantly, perhaps, it helps us to identify the conditions for incoherence in policy-making. His use of systematic interviews provides new insight into the calculations of politicians, key civil servants and military personnel. The insight here is deeper than the merely anecdotal. It is integral to an impressively sustained analysis of both the possibilities and the limits of the instruments of modern governance. That the effect of the deployment of these instruments was often unintended confirms the impression that the fog of government can be as dislocating as the fog of war.

Neumann claims that 'Westminster's position has been far more consistent than that of any other actor in the conflict'. What has been consistent is the objective of 'reducing its political, physical and financial commitment to the province'. As the old joke puts it, political handbooks can tell you how to acquire power. What they don't tell you is how difficult it is to get rid of power once you've got it. Those ministers and officials whom Neumann interviewed would probably acknowledge the truth contained in that joke. The quest for a stable constitutional settlement has proved to be an arduous one. 'Britain's long war', he concludes, 'is not quite over yet'. On the other hand, it has been Westminster's commitment to Northern Ireland and above all the professionalism of the security forces that has made a stable constitutional settlement a possibility. This book shows us why.

ARTHUR AUGHEY
Belfast

Acknowledgements

This study could not have been written without the wisdom, guidance and support of Dr Mike Smith, who was my supervisor at the Department of War Studies, King's College, London. In almost three years, I have come to respect and admire him both as a teacher and as a scholar, and without his academic expertise, particularly in the field of strategic studies, this work would never have got off the ground. His generosity in granting many hours of his time to debate my ideas was essential in shaping my argument, but it has also been a thoroughly enjoyable experience that has – time and again – motivated me to carry on. During the course of my studies there were many people who went out of their way to contribute to this study. I would like to thank all the interviewees – many of them sitting MPs and ministers – who gave of their valuable time to meet me. I am particularly grateful to Lord Lyell, who helped to facilitate many interviews that would otherwise not have taken place. I have also benefited from discussions with Malachi O'Doherty, Dr Andy Whyte, Dr Sydney Elliott and Dr Mike Page. I would like to express my warm appreciation for the assistance I received from the King's College Library; the British Library of Political and Economic Science; the University of London Library at Senate House; the Public Record Office at Kew; and the Political Collection of the Linen Hall Library in Belfast. Also, I would like to acknowledge the role of the Economic and Social Research Council for its generosity in awarding me a scholarship. Finally, I wish to thank my parents for their appreciation, encouragement and support over many years.

Abbreviations

AIA	Anglo-Irish Agreement
APG	Active, Permanent and Guaranteed
CLF	Commander Land Forces (Northern Ireland)
DED	Northern Ireland Department of Economic Development
DSD	Downing Street Declaration (1969)
DUP	Democratic Unionist Party
ECHR	European Court of Human Rights
EEC	European Economic Communities
EPA	Emergency Provisions (Northern Ireland) Act
EU	European Union
FEA	Fair Employment Agency
FEC	Fair Employment Commission
FO	Foreign and Commonwealth Office
GOC	General Officer Commanding (Northern Ireland)
HMG	Her Majesty's Government
IGC	Inter-Governmental Conference
INLA	Irish National Liberation Army
IRA	Irish Republican Army
ITN	Independent Television News
JDP	Joint Declaration for Peace (1993)
LEDU	Local Economic Development Unit
MoD	Ministry of Defence
MP	Member of Parliament
NATO	North Atlantic Treaty Organization
NIDA	Northern Ireland Development Agency
NIFC	Northern Ireland Finance Corporation
NIO	Northern Ireland Office
PRO	Public Record Office
PTA	Prevention of Terrorism Act
RIC	Royal Irish Constabulary
RIR	Royal Irish Regiment
RTE	Radio Telefis Eireann
RUC	Royal Ulster Constabulary
SACHR	Standing Advisory Commission on Human Rights
SAS	Special Air Service

SDLP	Social Democratic and Labour Party
SF	Sinn Fein
SPA	Special Powers Act (Northern Ireland) (1922)
UDA	Ulster Defence Association
UDR	Ulster Defence Regiment
UK	United Kingdom
USC	Ulster Special Constabulary
UUP	Ulster Unionist Party
UUUC	United Ulster Unionist Council
UVF	Ulster Volunteer Force

Abbreviations in figures, tables and footnotes

c.	circa – approximate date of publication
CAB	Cabinet Office
DEFE	Ministry of Defence
FT	Full Time
GB Reg.	Army regiments based in Great Britain
HC	House of Commons Hansard
HL	House of Lords Hansard

1
Introduction

> The mode and thought of men, the whole outlook on affairs, the groupings of parties, all have encountered violent and tremendous changes in the deluge of the world, but as the deluge subsides and the waters fall we see the dreary steeples of Fermanagh and Tyrone emerging once again. The integrity of their quarrel is one of the few institutions that have been left unaltered in the cataclysm which has swept the world.[1]

Winston Churchill's famous quote about the state of the world at the end of the Great War gives a flavour of the feelings of resignation and impatience that have been encountered by British politicians whenever they had to deal with what has traditionally been known as the 'Irish question'. And indeed, once again it might be too early to declare the conflict over. Arguably, what one has witnessed over the course of the current peace process may not be the ending of the conflict but the suppression of it into the politics of threat and coercion.[2] However, since the signing of the so-called Belfast Agreement in April 1998, the province has been closer to peace than ever before in the 30 years of violent conflict. There is no doubt, therefore, that the Belfast Agreement represents a turning point in the history of the Northern Ireland conflict, and one might contend that this provides a good opportunity to mount a systematic examination of the period in its entirety. In this respect, the role of the British government in the Northern Ireland conflict has been pivotal: first, because the conflict has taken place within the jurisdiction of the United Kingdom, and second, because it was the sovereignty of the British state that has been challenged by Irish Republicans who have tried to break away the six counties of Northern

Ireland from the United Kingdom. The question is therefore almost self-evident: how did the British government handle the problem?

The purpose of this study is not simply to provide a narrative of British policies, but to identify, trace the evolution and evaluate the success of British government strategies *vis-à-vis* the Northern Ireland conflict. As an essential part of this endeavour, the author will attempt to induce several hypotheses about the nature of the value system that has influenced the formulation of British government strategy. Chapter 2 is an attempt to outline the 'strategic tradition' of the British government in Northern Ireland, to derive its different elements, and to demonstrate what policy themes it has translated into. In Chapters 3–7, this framework will be applied to successive periods of British involvement, which are assumed to represent distinct segments in the evolution of British strategy. The internal make-up of the respective chapters will follow a topical rather than a chronological order, so that it becomes possible to pursue the respective strategic ideas as thematic units. The overall chronological order enables the reader to trace the evolution of British strategic thought in order to make lines of continuity (or discontinuity) visible. As a result, it will not only be possible to show how the strategy of the British government has evolved in the 1969–98 period, but also to assess the content of this change in a systematic and critical fashion (Chapter 8). In this chapter, the foundations of strategic theory are laid down, and a brief historical breakdown highlights major events in the British government of (Northern) Ireland prior to the first significant intervention of the British government in the current conflict.

However, before embarking on this project, it seems useful to clarify the meaning of some expressions, terms and names that will be used throughout this study. Northern Ireland is what sociologists call a 'deeply divided society'. It is less obvious, however, what name to use when one refers to the respective constituents of that society. The denominational division 'Protestant' versus 'Catholic' is just one of many possible fault lines, and although it might be very popular, it is not the most precise way to divide the population into two groups. Some authors have therefore referred to 'Unionists' and 'Nationalists', others have described them as 'settlers' and 'natives', or as 'Ulster British' and 'Ulster Irish'. Even though none of the solutions seems perfect, the author decided to use the terms Catholic and Protestant as well as Unionist and Nationalist interchangeably. Unionists are more likely to be Protestant, and they want Northern Ireland to remain part of the United Kingdom. Nationalists are mostly Catholic and in favour of a united Ireland. Moreover, since there are fewer Catholics in Northern

Ireland than Protestants, the respective groups will also be described as 'minority' and 'majority'. The terms Loyalism and (Irish) Republicanism are the more radical (and often militant) expressions of Unionism and Nationalism.

'Great Britain' is used to denote what is sometimes called 'the British mainland', that is, England, Scotland and Wales. The United Kingdom, on the other hand, consists of Great Britain and Northern Ireland. 'Ireland' means the geographical unit of the island of Ireland. The now independent part of Ireland is referred to as 'Republic of Ireland'; the six counties that have stayed with the United Kingdom after the Anglo-Irish Treaty of 1921 are 'Northern Ireland'. Other names (such as 'Ulster', 'the North', the 'North of Ireland', or the 'Six Counties') may nevertheless appear in quotes. 'Derry-City' is the name of the city, whereas 'Londonderry' will be used for the county. The government of the United Kingdom of Great Britain and Northern Ireland will be referred to as the 'British government', 'Westminster', or simply 'London'. Likewise, 'Dublin' and 'Irish government' are names used for the government of the Republic of Ireland. 'Stormont' is shorthand for the Northern Ireland Home Rule government as it existed between 1920 and 1972. Further, the official title of the 'agreement reached in multi-party negotiations' in April 1998 is the 'Belfast Agreement', even though the more colloquial term 'Good Friday Agreement' is equally popular.

Finally, it needs to be pointed out that – in this study – the use of the term terrorism is not meant to pass on any moral judgement about its perpetrators. Instead, the word is used to describe a violent tactic that intends to inspire fear and anxiety amongst a target group, thus serving as a 'message generator'.[3] If performed by a non-government actor, terrorism can be part of an 'insurgency', defined as 'an internal struggle in which a disaffected group seeks to gain control of a nation'.[4] Conversely, 'counterinsurgency' describes the constitutional, military, political or economic measures that represent the state's response to this challenge.

Strategic theory

The term 'strategy' has come to be widely used in popular discourse, and it often seems to have lost any real meaning. Particularly in business, it has become fashionable to employ 'the s-word' in every conceivable context. In the military, on the other hand, the term 'strategy' is traditionally employed in a strictly defined sense. Carl von Clausewitz, the famous Prussian general, described strategy as 'the use of engagements for the object of war',[5] and many generations of so-called military strategists have accordingly interpreted strategy as the art of applying military power in war. Yet, while thinking of strategy in terms of 'somehow long-term' (as business does) is too general to give the term any real meaning, defining strategy narrowly in relation to military power and war appears to be equally inadequate. Hence, what is strategy?

At its most basic level, strategy concerns itself with the 'use of available resources to gain an objective',[6] that is, strategy is about how to employ means to achieve an end. However, in contrast to some military strategists, who cannot conceive of any instrument different from military power, it is important to emphasise that the chosen means can be of any nature. This is what military strategists sometimes call 'grand strategy', namely, 'to coordinate and direct all the resources [available] towards the attainment of the ... goal defined by fundamental policy'.[7] Second, strategy needs to be seen as a scenario of at least two players. It is interactive, and there are always at least two participants involved in a strategic situation. Each player tries to maximise his utility by understanding (as well as anticipating) the behaviour of his opponent. Accordingly, T.C. Schelling defines strategic analysis as 'the art of looking at the problem from the other person's point of view, identifying his opportunities and his interests'.[8]

The idea of 'strategic analysis' is relatively new, and often misunderstood. M.L.R. Smith once remarked that the subject 'appears to fall between two stools. Too formalised to be an art. Too loose to be scientific'.[9] Indeed, whilst the strategic approach is flexible enough to allow for the uniqueness of a specific phenomenon, the adherence to a framework of assumptions enables the analyst to give the phenomenon in question a wider meaning. In this respect, strategic analysis represents a compromise between the looseness of the historical approach, which (in its purest form) postulates that social phenomena are always unique and incomparable, and the rigidity of frameworks like terrorism studies and counterinsurgency theory, which 'often draw together ... varied low level wars by trying to make theoretical generalisations primarily on the basis of tactical modality ... thus disconnect[ing them] from their historical and cultural backgrounds'.[10] In short, strategic theory enables contexts to develop whilst preserving an overarching rationale that organises the content in a systematic fashion.

As strategy is best understood as a set of assumptions rather than a fully fledged theory, the best way of approaching strategic theory is by making its implicit postulates as clear as possible. In the following, strategy will be looked at from three different angles: its relation to Realism, the assumption of instrumentality and the postulate of rationality in strategic analysis.

Strategy and Realism

Most commonly, strategic analysis is located within the realist tradition of International Relations. While there is no 'natural' connection between strategy and a specific branch of International Relations theory, it is nevertheless helpful to outline some well-developed concepts of Realism that are shared with strategic analysis. Of these, two themes seem particularly applicable: the power political approach and the assumption of moral neutrality.

As S.M. Lynn-Jones points out, Realism is 'not a single, unified theory'. Proponents of Realism disagree on many questions of international relations – some general propositions, however, are shared by almost all of them, including 'the belief that people generally pursue their own interests and that power determines who gets what in politics',[11] that is, the power political approach. Realists assume that social actors are selfish, and that the currency in which interests are traded is power, and that the application of superior power results in a successful outcome. Therefore, power can – most generally – be defined as an actor's capability to influence outcomes. Even though most realists would probably agree that physical (that is, military) power is the 'ultimate' form of power, objectives can be realised in many different ways. E.H. Carr's definition of power, for instance, includes both economic and ideological dimensions.[12] K. Waltz (and many other so-called Neo-Realists) measures state power in terms of so-called capabilities, such as military and economic capacities, size of population, political stability, or technological progress.[13] Like strategy, power is not necessarily confined to any specific form or action. Rather, it can be said that power is *any means an actor employs in order to influence an outcome.*

Although realists are well aware that the threat or the actual use of military power often results in physical violence, the loss of life, pain and deprivation, they accept military hostilities as one way of resolving disputes amongst selfish actors. This (seemingly indifferent) attitude leads to another assumption that Realism and strategic analysis share: moral neutrality. Realists are not concerned with passing judgements about the justice of a cause. The behaviour of an actor is examined in terms of the choices available, the calculation of interest and the efficiency of his actions, not primarily in relation to its moral content. This does not mean that Realists deny the existence of ethical or moral questions connected to the issues of war and peace, of conflict and conflict resolution. There undoubtedly are such issues, but neither realists nor strategists consider them to be their business. Hence, accusations of amorality – even cold-bloodedness – miss the point. As J. Garnett put it:

> [R]esearch into a subject in no way implies approval of it. It is a curious fact that when doctors study malignant carcinomas, no one assumes that they are in favour of cancer, but when political scientists examine war it is assumed all too frequently that they approve of it.[14]

If anything, Realism can be charged with conservatism. Because of its assumed moral neutrality, it tends not to question the status quo – its strength lies in revealing what is, not what ought to be.

Strategy and instrumentality

Strategic thinking assumes that means are subordinate to ends. In strategy, social actors take autonomous decisions on how to employ the tools at their disposal in order to realise their objectives. For instance, a government may introduce tax credits for high-tech companies as a means of facilitating growth in this sector of the national economy. The instrumental nature of this measure is fairly obvious. It serves to fulfil the ends of a policy that was consciously set by the government. In warlike situations, the reasoning is not altogether different. In fact, Clausewitz argues that 'war is nothing but the continuation of policy with other means'.[15] Consequently, whilst war makes it necessary to employ means that are unknown in periods of peace, war is nevertheless a function of policy. It serves a purpose that is defined by the actor that controls the means: '[War's] grammar, indeed, may be its own, but not its logic'.[16]

Moreover, war does not consist of an isolated 'act of force to compel our enemy to do our will',[17] as in Clausewitz's theoretical construct of 'absolute war'. In reality, all war is limited from the absolute – both by operational factors (such as technology, logistics, weather etc.), and by its objectives. The objective of war is therefore not necessarily the 'unconditional surrender' of the enemy, and the act of war itself is not a 'single blow' but a series of engagements. Hence, the conduct of war leaves enough time for all participants to change their strategy, and it eases the strictly hierarchical sense in which ends and means are related to each other. As a result, some strategists tend not to think of war as an archaic force, difficult (if not impossible) to control, but rather in terms of a sophisticated bargaining process – 'vicious' bargaining, but bargaining nevertheless.[18] In strategic theory, bargaining serves the purpose of carefully manipulating incentive structures, so that the cost of complying with one's demands becomes lower than continued resistance. In other words, 'If the enemy is to be coerced you must put him in a situation that is even more unpleasant than the sacrifice you call on him to make.'[19] Accordingly, strategic analysis is mainly concerned with 'the structure of incentives, of information and communication, the choices available and the tactics that can be employed ... It deals with situations in which one party has to think about how the others are going to reach their decisions.'[20]

The logic of bargaining is particularly significant in so-called low-intensity conflicts. Here, a strong side is typically pitted against a substantially weaker one, for instance, an established government against a revolutionary group. Rather than confronting the stronger side militarily, the weaker side's major political objective may be to gain popular support, whilst attempting to worsen the government's incentive structure through a campaign of force. While, from the perspective of the weaker side, a low-intensity conflict requires a highly developed idea of how to use the bargaining instrument, the stronger side could easily crush its opponent. This, however, rarely happens. In fact, governments – in particular democratic ones – often seem to be restrained in the use of force, and one of the aims of strategic analysis may be to find out why this is so.

Strategy and rationality

Strategic analysis examines the behaviour of human beings. However, by assuming rationality, strategic analysis sets a standard that no human being can possibly live up to. Hence, is it irrational to postulate rationality? F. Lopez-Alves has explained rationality as 'the endeavour to relate means to ends as efficiently as possible'.[21] Behaving rationally, thus, ideally assumes that actors are in possession of complete information about themselves and their fellow players, that they are unitary, and that they are perfectly aware not only of their declared values but also of their unconscious passions and preferences. As one can imagine, it is virtually impossible that such 'strategic man' actually exists. However, as Waltz would argue, the validity of a theory is not determined by whether its assumptions are true or not, but by the quality of the insights, explanations and predictions they lead us to.[22] In that sense, assuming rationality helps us to explain a substantial proportion of the reasoning of actors that *try* to maximise utility, even though they never completely succeed in doing so. Assuming anything different would be even less plausible. Accordingly, Garnett correctly distinguishes between two levels of strategic analysis:

> First, [strategy] is pursued at the purely rational level at which attention is focused on reasonable, conscious, artful behavior motivated by the cold calculation of interests; and second, at a level that examines the participants in a conflict in all their complexity.[23]

Garnett's two-level approach to rationality allows us to derive insights both on how an actor should have calculated his interests (if he was 'strategic man'), and to what extent his actual reasoning departed from the notion of rationality. Only by doing so does it become possible to find out about an actor's underlying cultural and ideological assumptions, and so understand his subjective rationality.

However, if the thinking of an actor was easily divisible into the purely rational part and the remaining strands, one could simply examine what the 'difference' between rational and actual thinking is made up of. Unfortunately, this (almost surgical) method of analysing a thought process is impossible, so that there is no other way but to make informed assumptions about the content of this unknown variable, and then to test and gradually refine them. Clausewitz, for instance, points to the role of elements like chance, uncertainty and moral strength in war; and he thinks that theory should not ignore them: '[Theory] must also take the human factor into account, and find room for courage, boldness, even foolhardiness. The art of war deals with living and with moral forces. Consequently, it cannot attain the absolute, or certainty.'[24] Although Clausewitz was far from developing a systematic notion of what constitutes a 'strategic tradition', he openly recognised the significance of factors that lie beyond 'objective' rationality. Maybe it is due to his emphasis on intangible influences that many strategists do not consider their field of study a domain of absolute rationality, but instead appreciate ideologies and value systems.

Historical background

Not least because history often shapes the value systems and ideological preferences of social actors, it is important to introduce the historical background to what happened in the 1969–98 period. In post-independence Ireland, historiography traditionally served the purpose of reinforcing the myth of a subjugated people united in their fight against an abusive and alien power. Only in the mid-1960s did a group of historians begin to question these assumptions. Many so-called Revisionists researched the economic and social history of Ireland; they looked at events within an international framework; and they discovered the diversity of social forces in Irish society. In turn, this more pluralist and less committed attitude has recently been attacked by a number of young Nationalist historians.[25] Whilst this author is openly sympathetic towards the Revisionist position, it is nevertheless his intention to be outspoken about matters of continuing debate.

Ireland before 1800

Nationalist historians believe that Anglo-Irish history started in the year 1170 when Strongbow and other Norman adventurers invaded Ireland at the invitation of the Gaelic chief of the province of Leinster. The so-called Old English, however, did not consider themselves to be missionaries of the Norman crown, and it is arguable whether they could be considered 'English' at all.[26] Instead, they arranged themselves with the leaders of the Gaelic tribes, and they only maintained a shadowy association to their homeland. Many of them became distinctly Gaelic, so that they were eventually referred to as '*hiberniores hibernis ipsos* – "more Irish than the Irish" '.[27] This (rather loose) relation between the two islands started to change only in the sixteenth century. The Tudors, and in particular Henry VIII, were committed to a centralising monarchy, and they saw themselves challenged by the rising power of the Old English House of Kildare. More importantly, Henry's split from Rome and the subsequent failure of Reformation to take root in Ireland transformed the hitherto insignificant island into a potential threat – a backdoor from which England's enemies could launch an invasion. Henry therefore tried to strengthen the ties between the Irish Earls and the Tudor dynasty. Only Elizabeth I, however, succeeded in defeating any opposition to the English crown. When she died in 1602, the monarchy 'could properly claim to have conquered most of Ireland, though English government still hardly impinged upon the lives of the mass of Irish people'.[28]

Shortly after Elizabeth's death, the Plantation of Ulster with settlers from Scotland and England began. While the establishment of a Protestant community in Ireland may be regarded as a deliberate policy to subjugate the island's population, the so-called Ulster Plantation can equally be seen in the context of the first English settlements in New England and Virginia, which reflected the pioneering spirit of that age.

In any case, the consequences of the Ulster Plantation were to spread the seeds of civil strife. Significantly, the so-called New English not only had a different religious allegiance from the Catholic majority, but they also took their land. When the thrust of the settlements was completed in 1610, 'there had been established a province with two mutually antagonistic communities'.[29]

This antagonism resulted in repeated bloodshed, such as the Catholic rebellion in 1641, the Cromwellian re-conquest of Ireland in 1649, and the Williamite wars that concluded with the battles of the Boyne and Aughrim (1690 and 1691). Each time, the two segments of the population of Ireland found themselves on opposing sides of the respective argument. Nevertheless, regarding the idea of English dominance, things were not as clear-cut. First, from the perspective of the English political elites, the wars of the seventeenth century were not so much about Ireland but about the question of who was to hold power in England. Also, the Williamite wars at the end of the century had a European dimension with Protestant England fighting alongside the Pope (!) and the so-called 'Grand Alliance' against the expansionist aspirations of France. Second, from the perspective of the Irish Catholic population, the wars were not about the principle of English control either. In the Williamite wars, the Catholics were happy to ally themselves with King James II, as long as this resulted in an improved position *vis-à-vis* the Protestant population.

For most of the following century, there was relative tranquility in Ireland. Some historians argue that the Anglo-Irish relationship in the eighteenth century was 'quintessentially a colonial one', that is, the Irish were subordinated to foreign domination and exploitation.[30] Others think that the power structures within Ireland as well as between the two islands were typical of the so-called *ancien régimes* all over Europe.[31] Whatever one's point of view, there can be no doubt that the Anglican elites within the Protestant population used the relative peace to establish a so-called Ascendancy, which dominated the structures of economic and political power.[32] In this regard, the winning of legislative independence for the Irish parliament in 1782 was the ultimate manifestation of Irish-Protestant self-confidence and patriotism. English central control, on the other hand, was largely informal. It was exercised through the Lord-Lieutenant, the administration at Dublin Castle and through a system of 'undertakers', which secured parliamentary majorities in return for patronage.[33] Incidentally, the eighteenth century was the first time the 'Irish question' – the question of what constitutional relationship should exist between Britain and Ireland – was effectively articulated.

The long peace of the eighteenth century ended only in its last decade. The Republican rebellion of the 1790s was encouraged by the revolutions in North America and France. Theobald Wolfe Tone, a Presbyterian lawyer who founded the Society of United Irishmen in 1791, articulated the principle of the unity of the Irish people regardless of their creed, as well as the idea of a separation from England. However, desperate for the support of the largely apolitical secret societies in which the Catholic peasantry was organised, Tone's United Irishmen needed to appeal to sectarian prejudices, which appeared to be far more effective in rallying the Catholic population than the battlecry for a Republic. The ensuing battles between the secret societies and the Protestant Orangemen (the Orange Order was founded in 1795) deepened the divisions, and the unrest which had been caused by the insurrection ultimately resulted in London resuming the direct government of the island.

The English government's initial response to the developments in Ireland was a mixture of reform and suppression. On the one hand, some of the anti-Catholic laws were repealed. On the other hand, though, Prime Minister William Pitt the Younger needed to crush the 1798 rebellion decisively if he wanted to avoid another blow to the integrity of the British Empire after his predecessor had suffered defeat in what were now the United States of America (USA). As no English troops were readily available, the government resorted to Protestant militias, and thus to the principle of *divide et impera*. As the then Lord-Lieutenant, Lord Cornwallis, put it: 'Religious animosities increase, and, I am sorry to say, are encouraged by the foolish violence of all the principal persons who have been in the habit of governing this island.'[34]

Ireland and the Union

The Act of Union (1801) abolished the Irish parliament in Dublin. Traditionally, historians have seen the Union as a final attempt to uphold the British connection, and to sustain Protestant supremacy within Ireland. The Union, it is argued, laid the roots for a conflict between supporters of the British connection and Nationalism, which 'deepened, extended, and intensified, not steadily, but in successive waves', and which 'reached its apotheosis in the proclamation of a Republic in Easter week, 1916'.[35] Contrary to this teleological interpretation, revisionists have regarded the Union as a relatively stable political arrangement which 'facilitated constitutional opposition and an apprenticeship in democratic politics'; most importantly, perhaps, 'it ensured a degree of internal and external security that was conducive to social and economic development'.[36]

Initially, Irish Catholics as well as leading members of the clergy supported the idea of the Union. Not only was it seen as guaranteeing external security and paving the way for economic improvements – the Catholics were also sympathetic to Pitt's endorsement of Emancipation, that is, the right of Catholics to take public office. Pitt thought that Catholic interests needed to be accommodated if Ireland was to be pacified. On this occasion, though, Emancipation failed, and when it eventually succeeded, in 1829, it had been preceded by a massive campaign by Daniel O'Connell, a Catholic lawyer from Dublin. Although he later campaigned for the repeal of the Union, O'Connell was not a Nationalist.[37] He believed in some sort of connection with England, and his willingness to work within the British framework was demonstrated by his coalition with Whigs and Radicals (1835–41), when Catholic lawyers and businessmen benefited from government patronage as much as the Protestants had done before.[38]

Only a few years later, the so-called Famine years came to symbolise everything that was wrong with the Union. Nationalists have come to regard the actions of the British government in terms of a systematic genocide. Accordingly, the debate about the Famine in Irish historiography has centred around the question as to whether the government's response to the potato blight in Ireland was adequate, and particularly, why London acted as it did. In fact, during the first winter of the Famine, Tory Prime Minister Robert Peel co-ordinated a swift and effective relief campaign. Only when Lord Russell succeeded him in 1846 did the government's attitude change abruptly. On the one hand, this resulted from the Whigs' strong belief in non-intervention and free trade. As a consequence, public relief schemes were abandoned, and the selling of Irish potatoes abroad continued.[39] Second, and perhaps more importantly, there was widespread confusion at Whitehall: ignorance, lack of knowledge and mismanagement led to English civil servants – in the words of a contemporary – being 'as fairly bewildered in the wilds of Connaught as if they had fallen among the aborigines of Timbucktoo'.[40] None of this confirms the Nationalist suspicion of government intent – nor does it diminish the government's responsibility for a catastrophe that had clearly been avoidable.

In the case of the Famine, as for most of the nineteenth century, London's response to a crisis in Ireland was one of initial disinterest, aloofness and crisis management. In this respect, Westminster's reaction to the Famine was not much different from its treatment of the potato blight in Scotland, which happened in the same decade.[41] In the words of C. Townshend: 'If British government in Ireland was in a sense despotic, it was a despotism tempered by both inefficiency and indifference.'[42] Whilst this provides an excellent case for independence, the problem was that no one at the time made it (notwithstanding the so-called Young Irelanders whose attempted rebellion in 1848 failed to attract any measurable support).[43]

This changed only in the last quarter of the century. Successive land acts failed to solve the economic problems of an island that was geographically remote and largely dependent on agriculture. Isaac Butt and Charles Stewart Parnell (both Protestants) managed to transform the latent social discontent of the Catholic masses into a question of self-governance, and by 1880, Parnell was the undisputed leader of a unified Home Rule Party that fought for the restoration of legislative independence. From a British perspective, the Irish question had several dimensions. First, it was one of party political significance as both Tories and Liberals needed Irish support in the House of Commons if they wanted to form stable governments (when Parnell had eventually aligned himself with the Liberals, the Tories decided to form an alliance with the Irish Unionists). Second, a new settlement for Ireland was perceived as a precedent for the British Empire at large. It was, as D.G. Boyce maintains, 'inextricably bound up with the future of the British constitution, and more important, the British nation'.[44] Finally, the Irish question was one of how to strike a fair balance between the interests of the different communities.

At the end of the nineteenth century, British politicians had found two main answers to the Irish question. One was Home Rule, which would have granted Dublin independence in a number of policy areas, but maintained the constitutional link to the United Kingdom. This idea was advocated by the Liberal Party and Prime Minister William Gladstone, who introduced Home Rule Bills in 1886 and in 1893. The 1886 Bill split the Liberal Party and thus failed to receive a majority in the House of Commons. The second Bill passed the House of Commons but was rejected in the House of Lords.[45] The second answer was what historians have called 'constructive Unionism'. Instead of self-government, London would address the major social and economic grievances directly, thus trying to 'kill Home Rule with kindness'.[46] This policy was advanced by the Conservative governments of Robert Salisbury and Arthur Balfour (1886 to 1905), and it included a final solution to the land question which '[converted] the tenant farmers into peasant proprietors'.[47] Throughout the Union period, however, neither Liberals nor Tories hesitated to introduce Coercion Bills when they found tougher measures necessary to suppress the civil unrest which resulted from sectarian strife. While Tories and Liberals disagreed on the significance of the constitutional question, one may therefore conclude that both parties practised a moderate mixture of coercion and conciliation when in power.

When the Liberals returned to power, Home Rule was back on the agenda. The introduction of a modest Home Rule Bill in 1912 was sufficient to alarm the Unionists in Ulster, albeit not enough to satisfy the aspirations of Herbert Asquith's allies, the Irish Nationalists. With Unionists and (then) Nationalists forming paramilitary organisations in order to defend their respective causes, the following years saw the radicalisation and militarisation of the conflict over Home Rule. Under these circumstances, the partition of Ireland into two Home Rule areas appeared to be the only possible means of appeasing the Protestant Northeast of the island whilst maintaining the goodwill of the Irish Nationalists. Still, none of the suggested solutions (under headings like 'county option', 'temporary exclusion' or 'home rule within home rule') seemed to please both communities at the same time. Arguably, civil war was prevented only by the outbreak of the First World War, which, in Asquith's words, 'dwarfed the Ulster and Nationalist Volunteers to their true proportion'.[48]

After the Easter Rising of 1916, a moderate solution along the lines of the suggested Home Rule Bill appeared even less likely. As support for the constitutional Nationalists dwindled, the more radical party *Sinn Fein* became the predominant force in Irish Nationalism. In contrast to the Republican view,[49] the British government continued its programme of constitutional proposals. Yet, it is equally true that the increased violence compelled policymakers in London to move towards repression. This dual strategy of coercion and conciliation was signified by the simultaneous implementation of, on the one hand, two Home Rule areas and the deployment of the Blacks and Tans, the notorious auxiliary force of the Royal Irish Constabulary (RIC), on the other. In 1921, this strategy ultimately failed.[50] The Anglo-Irish Treaty of December granted dominion status to the 26 counties of the 'South' and left the constitutional status of the Home Rule area of (what was now) Northern Ireland untouched.

Northern Ireland, 1921–69

According to the Government of Ireland Act (1920), the Northern Ireland government at Stormont held powers in a wide range of so-called 'transferred' matters which included, amongst others, security and electoral arrangements. Although the supreme authority of the British parliament was reaffirmed in Section 75 of the 1920 Act, Westminster refrained from legislating in matters that were considered to be the responsibility of Stormont. As a result, the Northern Ireland government was what I. Budge and C. O'Leary describe as 'a self-governing province with some of the trappings of sovereignty'.[51] This lack of legislative control was of no worry to various British governments. On the contrary, the settlements of 1920 and 1921 removed the Irish question from British politics, and British decision-makers were determined not to allow it back on the agenda. At Westminster, the unspoken consensus was that the best policy was to leave Irish matters to the Irish, that is, to exercise as little control as possible. As Boyce put it, there was a 'desire to avoid opening up an issue that could bring nothing but trouble to the British government, perhaps even landing it with the unenviable task of resuming the government of Northern Ireland'.[52] The parameters of this policy did not change, even when it became obvious that the Unionist Party had secured the existence of the beleaguered province by establishing a system of government that systematically excluded the Catholic minority from positions of power and influence.[53] Contact between Westminster and Stormont – most commonly through Home Office or Treasury – was restricted to what was absolutely necessary. Moreover, as a result of (Southern) Irish independence, the number of Irish seats in the House of Commons decreased to a mere dozen, so that the party political significance of the Irish vote withered. The party ties – particularly between Conservatives and Unionists – gradually loosened, and a new generation of politicians was neither interested in Northern Ireland nor familiar with Irish affairs.[54]

Only in the years of the Second World War were British ministers reminded of the existence of Northern Ireland, and on this occasion, it helped to increase Stormont's standing at Westminster. The province's willingness to participate in the war effort contrasted positively with the neutrality of the Dublin government. In addition, Northern Ireland's geographical position turned out to be of military significance, as it provided a supply base for the United States and Canada when mainland British ports were cut off. This was recognised in a number of policy documents (see Chapter 2), and it facilitated the Ireland Act (1948), which guaranteed Northern Ireland's constitutional position as part of the United Kingdom as long as Stormont wished. Still, Westminster's active role in the government of Northern Ireland remained so small that some historians manage to tell the history of the province in the 1945–69 period without a single reference to the British government.[55]

P. Bew *et al.* argue that, when Harold Wilson became Prime Minister in 1964, Northern Ireland had become irrelevant to Westminster, both politically and economically. Accordingly, there was no such thing as a coherent policy with regard to the province when the Irish question returned to the centre of British politics in the second half of the 1960s.[56]

The start of the Troubles had not been anticipated by the British government. London's initial reaction to the street marches, protests and civil disturbances in the second half of the 1960s was a mixture of disbelief, uncertainty, and – above all – reluctance. Although Wilson had promised a more pro-active policy in relation to Catholic grievances before 1964, he soon returned to the non-interventionist policy of his predecessors.[57] It was agreed that, if anything, the London government would try to work through the Stormont government of Terence O'Neill, who was perceived to be a genuine reformer. As one Cabinet member, Richard Crossman, declared: O'Neill was 'the man we were relying on in Northern Ireland to do our job of dragging Ulster out of its... Catholic–Protestant conflict'.[58] The fervent opposition he encountered amongst radical Protestants only seemed to confirm the view that O'Neill occupied the middle ground between extremist Protestants and radical Catholics. Accordingly, Wilson described his approach in dealing with Stormont as 'cautious', and indeed, even the reforms the Westminster government pressed for after the violent clashes of October 1968 were too modest to 'have the effect of either securing peace or securing O'Neill's position'.[59]

Although the Home Office was made to draw up detailed contingency plans if London had to assume the direct rule of the province, active intervention was considered only as a last resort. The principal aim of the British government was, as Home Secretary James Callaghan put it, not 'to get sucked into the Irish bog'.[60] The way in which the British government has subsequently attempted to get out of the 'Irish bog' is the subject of the main part of this work.

2
The Strategic Tradition of the British Government in Northern Ireland

In the preceding chapter, it was shown that strategy does not operate in the domain of pure rationality, but that in addition to the 'cold calculation' of interest there are also values and ideologies that determine the behaviour of an actor. Accordingly, the aim of this section is to construct the 'strategic tradition' of the British government in Northern Ireland, that is, to explain its main assumptions and motivational patterns, and to demonstrate how they have translated into so-called policy themes, which can then be traced throughout the conflict. Of particular interest are the influences which have determined the government's use of the main instruments at its disposal, that is, the principles that have guided the government's views about the province's constitutional status *vis-à-vis* Great Britain and the Republic of Ireland (the constitutional instrument), the assumptions that have determined London's decisions on how to enforce the rule of law (the military instrument), the values that have guided the government's views on the distribution of political power within the province (the political instrument) and the beliefs that have determined London's judgements in setting the economic and social framework (the economic instrument).

The constitutional instrument: Ireland as a place apart

In attempting to construct the British government's constitutional approach to Northern Ireland, Irish Republicans have traditionally employed the colonial paradigm. They claim that Great Britain continues to have some 'selfish' interest in maintaining a presence in Ireland. Even though a small number of Republicans still believe that Britain's supposed interest in Ireland is of an economic nature, the size of the annual subvention to the province seems to have convinced most supporters of the colonial analogy that Britain's interest in Northern Ireland must lie elsewhere. Attention has therefore focused on military or geopolitical considerations. First, with the Republic of Ireland not being a member of the North Atlantic Treaty Organization (NATO), Northern Ireland represents a key territorial link between Western Europe and North America. Thus, it is maintained, the province remains vital to British security.[1] Second, Republicans contend that the British presence is a safeguard against a revolution in Ireland, which, it is argued, would inevitably occur once the divisive influence of the British Crown had been withdrawn. It follows that the existence of Northern Ireland prevents Ireland from becoming the 'British Cuba', that is, the backdoor from which revolution would spread to Great Britain.[2] Third, according to Republicans, Northern Ireland serves as a 'training ground' for the British Army, where new weapons and tactics are tested and the troops are provided with essential battlefield experience.[3] To substantiate these claims, Republicans cite evidence in the form of a 1949 British Cabinet document, which classified Northern Ireland 'as a matter of first-class strategic importance'. It stated that 'it seems unlikely that Britain would ever be able to agree to Northern Ireland leaving His Majesty's jurisdiction ... even if the people of Northern Ireland desired it'. Furthermore, a 1951 paper, which originated from the Commonwealth Relations Office, reaffirmed that Ireland was still considered 'a potential base for attack on the United Kingdom', and that 'a part of the island [should therefore]... remain part of the United Kingdom'.[4]

The Republican argument – whilst powerful at first sight – is far from compelling in its original context, namely, the history of the British Empire and Westminster's motivations in its dissolution. The 1949 and 1951 documents were drawn up at a time when the British government assumed that it was possible to hold on to large parts of the Empire. Independence was granted only when the government believed it to be inevitable, and London was anxious to safeguard the economic and military interests of a Great Power. With Britain's post-war political and economic decline from Empire, the emergence of nationalism in many colonies, and the rise of anti-colonialism at home, this policy became increasingly untenable. Arguably, the failure to regain the control of the Suez Canal in 1956 could be singled out as the one event which signified the end to Britain's imperial aspirations. Westminster realised that 'the world was changing', and that there was nothing to be gained from 'maintaining an imperial position if it involved any expensive struggle'.[5] In the following years, London adopted a pragmatic attitude in relation to its Empire. The transition towards independence had to be smooth, and where Westminster still believed to have some interest, it made sure that 'friendly' governments took over. Even in what had earlier been classified as 'strategic fortresses' (i.e. overseas possessions whose value to Britain would always trump the right of self-determination), the British government eventually agreed to independence if – as in the cases of Cyprus or Kenya – the maintenance of British military bases was guaranteed.[6] Hence, if the colonial logic had applied to Northern Ireland, there was no reason as to why the British government would not have agreed to let the province go by the time the Troubles had broken out, if only in return for some military bases. As Hugh Rossi, who was minister at the Northern Ireland Office (NIO) in 1979–81, summed it up: 'From the time of the Spanish Armada down to World War II, Great Britain had a great strategic interest in a strong military presence in Ireland. By the 1960s, the geopolitics of the world had rendered this impractical and unnecessary.'[7]

Contrary to the idea of a 'British Cuba', the Irish appetite for revolution has traditionally been less distinct than Irish Republicans (or members of the right wing British Monday Club)[8] would have imagined. In the first years of the conflict, members of the British government regarded the Republic of Ireland as a conservative Catholic theocracy rather than a hotbed for Communist rebellion. Referring to Protestant fears, Stanley Orme (an NIO minister in the mid-1970s) asserted that the Republic was seen as 'a theocratic state bound ... to the backward-looking social morality of the pre-Reformation Roman Catholic Church'.[9] With the entry of the Republic of Ireland into the European Economic Communities (EEC) in 1973, the idea that the Irish were inclined to decide upon a radical change of their political and economic system seemed to have lost any attractiveness to the British government, and instead of being a potential enemy, the Republic was now regarded as a partner on the European stage.[10] When Northern Ireland Secretary James Prior once referred to the danger of a Marxist 'British Cuba', this comment was thought to impress his largely Irish American audience, many of whom were supporting the armed struggle of Republicans in Northern Ireland out of nostalgia. The statement did not reflect London's attitude towards the province, nor was it his own view.[11]

The claim that Northern Ireland served as a 'training ground' for the British Army ignores the fact that the British defence establishment has traditionally been critical of the Army's deployment to the province. As early as 1970, the Defence Secretary, Lord Carrington, complained that 'the maintenance of the garrison of Northern Ireland at its present level involved heavy expenditure and imposed a serious strain on the

Army'.[12] In 1977, MPs were told by a senior Ministry of Defence (MoD) official that 'Britain's position in Nato could be jeopardised' if troop levels in Northern Ireland were not reduced.[13] Roland Moyle (an NIO minister in the mid-1970s) put it as follows: 'Our defence people were taking the view that the job of the British army was to defend the North German plain from the Red Army, not chasing around the backstreets of Belfast.'[14]

If London had, thus, no apparent interest in Northern Ireland, does it follow that the province was regarded as an integral part of the United Kingdom? Traditionally, British prime ministers have been anxious to emphasise that Northern Ireland was – as Prime Minister Margaret Thatcher famously remarked – 'part of the United Kingdom as much as my constituency [in Finchley, North London] is'.[15] Below the surface, however, Westminster's attitude towards Northern Ireland has been more ambiguous. To Westminster, the Unionist idea of being British was alien, and at times, it seemed to contradict what it believed to be the very essence of Britishness. London's concept of Britishness entailed the presumed virtues of British political culture, such as fairness, tolerance, moderation and the rule of law. Unionists, on the other hand, appeared only to appreciate the symbols of Britishness (the Queen, the Union Jack), but not what they stood for. They were regarded as backward bigots who abused their supposed Britishness for selfish reasons, to establish a false sense of superiority over their Nationalist neighbours, and to extract political and financial support from the government at Westminster. Simply put, they were – in the words of Prime Minister Wilson at the height of the Loyalist strike in 1974 – 'people who spend their lives sponging on Westminster and British democracy and then systematically assault democratic methods'.[16] Even Thatcher, who described her instincts as 'profoundly Unionist', believed that the Unionist definition of Britishness was 'too narrow'.[17] There was therefore little emotional attachment that would have resulted from the 'Britishness' of the Unionists, and the pledge to maintain the constitutional status of Northern Ireland as part of the United Kingdom was upheld for reasons that had little to do with a shared sense of national identity. In fact, in the course of more than 30 interviews for this study, not a single NIO minister or senior civil servant expressed any enthusiasm about Northern Ireland's continued membership in the United Kingdom, whilst several privately shared the view of Lord Gowrie (an NIO minister in 1981–83), who once stated that 'if the people of Northern Ireland wished to join with the South of Ireland, no British government would resist it for twenty minutes'.[18]

Furthermore, instead of seeing the conflict as one of divided loyalties and overlapping territorial claims, the British government conceptualised the situation as being peculiar to Ireland and the Irish. This attitude sometimes amounted to crude assumptions about the 'Irish character', which was regarded as passionate, uncivilised, unreasonable and – in any case – incomprehensible to the English mindset. According to Reginald Maudling, who held responsibility for Northern Ireland under Prime Minister Edward Heath, it was 'very hard for an Englishman to understand the feelings of those who live in Northern Ireland. The history of their struggles is a long one, and they tend to cherish every moment of hatred in it.'[19] Significantly, London's definition of Irishness included Protestants and Catholics alike, both of whom were thought to be engaged in rituals which 'take on an almost Balkan immediacy'.[20] Historical analogy appeared to support the contention that British interventions in Ireland were destined to fail, and that London's efforts – no matter how well-intended – were likely to do more harm than good in an environment that was predominantly characterised by its irrationality. Wilson's Northern Ireland Secretary Merlyn Rees, accordingly, believed that it was impossible for the '[t]he English disease' to find a solution to the Irish problem.[21] In short, Westminster had convinced itself that the people and the culture of the province were foreign to what it believed to be the British way, and that – if not for a rather unfortunate accident of history – Northern Ireland really belonged to the rest of the island of Ireland. The British government believed itself to be an outsider in what was an Irish conflict, and the best it could do was to assist the Irish in bringing about a solution themselves.

Consequently, the option of a withdrawal from Northern Ireland was not a taboo. Indeed, it was seriously considered by both Labour and Conservative governments. Yet, all the governments during the 1969–98 period eventually arrived at the same conclusion: that using the constitutional instrument in order to pursue a policy of Irish unity would lead to sectarian strife and civil war, and that the consequences of 'walking out' were 'to leave the Irish to murder one another'.[22] It is not entirely clear what mechanics were anticipated in that case, but London appeared to assume that the withdrawal of British troops would be followed by a Protestant genocide of the Catholic minority, thus provoking a military intervention of the Republic of Ireland.

This, however, was not a sufficient explanation in itself. After all, British withdrawal from India, Palestine and Cyprus had equally led to civil strife, and London had stuck to its original decision nonetheless. The difference between the former colonies and Northern Ireland was its closeness to Great Britain, and Westminster's constant awareness of the province's proximity resulted in a strengthened sense of responsibility.

This link (between closeness and responsibility) could be established through a variety of mechanisms. For example:

- *Media scrutiny*: the Northern Ireland conflict received more domestic and international press coverage than any of the emergencies in remote parts of the world. Cabinet members were fully aware that '[e]very action was carried out in the glare of television publicity',[23] and that the government would be held accountable.
- *Geography and history* which have produced strong economic and cultural ties between the two islands, not least in the form of a large Irish community in Great Britain (according to the 1991 census, 830 500 inhabitants of Great Britain were born in either part of Ireland; having at least one Irish parent, almost four million would qualify as Irish citizens).[24] Westminster therefore believed that heightened instability in Northern Ireland was likely to spill over to the British mainland, and that it was – in Wilson's words – the government's duty 'to prevent the spread of factional violence in Britain itself'.[25] In 1975, Callaghan (then Foreign Secretary) referred to the British withdrawal from Cyprus and Palestine, stressing that to act in a similar fashion would place 'the security of Britain as well as Ireland at risk'.[26]
- *Common institutions*: Northern Ireland was part of the domestic framework, and its citizens were equal under British law. The military campaign of the Provisional IRA was therefore a direct challenge to the British political system: to ensure that democracy and the rule of law were upheld was a point of principle and a matter of asserting parliamentary democracy. According to Northern Ireland Secretary Patrick Mayhew: 'In this country, we are used to defending democracy and the rule of law. The price is always high, and always worth paying.'[27]

If closeness produced responsibility, it also served to guide London's efforts to keep the province at arm's length. A 'responsible' government would prevent the conflict from disrupting Westminster politics and from becoming a contentious issue in parliament; it would protect its (mainland) citizens from any conflict-related instability or violence; and it would attempt to limit the extent to which Northern Ireland made the government vulnerable in its dealings with other countries. In essence, a responsible government would try to contain the negative effects of the conflict to Northern Ireland. As a result, the proximity of the province and the sense of responsibility it had induced resulted in two – seemingly contradictory – lines of thinking: there was an incentive to distance Northern Ireland from Great Britain, yet at the same time there was a disincentive to bring this process to its apparently logical conclusion, that is, to withdraw from the province.

Historically, British government thinking about Northern Ireland has translated into three constitutional concepts. The first was the so-called consent principle, which makes the province a *conditional* part of the United Kingdom. It means that Northern Ireland remains within the United Kingdom as long as that is the wish of its inhabitants (before 1969: a majority of the Stormont parliament). In practice, the same principle would presumably apply to other parts of the United Kingdom, but only in the case of Northern Ireland has London spelled out explicitly that its attitude in relation to the constitutional status of the province was neutral. To do so, one may argue, was entirely unnecessary, as it was unlikely that London's reasons for preserving the Union (the 'civil war scenario') were to change once there was a majority of one in favour of unification with the Republic. Don Concannon (an NIO minister in the late 1970s) is one of very few British politicians who have admitted openly that the consent principle was in fact a 'paper guarantee', and that '[e]very-one knows that the guarantee is not the piece of paper but a million [Protestant] souls who are prepared to get off their backsides and do some-thing about it'.[28] Critics have also maintained that London's emphasis on majority consent as the only reason for maintaining the Union has not only been inexpedient, but that it has led to an exacerbation of the sectarian divide. As J. Ruane and J. Todd explain: 'The communities... are partially defined by their constitutional preference and each feel trapped...by the fixed constitutional preference of the other... [E]ach finds in the majoritarian guarantee an added reason for maintaining communal solidarity and increasing communal demographic strength.'[29]

The second constitutional theme was devolution. The idea of a regional government appears at odds with the reality of Britain as one of the most centralised states in Europe. Northern Ireland, though, was regarded as a special case, and even a majority of the Conservative Party – which had strong objections against devolution in Scotland and Wales – were keen supporters of a Home Rule parliament. In fact, unlike Scotland and Wales, where devolution was seen as a means of undermining the integrity of the United Kingdom, self-government in Northern Ireland was welcomed by many Unionists within the Conservative Party because the motive was thought to be the opposite from what it was in Scotland and Wales. According to Michael Alison, an NIO minister in 1979–81:

[I]n Northern Ireland the land neighbour from which it will want increasingly to separate itself will be the Republic [of Ireland]. That is the aim of those who want to promote the Union. So there is nothing dangerous from the point of view of identity and membership of the United Kingdom if Northern Ireland pursues the course that was objectionable in Scotland and Wales.[30]

The underlying reason for Westminster's 'love affair' with devolution in Northern Ireland was that it allowed London to keep the province at maximum distance without raising any questions in relation to its constitutional status as part of the United Kingdom. For almost 50 years, the existence of Stormont guaranteed that the British government was reminded of its unwanted province only when it came to paying the yearly subvention.

The third concept was the inclusion of the Republic of Ireland in the government and/or management of the province. This could happen for a series of practical reasons, such as to facilitate cross-border co-operation in security, to pre-empt Dublin's criticism of the treatment of the minority in Northern Ireland, or to engage the minority community with which the Irish government had formed a special relationship. More fundamentally, however, London believed that Irish matters were best left to the Irish, and that the Dublin government ought to share some of the responsibility for what was believed to be an Irish affair. As Gowrie put it: 'The government of Ireland cannot be done without Dublin.'[31] Accordingly, the so-called 'Irish dimension' was first reflected in the 1920 Council of Ireland which provided for the eventual unification of the two Home Rule areas. Even so, Unionists have rejected the all-Ireland approach, and it has traditionally been a sensitive issue to determine to what extent intergovernmental co-operation could be formalised without being interpreted as a 'slippery slope' that would be followed by further concessions to the Nationalist aspiration and, ultimately, lead to the unification of both parts of the island of Ireland. In this regard, Unionist suspicions were bound to be fuelled by London's 'neutrality' with regard to the province's constitutional status as part of the United Kingdom.

The military instrument: minimum force versus internal conflict

The second element of the British government's tradition in Northern Ireland, the military instrument, needs to be explained with reference to the postulate of 'minimum force' as well as four political and ideological challenges that have determined the actual 'level of force'. Before doing so, however, it is necessary to clarify the two concepts as such.

- The term 'level of force' attempts to describe the intensity of the overall security effort. In this work, it is thought of as an open-ended scale with 'minimum force' at its lower end. Rising 'levels of force' are typically reflected in the operational intensity of the security forces (e.g. number of house searches, helicopter operations, etc.), increasing Army force levels (numerical strength of the security forces), greater physical visibility of the military machine (security installations, presence of the military) and the reliance on emergency legislation.[32]
- The principle of 'minimum force' derives from British common law, which postulates that every member of the security forces is a so-called 'common law constable'. His legal status is equal to any civilian, and the appropriate level of force to be used by the security forces is determined by what is 'reasonable in the circumstances'. This interpretation of the security forces' role has translated into the duty to respond to force, yet only with what is absolutely necessary in order to restore law and order.[33]

The first challenge to minimum force relates to the circumstances under which the principle was applied in Northern Ireland. Throughout the Northern Ireland conflict, the idea of 'minimum force' has guided the security forces' efforts, yet in contrast to Great Britain, where the state's monopoly on the use of force has been widely accepted and rarely challenged, in Northern Ireland, no consensus with regard to the security forces' activity existed, and the execution of state authority was actively resisted by at least one community at a time. For London, the fact that its authority was defied within its immediate jurisdiction was difficult to rationalise. Whereas the rejection of British authority in remote parts of the Empire could be understood as a logical – if not inevitable – reaction to foreign rule, Northern Ireland citizens were represented at Westminster; they were equal under British law, and all the channels of participation and institutions of government under the Westminster constitution were open to them. They were members of one of the most advanced liberal democracies in the world, and there was no reason to engage in what Callaghan believed to be 'this nonsense on the streets'.[34] In a similar vein, Prior was keen to point out that whatever the insurgents' political aims, their violent expression could not be accepted: '[W]hile the Government are prepared to recognise and accommodate the sense of Irish identity among the minority..., they cannot accommodate any identity, whether Unionist or nationalist, expressed through violence or through rejection of the law and the institutions of the country.'[35] From London's point of view, the use of force to pursue political objectives in the United Kingdom was anti-democratic rather than just anti-foreign. It was an attempt to defy the Westminster system of government, and it set a dangerous precedent. As a result, the government's campaign to preserve its authority was a matter of principle, the significance of which went far beyond the question of what national state the province would belong to.

Second, the hybrid nature of the conflict in Northern Ireland necessitated separate types of response. It continues to be a matter of debate as to whether the 'Troubles' were caused by two ethnic groups with mutually exclusive national identities (Unionists versus Nationalists), or whether the conflict originates in the 'foreign occupation' of Ireland (the British government versus the Irish people). Irish Republican thinking is based on the latter, whereas the British government has justified its presence by referring to the former, thus regarding itself as an 'honest broker' between the two sides. In practice, though, the British government has encountered both types of conflict: civil disorder, which resulted from sectarian tensions between the two communities, and a campaign of insurgency that was forced upon the British government by the Irish Republican Army (IRA) and its demand that Northern Ireland should be united with the rest of the island. London needed to acknowledge, therefore, that the security forces had to carry out a 'twofold task', namely that of 'maintaining order and preventing communal strife and of eradicating terrorism'.[36] This implied that, on the one hand, the British government needed to deploy the security forces as peacekeepers, who restored law and order and posed as a buffer between the 'warring factions'. To perform this function, the security forces had to be accepted as impartial by Catholics and Protestants alike. In Wilson's words, they needed to be 'firm and cool and fair'.[37] Since any use of what could be perceived as excessive force would have jeopardised the security forces' role as neutral arbiters, this requirement was perfectly coherent with the principle of minimum force. On the other hand, however, the government was engaged in a counterinsurgency campaign. Not only was a substantial proportion of the IRA's activities directed against the government and its agencies, it also inflicted considerable material and physical damage on the civilian population. As a consequence, the British government was obliged to respond to the IRA's campaign, even if it disapproved of its interpretation of the conflict. Further, since the IRA and its supporters were firmly based in the Catholic community, the need to counter the Republicans was bound to violate the principle of even-handedness.[38]

Third, in addition to the level of threat, the level of force was determined by conflicting pressures of the two communities. Contrary to the resolution of conflict in far flung territories of the Empire, where local opinion mattered only up to the point of withdrawal, there was no 'exit strategy' in Northern Ireland. As Prime Minister John Major put it: 'The British government...cannot walk away from a part of its own country.'[39] London had convinced itself that the prospect of 'holding' the province with purely military means – that is, if an overwhelming majority of its inhabitants resisted the way in which it was governed – was not desirable; and the possibility of both communities fighting concurrent campaigns against British rule was Westminster's worst nightmare – it would have ignited the civil war scenario the prevention of which the British government saw as its main responsibility towards the province (see above).[40] London's favoured 'political solution' – a devolved cross-community settlement – depended on the lasting consent of both communities. The two sides, however, had made the adoption of a particular military approach a condition of their participation in talks, so that the level of force was to become a 'bargaining chip' between the government and the two communities. Given that the minority community was more likely to be the subject of attention by the security forces, Nationalist politicians have consistently favoured a more subtle approach, which entailed the abolition of emergency powers and the downscaling of military operations. Unionist leaders, on the other hand, have been anxious to call on London to 'get tough' on the IRA, which included demands for 'shoot-to-kill' operations by the security forces, internment without trial, or the removal of a suspect's right to silence.

Finally, the principle of minimum force was challenged by public opinion in Great Britain and – to a lesser extent – abroad. Like every government policy in a democratic setting, the British government's actions in Northern Ireland were scrutinised by the wider public, and the British government was ultimately held accountable by the British electorate. To London, it was obvious that the continued involvement in the province hinged on the British public's acquiescence, and that, therefore, public opinion in Great Britain had to be part of the strategic calculus. For example, as early as February 1971, the Cabinet worried that 'public opinion in Great Britain was beginning actively to resent the situation which was developing in Northern Ireland; and many people would favour abandoning the Province to its fate'.[41] Regarding the level of force, London's dilemma arose from the fact that public opinion on the mainland was highly ambiguous. One section of the electorate appeared to suggest that there was not much point in using any force at all, and that 'the boys' – that is, the British soldiers who were stationed in the province – should be brought back home in order to avoid further casualties in what was believed to be a lost cause. As a result, many opinion polls showed a substantial proportion of those questioned in favour of 'withdrawing the troops immediately'.[42] In addition, liberal and left-wing commentators in Great Britain, as well as public opinion in the United States, were highly critical of the security forces' use of emergency powers, the deployment of special forces and the erosion of civil liberties which was enacted on both sides of the Irish Sea in response to the 'terrorist threat'. Even so, to understand the dynamics of public opinion fully, one has to consider two additional trends. As R. Rose *et al.* pointed out in 1978, large sections of the British public had come to see the conflict as 'boring', and most atrocities in Northern Ireland were consequently regarded with indifference; they failed to cause any strong reaction on the British mainland other than reinforcing the cliché that 'the Irish' were unreasonable.[43] Yet, whenever the IRA committed atrocities in England, there emerged an equally strong notion of defiance, that is, that one must not 'give in to terrorists'. When asked what effect IRA bombs on the mainland had, only 28 per cent of the respondents to a 1984 MORI poll declared that they were more likely to support British withdrawal, whilst a majority (53 per cent) favoured 'tougher action'.[44] Likewise, after the Bishopsgate bomb in April 1993, the Dean of St Paul's Cathedral declared: 'This great city has faced plague, pestilence, fire and the Blitz. The IRA have no more hope of killing the spirit of London than Adolf Hitler had.'[45] If the IRA was indeed on a par with the pestilence and Hitler, its defeat was a national mission that allowed for extraordinary measures. Thus, in the same way in which the government regarded the IRA as an anti-democratic challenge to the rule of law and the British constitution, a significant section of the British public felt that the IRA had to be put down as a matter of preserving the integrity of the nation.

Three policy themes have emerged as a result of British thinking on the use of force. First, there could be no 'military solution'. To coerce the population, or to 'put down' any violent expression of opposition to state authority with military means alone was incompatible with the principle of minimum force, and it contradicted the government's self-declared role of a 'third party' to mediate between the warring factions. Most fundamentally, it was regarded as counterproductive. Any lasting solution had to be 'political', that is, an agreed settlement that was brought about 'by proper parliamentary, constitutional and electoral processes, [because] this is the British way of doing things'.[46] At the same time, though, it was clear that the impact of violence was disruptive and destabilising. To achieve the pacification of the province, it was therefore necessary to use the military instrument in order to reduce the level of violence to 'an acceptable level',[47] namely one which allowed the primacy of constitutional politics to be re-established. This consensus, however, was weakened by Westminster's tendency to remove itself from the execution of the military instrument, which meant that the government exercised less political control of the security forces than necessary. There was an inclination to delegate controversial security decisions from Cabinet or ministerial level to other actors or institutions who were thought to judge a particular question on a purely technocratic basis. By doing so, the government avoided responsibility, it distanced itself from events in the province and protected itself from accusations of partisanship. At the same time, the logic of outsourcing increased the tendency to regard security matters in an isolated manner, and it hampered the use of the military instrument as a means of bargaining.

The second theme was the maintenance of civilian government and the preservation of basic principles of British justice in order to allow for what John Cope (an NIO minister in 1989–90) believed to be 'as normal a legal process as possible'.[48] While some Unionist commentators have repeatedly pressed for the introduction of martial law,[49] they have failed to understand that the preservation of democratic procedures was essential to the government's justification of its involvement in Northern Ireland. From London's point of view, it was a case of providing evidence that British institutions and the rule of law – with an independent judiciary, public trial in an open court, representation by a lawyer and the automatic right of appeal – were superior to the 'kangaroo courts' of its enemies, and that the 'terrorists' were engaged in criminal activities rather than pursuing a legitimate cause. Simply put, there was no point in embarking on a mission to assert the authority of constitutional government if its defence involved the abolition of what one wanted to preserve. Northern Ireland Secretary Peter Brooke expressed this view very strongly:

> [O]ur response to terrorism must be conducted within the framework of the rule of law. It is, quite simply, because our adherence to the rule of law, in the face of the most atrocious provocation, as well as to democratic procedures and the principles of justice that sustain our civilisation, demonstrates why terorrism should not win and why it cannot win. For terrorism, by its very nature, represents a relapse into barbarism and savagery that unites the entrie civilised world in determined and unquenchable opposition.[50]

One may argue that this approach was bound to result in some degree of self-deception, as some civil liberties needed to be curtailed in order to meet the requirements of the security forces. In fact, to determine the degree to which the principles and the ordinary processes of the rule of law could be foregone in the name of effective counter-insurgency was to be London's main dilemma in formulating a coherent military strategy.

The third theme was the replacement of military troops from Great Britain with local police. The idea of police primacy cannot be ascribed to a singular influence. It may have reflected the government's alienation from the province, the belief that Irish problems are best left to the Irish, and the conviction that the British – whether soldiers or politicians – could do no good on Irish soil. It also appeared to make London's engagement more sustainable in the long term, particularly with regard to public opinion in Great Britain and the need to fulfil other commitments elsewhere. Most importantly, it helped to reinforce the notion of the IRA as an anti-constitutional challenge to civilian government. In implementing this principle, however, the British government ignored that the security forces in Northern Ireland were predominantly recruited from the Protestant community, and that law enforcement was therefore likely to be seen as one-sided. The British government was largely indifferent to the sectarian dynamics of the conflict, mainly because there was a strong belief that the professionalisation of the RUC (as well as the impartial ethos of the British Army) would soon make the sectarian composition of the security forces irrelevant.

The political instrument: British political culture in a divided society

Like security policy, British government thinking *vis-à-vis* the distribution of power within Northern Ireland was strongly influenced by the tenets of British political culture (defined as 'the emotional and attitudinal environment within which ... [the British] political system operates').[51] Most fundamentally, the substance of both the Westminster constitution and British political culture can be found in their approach towards resolving conflict. The Westminster system, with its lively and controversial debates at the House of Commons, appears adversarial, yet in almost dialectic fashion, the underlying principle of conflict resolution in British political culture is the search for co-operation and compromise, the quest for 'give and take'. At the end of every process of discussion and mutual persuasion, it seems, all the participants get together, hammer out their differences and find a solution that respects the integrity of everyone involved, even if that compromise fulfils everyone's aspirations only to a certain extent. British political culture is, therefore, pragmatic rather than dogmatic, and the use of violence for political purposes is outside its bounds. Further, the British constitution is the result of centuries of piecemeal change, starting with the Magna Carta in 1215 and interrupted only by the English Civil War in the seventeenth century. Unlike many other liberal democracies, where the change from aristocracy to democracy had been abrupt, the term 'revolution' is alien to the British political tradition. In Britain, political challenges have been absorbed by a constitutional apparatus that is based on a 'system of tacit understandings' rather than a rigid code, and that has therefore proved flexible enough to adapt to change whilst preserving its symbols and institutions. In P. Norton's words, the British constitution is a 'living organism in a condition of perpetual growth'.[52]

The practical reason as to why the different political actors have traditionally been willing to compromise is the fact that a majority of the electorate considers itself to be 'moderate'. For any political party, this means that it has to reach out beyond its core supporters and appeal to the political centre if it wants to win a majority and political power.[53] The controversy that precedes the eventual compromise is seen as part of the 'political game' – as competition rather than confrontation – and it helps to map out the main planks of an agreement. Accordingly, former Prime Minister Lord Balfour declared in 1927 that '[o]ur whole political machinery presupposes a people so fundamentally at one that they can safely afford to bicker; and so sure of their own moderation that they are not dangerously disturbed by the never-ending din of political conflict'.[54] Equally important, there has been a high degree of consent between governors and the governed in relation to the way in which political power was exercised through the mechanisms of the existing political system. The extent to which political culture and institutions in Great Britain are linked even led some observers to conclude that 'the crown; the flag; the rule of law...and parliamentary democracy' embody the essence of what one refers to when speaking about 'Britishness'.[55] Despite its elitist orientation and the dominance of what some might claim to be 'English norms', Westminster has therefore enjoyed a high degree of legitimacy amongst the electorate.

It is not difficult to identify the principal tenets of British political culture in London's thinking about how to bring about a 'political solution' of the Northern Ireland conflict. In fact, the government's political ideas were firmly based on the 'British ideal', and even though London gradually recognised that the reality of the Northern Ireland situation was different from Great Britain, it thought of British political norms as something that people in Northern Ireland had to be educated towards. The most significant British idea was that of a 'moderate centre' which had to be mobilised against the 'men of violence' who were, regardless of their motives, the 'enemies of law abiding citizens everywhere'.[56] Heath declared, accordingly, that 'find[ing] a lasting political settlement that would unite moderate opinion across the religious divide' was the underlying motive of all his government's actions in Northern Ireland.[57] The notion of a 'moderate centre' rested on the assumption that the vast majority of the province's inhabitants were 'peaceloving' and 'decent' people who wanted to pursue their jobs and lead a happy life, no matter what religious denomination they belonged to. At the fringes of society, however, there were small groups of dangerous criminals who exploited old antagonisms for their own ends. In London's view, Northern Ireland society consisted of the 'bad' – that is, those who committed, approved of, or stirred up violence – and the 'good', that is, the moderates who condemned violence, and who were prepared to work together in order to uphold the rule of law. In a passionate plea at the House of Commons, Callaghan declared:

> There may be 250 or 500 men in Northern Ireland today who are intent on dragging the country down so that it lives under the shadow of the gun. The question is not … what those few hundred will do, but what the rest of the people … will do. Will they allow themselves to live under the shadow of the gunman and permit themselves to be divided … into two groups, separated by a mile of misunderstanding?[58]

Thus, in a remarkable similarity to Irish Republican ideology, the British government thought the sectarian divide to be imagined rather than real. In contrast to the Republicans, however, who made 'British Imperialism' responsible for the division of society, London believed that it was the result of the work of 'demagogues' and 'terrorists'.

The solution was simple. In truly British fashion, the protagonists of moderate opinion from both sides had to sit around a table, clear up misperceptions, iron out their differences, and then develop a positive vision for the future of their country, which – from London's perspective – appeared to be based on the absence of violence, co-operation and economic prosperity. Consequently, the constitutional question was regarded as a matter of lesser importance: 'The real issue of politics in

Northern Ireland is how, within the existing boundaries, two communities can live together. That is what really matters.'[59] It followed that the British government was an 'outsider' whose only interest was 'to try and bring about peace. To try and stop the violence in any way we could.'[60] In that sense, London assumed its 'moderate' allies from both sides of the sectarian divide to treat each other with fairness and respect: they were 'men of goodwill' who had a common interest in building a powerful alliance against the 'enemies' of society and constitutional government. The 'men of violence', on the other hand, had no constructive role to play. On the contrary, the purpose of bringing the 'moderates' together was to defeat the extremist elements which prevented Northern Ireland from becoming a 'normal' society.

Crucially, however, the 'men of violence' were not seen as a static group. London had always assumed that the 'men of violence' could be converted to the 'moderate centre'. The term 'dove' was, accordingly, believed to describe a stage in the evolution of a paramilitary organisation at which a significant section within that organisation was thought to be willing to give up violence in favour of constitutional means.[61] Once a terrorist organisation was thus believed to be ripe for 'democratisation', London's attitude was determined by two – somewhat conflicting – influences.[62] On the one hand, the British government believed that any conversion towards peaceful politics had to be encouraged. As a lesson from its colonial past, the British government thought that one had to react with pragmatism once the paramilitaries seemed to be willing to compromise. Heath, for example, stated that the British government had never had any reservations about negotiating with the 'rebel leaders' if doing so helped 'to put an end to terrorism and establish a peaceful regime'.[63] On the other hand, Northern Ireland was part of the domestic realm, and if London wanted to retain the integrity of its institutions and maintain the credibility of the democratic process, it needed to demonstrate that extremists would 'not be allowed to bomb [their] way to the conference table',[64] that those who used violence were criminals, and that the 'true' moderates must not be betrayed by compromising with the 'men of violence'.[65]

British government thinking *vis-à-vis* the political instrument translated into two themes. The first was the notion of the British government as an 'honest broker' between the two sides. As London thought of itself as an outsider who had no stake in the inter-communal power struggle except the desire for peace and reconciliation, it believed itself in a perfect position to play the role of a mediator between the conflicting aspirations of the two communities. Accordingly, the British

government would make sustained efforts to balance both sides'
interests, and tease out the 'middle ground' where agreement could be
found. London's claim to be a disinterested outsider, however, was difficult to accept by the two sides. Nationalists found it hard to regard an
actor as neutral which, from the point of view of Irish Nationalism, was
the major obstacle to Irish unity, and whose symbols were regarded as
alien, exclusive and oppressive. Unionists, on the other hand, objected
to the structural asymmetry of London's role that allowed for the close
political co-ordination with Dublin and 'secret talks' with the representatives of paramilitary groups, but that made it impossible for
Westminster to side with their self-declared allies, the Unionists.[66]

The second theme was the idea of a cross-community settlement that
would produce political stability. Whilst any modification of majority
rule was remarkably un-British in that it meant the virtual abolition of
the adversarial Westminster model, the British government recognised
that '[s]imple majority rule ... would leave the minority in perpetual
opposition',[67] which implied that Nationalists had to be given a permanent role in the political system for democratic government to be effective and stability to emerge. In fact, the British government saw any
form of co-operative (or power-sharing) government as a means of *overcoming* the sectarian status quo; it was a temporary 'bridging operation'
until 'normal' politics would be established.[68] In the meantime, London
hoped, the 'men of goodwill' from both sides would work together in
order to strengthen the 'moderate centre' and defeat the 'men of violence'. Even so, the practical difficulties with this approach were numerous. Most significantly, the requirement of mutual consent meant that
both sides – Unionists as well as Nationalists – were at liberty to veto the
terms of any settlement. Had Westminster's assumptions about the
'moderate centre' been accurate, this would not have posed a problem.
In reality, though, the (sectarian) pattern of inter-party competition in
Northern Ireland suggests that the two main 'moderate' parties, the
Ulster Unionist Party (UUP) and the (mainly Catholic) Social
Democratic and Labour Party (SDLP), need to reach out to the fringes of
their respective blocs in order to broaden their appeal.[69] As a consequence, there is no natural inclination to move towards the centre, as in
Great Britain, and the traditional values of British political culture –
moderation and compromise – are therefore of questionable value.
Moreover, London's idea of a cross-community settlement ignored the
cause of the division it wanted to heal. With the notable exception of
the inter-confessional Alliance party, all the major parties in Northern
Ireland can be defined with reference to the constitutional issue, and the

political actors in the province consequently see each other primarily in terms of their respective stance on the constitutional question.[70] Whilst the British government anticipated that the constitutional issue would wither away once the parties of the 'moderate centre' had started to co-operate, the overriding importance of the constitutional question to both elites and society at large suggests that any attempt at power-sharing would be overshadowed by the incompatibility of each side's ultimate aspiration. Incidentally, the absence of any national consensus was the main reason why A. Lijphart (who had created the concept of the 'consociational democracy') believed the conditions for co-operative government in Northern Ireland to be 'overwhelmingly unfavorable'.[71]

The economic instrument: peace through prosperity

The final element in the British government's strategic tradition is its approach towards economic policy. To develop this notion, it is necessary to review the fundamental assumptions on which British economic policy in the post-war period rested. Amongst historians, it is almost universally agreed that the Second World War gave rise to a new consensus on economic policy, the most prominent concepts of which were the Welfare State and the 'managed economy'. At the end of the war, most Britons came to believe that the state had a significant role to play in the process of reconstruction, and many soldiers – who had served their nation on the battlefields of Europe – looked upon the state to provide them with the means for a new beginning. This mood had set in once victory was assumed to be certain, and arguably, it contributed to Labour's election victory in 1945.[72] The 1942 Beveridge Report (on 'Social Insurances and Allied Services') set out the agenda for the years to come. It declared the defeat of the 'giants' of 'Want, Disease, Ignorance, Squalor, and Idleness' as its aims, and it resulted – most prominently – in a system of social insurance that would cover every citizen, as Churchill put it, 'from cradle to grave'. The new spirit ran contrary to the ideas of *laisser faire* which many had made responsible for the economic and political catastrophes of the 1920s and 1930s. At the end of the war, the tenets of Keynesian economic management had therefore become the accepted orthodoxy. Keynes' economic philosophy justified the state's right of intervention in the markets, the idea of increased state spending as a means to counter recessionary tendencies, and the maintenance of a large public sector. In doing so, the government's objective was to ensure prosperity and – most significantly – full employment. In addition, politicians at the time also stressed the 'human benefits of being engaged in productive employment', and Beveridge pointed to the fact that meaningful employment was 'a provision for human happiness'.[73] Equally important was the provision of public or publicly funded housing. As in the cases of social security and unemployment, the immediate need for government action arose from wartime destruction, yet at the same time it was regarded as a means for building a better society by 'removing the slums' (particularly in Northern England and Scotland), and providing every community with a 'decent' standard of housing was seen as a precondition for social peace and individual self-fulfilment.[74]

The reason as to why the Welfare State and the 'managed economy' survived several changes in government can be found in its ideological outlook. It was social democratic rather than socialist, and in that sense it united the pragmatic wing of the Labour Party with the mainstream of 'One Nation' Conservatism. The doctrinaire socialists within Labour, on the other hand, despised the economic consensus as 'an inadequate bandage for the wounds inflicted on the poor by capitalism'.[75] In his analysis of the post-war reforms, S. Pollard confirmed that 'the major redistribution achieved by the social services was horizontal...and this aspect of it met with widespread approval, for, after all, the net contributor and the net beneficiary was commonly the same person at different stages of his career'.[76] Understanding the Welfare State as a means of creating an 'egalitarian society' would be a serious misperception. Its aim was to eradicate poverty, and to make the provision of public services more efficient. When in government, neither Conservatives nor Labour showed great willingness to upset the general consensus by engaging in redistributive policies that would have questioned the nation's social fabric. As A. Sked concluded: The 'whole ethos [of the Welfare State] has been one designed to support rather than to undermine the social system'.[77]

London's thinking in relation to the economic situation in Northern Ireland was remarkably similar to the postulates that had shaped the post-war consensus in Great Britain. The premise of London's economic policy in Northern Ireland was the assumption that there was a link between peace and prosperity. In London's view, both the disharmony between the two communities and the seemingly irrational significance that Protestants and Catholics had attached to the constitutional question related to the fact that – compared to the rest of the United Kingdom – living standards in Northern Ireland were low and unemployment was high. As early as September 1969, Callaghan told his Cabinet colleagues: 'If even 1500 jobs could be created in Londonderry, this would go a long way towards transforming the political situation.'[78] More than two decades later, Mayhew approvingly quoted his predecessor at the time of the Great War, Augustine Birrell, who had 'once wistfully reflected that, if he could only get the jobs, most of his other Irish problems would subside'.[79] Given this analysis of the problem, it came as no surprise that the main economic tools in resolving the political *malaise* of Northern Ireland included the provision of additional employment, the creation of social and leisure facilities, and housing. As Prior stated: 'Thatcherism didn't exist in Northern Ireland...It was the one part of the United Kingdom where Keynesianism was still rampant'.[80] Of course, this set of priorities necessitated massive financial support. Westminster was fully aware of the financial burden Northern Ireland would continue to represent, but it had obviously decided not to let this implication determine its use of the economic instrument. Peter Viggers (the NIO's minister for industry in 1985–89) now admits that he was 'embarrassed by the size of my departmental budget: I had a huge budget, and I was not inhibited in any way by money. I was urging a harsh, tough business-like line, but I was almost on my own in that.'[81]

Like the post-war consensus, British thinking in relation to the economic situation in Northern Ireland was reluctant to address the issue of economic inequality. Whereas in Great Britain inequality was largely defined in terms of the class cleavage, people in Northern Ireland conceptualised inequality predominantly in terms of the sectarian divide. Throughout the 1969–98 period, the relative deprivation between Catholics and Protestants with regard to every economic and social indicator (such as unemployment, income, living standards, etc.) remained highly significant with Protestants in a more favourable position overall.[82] Although the argument about whether direct and/or indirect discrimination was the primary cause for this differential is continuing,[83] there can be no doubt that the result – namely the difference between the two communities in terms of economic status – has been a persistent grievance which contributed to the sense of political injustice, disadvantage and alienation felt by many members of the Catholic community in Northern Ireland.[84] On behalf of the British government, there was a clear sense of unease when it came to formulating economic policies that were geared towards advancing the opportunities and rights of groups rather than individuals. One approach to relative deprivation was, therefore, to ignore the evidence, and to refuse to admit that there was a problem. Callaghan, for example, believed that '[c]omplaints about employment are heard just as much among the majority'.[85] Westminster clearly hoped that the keenly anticipated outbreak of prosperity would gradually level out the differences between Catholics and Protestants, and that the issue would consequently go away without the need for London to intervene pro-actively. The first Northern Ireland Secretary, William Whitelaw, stated that his aim was to 'work towards measures that benefit Northern Ireland as a whole rather than favouring one community or another',[86] thus regarding the issue of economic equality as a zero-sum situation in which gains for one community were possible only at the expense of the other.

London's tradition in using the economic instrument was reflected in two policy themes. The first was the need to engage in resolute state action in order to create employment. The British government would not have any ideological reservations about providing the necessary funds to create additional employment in the public sector. Nor would Westminster shy away from attempts to secure investment from abroad by offering generous subsidies. Throwing money at the province, however, did little to address the question of inequality, and – as many authors have pointed out – this approach transformed Northern Ireland into a 'workhouse' economy where dying industries were kept alive by the state and large amounts of public money were given to 'branch plants' that were susceptible to closure in times of recession.[87] Second, the British government was reluctant to implement policies that would challenge the economic and social status quo between the two communities. Concepts like 'affirmative action' (any active effort to improve employment or educational opportunities for any one minority or marginalised group) or 'preferential treatment' ('positive discrimination' or quota systems)[88] remained alien to the British tradition of using the economic instrument. Basing its policies on individual safeguards against direct discrimination, London ignored the fact that the existing imbalance in economic opportunities had not primarily been a result of overt discrimination, and that – as P.A. Compton points out – 'in the deeply divided society of Northern Ireland…the "rights" of the community may rival those of the inidividual in political importance'.[89] Somewhat paradoxically, the British government accepted that the *political* situation in Northern Ireland necessitated the alteration of simple majority rule (see above), yet it refused to recognise the sectarian logic in relation to the *economic* situation.

Conclusion

The aim of this chapter has been to outline the main ideas that have guided British strategic thinking in relation to Northern Ireland. It needs to be emphasised that the boundaries between the different elements of the strategic tradition of the British government are largely artificial. In some cases, a similar idea might have influenced the use of different instruments. The idea of Westminster as a 'neutral arbiter' in an inter-communal conflict, for example, can be found as an influence in deploying the security forces, in its self-declared role as a political medi-ator between the two communities, and as an explanation for failing to address the issue of inequality in the area of social and economic policy.

The division of the strategic tradition into different elements made some contradictions in British government thinking obvious. For exam-ple, whereas London's ideas about 'Ireland as a place apart' dictated that the constitutional instrument had to be used in order to keep Northern Ireland at maximum distance to the British mainland because the Irish were seen as 'irrational', Westminster's political calculus assumed that the tenets of British political culture were transferable to the province. Likewise, the British government accepted that the sectarian dynamics in Northern Ireland would determine the access to political power, but it was not prepared to apply the same line of thinking to the economic instrument. Most fundamentally, perhaps, the British government fuelled constitutional ambiguity and instability by making Northern Ireland a conditional part of the United Kingdom, yet politically, London sought to introduce a system of government that required trust and stability for both sides to be willing to share power.

The description of the different elements of the strategic tradition showed that there was little in British government thinking on Northern Ireland that merits the term 'grand design'. On the contrary, it assembled a number of ideological strands from different sources in order to suit the perceived circumstances, and – with the possible excep-tion of the economic instrument – it rarely looked beyond the short or medium term. It can therefore be described as 'managerial', that is, prag-matic within the existing ideological and constitutional parameters. Despite the obvious importance of the constitutional question to the nature of the conflict, and although Westminster thought of Northern Ireland as a natural constituent of Ireland rather than an integral part of the United Kingdom, there was no strong inclination to take up the con-stitutional issue, or to formulate a clear ideological preference on whether the province should belong to a united Ireland or remain with the United Kingdom. In relation to the 'big questions', the attitude of the British government was largely agnostic, and the formulation of strategy was therefore susceptible to the immediate impact of events 'on the ground'. As Rees put it: '[I]t is wrong to look at the many problems in Northern Ireland as if there were some ready-made textbook solution. What the government will do is to respond positively to a developing situation.'[90] This approach allowed for flexibility, yet it could equally lead to a lack of overall consistency and perpetual empiricism. As P. O'Malley once pointed out: 'None of the parties to the conflict trusts Britain, and with good cause. Because she will not declare herself, no one knows where she stands.'[91]

The value system that has been outlined in this chapter is not static. It will therefore be of interest to find out how stringent certain ideas were implemented in particular periods of London's engagement, and why some assumptions featured less prominently in the formulation of British government strategy than others. In fact, finding out how and in what way British strategic thought in relation to Northern Ireland has evolved in the course of the 1969–98 period is the main purpose of this study, and it will be pursued in the following chapters of this work.

The Evolution of British
Government Strategy in
Northern Ireland

3
Avoiding Responsibility? London on the Defensive, 1969–72

The years 1969–72 represented a period of rapid, if not dramatic, change. In August 1969, London – in its first significant intervention – agreed to deploy the Army to Northern Ireland in order to prevent inter-sectarian violence. Within two and a half years, the troops themselves had become the targets, and Westminster thought it necessary to abolish the structures of self-government and assume the direct rule of Northern Ireland.

The border is not an issue? The emergence of an Irish dimension

In early August 1969, there had been pressure on the British government to abolish the Home Rule structures in Northern Ireland and replace them with the direct rule of the province from London. Both within and outside the United Kingdom, Westminster was increasingly held liable for a situation for which it perceived itself not to be responsible.[1] Even so, rather than exercising the supreme authority of the United Kingdom government under Section 75 of the Government of Ireland Act (1920) (i.e. to take over the government of the province), the government concluded that 'it would be better to avoid direct intervention'.[2] At this point, British Cabinet members still believed it possible to 'use the Northern Ireland Government as agents'.[3]

Given London's assumptions about Ireland as 'a place apart', the decision to keep Stormont in place was well within the traditional framework of the British strategic tradition. First, there was a feeling amongst Cabinet members that they did not possess the necessary knowledge about Northern Ireland to take over political responsibility. Home Secretary Callaghan (with whom the responsibility for Northern

Ireland lay) confessed that most MPs 'knew less about Northern Ireland than we knew about our distant colonies, on the far side of the earth',[4] and Denis Healey, the Defence Secretary, admitted that 'we shall be as blind men leading the blind if we have to go in there knowing nothing about the place'.[5] According to Prime Minister Wilson, this had resulted from 'years of neglect'[6] under the Tories, but it had actually continued under his Labour government. In fact, as shown in previous chapters, mutual neglect was the foundation on which the post-1920 constitutional relationship between Northern Ireland and Great Britain had rested. Second, most members of the Cabinet conceptualised the conflict in historical terms, and one lesson that the government thought to have learned from Anglo-Irish history was that British interventions in Ireland caused more harm than good. The assumption was that – once politically drawn into Ireland – the British government would take over an open-ended commitment in a conflict to which there was no solution. The British press analysed the conflict in similar terms, and the newspapers were full of reminders that 'the English [might] have long since forgotten all about the Coercion Acts, the Irish revolution and the Black and Tans. The Irish have not'.[7] At the Cabinet meeting on 19 August 1969, Healey therefore cautioned the demand for greater political intervention. Tony Benn, another Cabinet member, noted that 'although ... [Healey] had sympathy with the Catholics, he had to point out that ... we should be once again in the 1911–14 situation' (see Chapter 1).[8] Third, and most importantly, there was genuine fear that the majority community would resist the abolition of Stormont, and that Protestant extremists, such as the followers of the Reverend Ian Paisley, would launch a civil war if the government was seen as giving in to the Catholics. Crossman, a member of the Cabinet committee on Northern Ireland, noted: 'Callaghan and Healey reminded us that ... the Protestants are the majority and we can't afford to alienate them'.[9] Radical constitutional action, such as a unilateral declaration of withdrawal from Northern Ireland, was therefore ruled out. As Benn observed: 'Britain cannot walk out of Ulster entirely, although we had considered it as an alternative ... [Michael Stewart, the Foreign Secretary] thought that awful as it would be to take over responsibility, it would be less awful than walking out.'[10]

Accordingly, Westminster's constitutional response in 1969 is best understood as an attempt to revitalise the Home Rule structures which had allowed the British government to abdicate its political responsibility for the province without raising the question of withdrawal. Westminster's objective was to restore a reformed *status quo ante*, so that the troops could be withdrawn and Northern Ireland be re-insulated from Great Britain. This strategy was set out in the so-called Downing Street Declaration (DSD), which was agreed by Wilson and Northern Ireland Prime Minister James Chichester-Clark on 19 August 1969. It affirmed that the border was 'not an issue', and that Northern Ireland would 'not cease to be part of the United Kingdom without the consent of the people of Northern Ireland'.[11] Furthermore, the Home Rule parliament at Stormont would henceforth 'take into account at all times the views of Her Majesty's Government in the United Kingdom'.[12] The only substantial transfer of power – the Army's General Officer Commanding (GOC) assumed control of the local security forces – came about as a consequence of the troop deployment. The need for greater formal control was substituted for a mixture of public commitments and threats. London promised to protect the Catholic minority from further violence, and it guaranteed that Catholics would be treated fairly by the Northern Ireland government. Conversely, the Stormont government was publicly put 'on probation', that is, the continued existence of the Home Rule institutions depended on it carrying through a programme of reform which ensured 'British standards of citizenship'.

As it turned out, the government's 1969 strategy was impractical, irresolute and inconsistent as a means of providing a durable solution. The decision to allow the Unionist government to reform itself demonstrated that London's overriding priority was to maintain the existing constitutional relationship and avoid a possible 'Protestant backlash'. In practice, though, Stormont lacked the determination to carry through an agenda that would have limited its power, or which could be seen as such by its hardline Unionist supporters. As a result of Westminster's retreatist attitude towards Northern Ireland as well as the relatively unchallenged position the Unionists had thus been in until 1969, the Stormont government had come to define the relationship with London as a zero-sum game in which any attempt to influence the way in which Northern Ireland was governed was interpreted as outside interference, particularly when it appeared to benefit the Catholic minority.[13] In this regard, the British government's threat (i.e to abolish Stormont altogether) was not very effective as a means of coercing good behaviour. The Northern Ireland government was well aware of London's reluctance to take over the government of the province, and the press (rightly) assumed that Westminster would take this step 'only as a last resort'.[14] The threshold for intervention had been set very high, and as there were no lesser sanctions with which Stormont could be coerced, Chichester-Clark and his colleagues had considerable scope to water down Westminster's demands. Simply put, Westminster threatened 'massive retaliation' when a more flexible instrument would have been needed, and the commitment the DSD had given to the Catholic community was consequently difficult to carry out. As a substitute, Callaghan embarked on a series of high-profile visits to Northern Ireland, where he was widely perceived as a 'major-league performer showing the parish-pump locals how to run their affairs'.[15] This suited his personal ambitions and showed the British public that the government was 'doing something' about Northern Ireland, yet at the same time it undermined the authority of the Unionist government. It thus weakened the instrument it was supposed to revitalise, and it contributed to the fragmentation of the Unionist Party whose leaders, such as the then Minister for Development, Brian Faulkner, despised 'these rather superficial circuses and messianic visits'.[16] In addition, the continued existence of Stormont as the only source of political power in the province maintained an asymmetry in military and political control which provided fertile soil on which the national question was to resurface. Whilst telling the Army to act impartially, the British government tied its political authority to the Unionist government which had been made responsible for most of the grievances the civil rights movement of 1967 and 1968 had been protesting against. As a consequence, Westminster compromised its role as an 'honest broker' in what had started as an inter-communal conflict.

From June 1970, the Conservative government under Prime Minister Heath and Home Secretary Maudling continued to operate within the DSD framework, albeit in a dramatically changed environment. Carefully preserving the myth that the Conservatives bear full responsibility for the tragic events that followed, Callaghan has since argued that if the 'change which I initiated had been followed up vigorously after 1970 when I left office ... the worst of the troubles might have been avoided.'[17] Arguably, and contrary to his claim, it was precisely *because* Callaghan's strategy was maintained that the overall situation further worsened. Like Callaghan, Maudling hinted at Direct Rule if the Stormont government did not continue the course of reform, and he reaffirmed Westminster's role as a protector of the minority.[18] However, the new government was now faced with a military campaign that had unfolded an entirely different dynamic. The IRA had succeeded in bringing about a repressive reaction on behalf of the security forces, which gradually exposed the fatal imbalance of political and military control that had been formalised in the DSD, and it skilfully escalated its campaign up to the point when, in early

1971, it felt confident enough to launch an all-out offensive against what it perceived to be the 'British forces of occupation'. In addition, the constitutional Nationalists of the SDLP withdrew their representatives from the Stormont parliament in July 1971, thus depriving the Home Rule structures of any remaining legitimacy. On the Protestant side, London needed to acknowledge that the ruling Unionist Party was gradually disintegrating under the conflicting pressures from Westminster and the party's more radical wing, the latter of which appeared likely to assume power and establish 'a regime whose policies we [the British government] could not accept'.[19] With almost 15 000 British troops in the province and growing discontent about the crisis management policy of the British government, the projected costs of proceeding along the lines of the 1969 strategy had therefore clearly outweighed the assumed benefits. To some extent, the existing Home Rule arrangement had lost its value, and indeed, even before the failure of internment without trial in early August, the Cabinet had con-cluded that 'the situation was such ... that we now had seriously to contemplate the possibility that we might be compelled to institute direct rule'.[20]

The failure of internment without trial compelled London to abandon its 1969 strategy, which rested on the ideas expressed in the DSD. For the first time, London acknowledged that 'past policy on Northern Ireland is in ruins', and that 'a new initiative is imperative'.[21] On 2 September 1971, the Central Policy Review Staff supplied Heath with a list of alternative courses of action. It included the re-partition of the province, the joint government of the province by Dublin and London, and a devolved 'coalition' government between representatives of minority and majority.[22] The re-partition of Northern Ireland was instantly eliminated from the list, as it 'would prove impracticable in a city such as Belfast, where the two communities were closely intermingled; and it would encounter the most bitter opposition'.[23] Joint government was believed to be unacceptable to the majority, as it implied not only the abolition of Stormont (as in Direct Rule), but also the sharing of sovereignty with the Republic of Ireland. The prospects of a coalition – or power-sharing – government were judged to be unrealistic given the conflicting national aspirations of the two communities (see below). However, in a crucial change of approach, London also made it clear that modifications of the province's internal constitution would now be seen as a separate matter from the guarantee to maintain Northern Ireland's overall constitutional position as part of the United Kingdom. On 21 September, the Cabinet concluded that 'it was important to distinguish between the constitutional status of Northern Ireland...and the constitutional arrangement *within* the Province...[T]here was no aspect of the constitutional arrangement which could not properly be brought under review' (emphasis added).[24]

There are some indications that this change had been caused by the growing influence of the Irish government. In London's view, the decision to intensify the co-operation with Dublin was nothing but a natural response. Heath believed that it was healthy for 'the two parts of Ireland' to maintain strong economic, social and cultural links, and he interpreted the previous absence of such co-operation as 'a major factor in the...lack of understanding between the two communities within Northern Ireland'.[25] Yet, in addition to instinct, the intended *rapprochement* was determined by sheer necessity. After the failure of internment, the Irish government was the only representative of constitutional Nationalism that continued to communicate to the British government. Thus, if London wanted to succeed in re-engaging the minority, it needed to win over the Dublin government as an ally – particularly since Dublin's interests were not perceived as being substantially different from one's own. Far from acting upon its constitutional imperative of furthering the 're-integration' of the national territory, the Irish government had been anxious to stop the conflict from spilling over into the Republic of Ireland, and Prime Minister Jack Lynch was praised by London as 'exerting as much influence towards moderation as the political situation in the Republic allowed him'.[26] Whilst some of Lynch's speeches undoubtedly aimed at appeasing Nationalist sentiment, Dublin had – in practice – pursued a reformist agenda on behalf of the minority. Its objective was to bring about the removal of Stormont, and to establish a channel that formalised a say for the Irish government in Northern Ireland affairs.[27] Crucially, Lynch had also started to lobby in favour of power-sharing when London still considered it sufficient to include a small number of prominent Catholics in an otherwise unreformed Stormont.[28]

It should have come as no surprise, therefore, that the Anglo-Irish summit on 6 September 1971 was followed by a series of significant changes in rhetoric as well as substance. One such change concerned the gradual co-option of power-sharing as a way of accommodating the Nationalist minority (see below). Another related to the explicit expression of British neutrality. In contrast to Maudling, who had believed in the strong reaffirmation of Northern Ireland's constitutional status as part of the United Kingdom, Lynch managed to impress upon Heath that 'the only way to bring back the disaffected Northern Catholics into public life was to give them even the slightest ray of hope about the British attitude to reunification'.[29] Accordingly, the British government rephrased the consent principle in favour of Nationalist aspirations, thus making it obvious that there was no principal objection to Irish unity on the British side. On 15 November, Heath thus became 'the first British Prime Minister to declare that Britain has no selfish interest in Northern Ireland'.[30] At the Lord Mayor of London's annual banquet, he declared:

> Many Catholics in Northern Ireland would like to see Northern Ireland unified with the South. That is understandable. It is legitimate that they should seek to further that aim by democratic and constitutional means. If at some future date the majority of the people in Northern Ireland want unification and express that desire in the appropriate constitutional manner, I do not believe any British Government would stand in the way ... .[31]

Two weeks later, the Home Secretary reinforced this message by giving an even stronger affirmation of British neutrality. In the House of Commons, Maudling declared:

> [I]f, by agreement, the North and the South should at some time decide to come together in a United Ireland, if, by agreement, this should be their wish, then not only would we not obstruct to that solution but, I am sure, the whole British people would warmly welcome it.[32]

Arguably, this statement almost abandoned the idea of British neutrality. It is important to note, however, that Maudling's somewhat surprising change in rhetoric indicated no fundamental shift in British policy. As he explained:

> The issue ... is not the border because everyone knows that the border will not be changed in the foreseeable future ... The real issue of politics in Northern Ireland is how, within the existing boundaries, two communities can live together. That is what really matters.[33]

While it is easy to date back the 'greening' of British rhetoric, it is almost impossible to determine the exact instance, or occasion, on which the issue of suspending the Home Rule arrangement emerged. What seems clear, however, is that it was no immediate reaction to the events on

'Bloody Sunday'. As shown above, the government had started to consider the idea seriously in the summer of 1971, and it remained implicit in many of the constitutional ideas that were formulated in the months thereafter. Moreover, one may argue that the immediate chain of events, which triggered the abolition of Stormont in late March 1972, originated in a memorandum by Maudling, which was submitted to Cabinet members as late as 3 March 1972. It argued that 'there is [no] possibility of persuading Catholics to go back to the old system', and that 'the dangers of continuing with the present policy are now greater than the dangers of trying to make a new start'.[34] Outlining the proposed initiative, Maudling believed it to be essential that the British government reasserted full control of law and order, not least because there was little 'chance now of getting the minority community … to accept that the administration of law and order by Stormont [was] … impartial'.[35] He also recommended a Northern Ireland Cabinet 'with minority representation chosen by the minority', thus going significantly further in the direction of power-sharing than some of his earlier ideas (see below). Maudling clearly understood that these demands were almost impossible for the Faulkner government to fulfil. Indeed, he pointed out that 'Mr Faulkner himself has openly said that he would not carry on if law and order were transferred from Stormont to Westminster'.[36] Hence, whilst hoping that the abolition of Stormont could be avoided, he started to make the case for doing so:

> [T]here is a lot to be said for a clean break with the old system and an interim period of government while the new system is being worked out and implemented … Distrust of Mr Faulkner is so widespread, not only in the minority community, that it is difficult to see how the necessary consultations and agreement could be achieved while his Government remained in power.[37]

Even so, Cabinet support for the abolition of Stormont remained far from enthusiastic. This was partly because members of the government were reluctant to create the impression that London had conceded one of the IRA's major demands, but also because it was considered to be 'penalising the Protestant community, which professed a strong loyalty to the Crown and had behaved with commendable restraint in recent months'.[38] Most significantly, though, the British government was anxious to avoid what became known as 'the Protestant backlash'. There were, for example, persistent worries about the loyalty of the Northern Ireland Civil Service and the Royal Ulster Constabulary (RUC).[39] Even as late as 23 March 1972 – one day after Faulkner had rejected the reform proposals – some members of the Cabinet hoped that the end of the Home Rule arrangement could be avoided, arguing that 'the Unionist reactions … might be so violent as to provoke a state of virtually civil war, while the IRA might be provoked into extending their campaign of terrorism in Great Britain'.[40] The 'civil war scenario', which has traditionally prevented the British government from abandoning the province altogether, had thus prolonged the life of the Stormont government by some weeks. It was equally clear, though, that the price of maintaining the Home Rule arrangement had by now become unacceptable, and that radical change was unavoidable for London's wider aim of re-insulating Northern Ireland from the British body politic to be achieved.

A swift exit? From peace-keeping to counterinsurgency

Like London's constitutional approach to the province, the government's military strategy underwent dramatic changes in the 1969–72 period. In 1969, the supposed lessons of history dominated the minds of the Cabinet, and these were that British soldiers could do no good on Irish soil. Wilson believed that '[i]n Roman Catholic circles British troops, recalling Black and Tan memories, could be evocative', and the decision to introduce them 'would unite both sides against them'.[41] London's military strategy before 15 August 1969 was therefore guided by its desire to avoid the deployment of British troops, to agree to it only as a last resort and to make clear to the Stormont government that it had to exhaust its own resources before any request for British troops could be considered. This approach proved highly ineffective. It contributed to a further erosion of the local security forces' credibility, and it thus made the eventual introduction of the Army inevitable. On 14 August, London eventually agreed to Stormont's request to send British troops 'in aid of the civil power'.

Although the British soldiers were hailed by the Catholics on their arrival, London had convinced itself that the peace could not last for long. As early as 19 August, Healey warned that 'there were already signs that the honeymoon was ending'.[42] As soon as the troops were on the ground, the government's priority was therefore to ensure their swift withdrawal. In Cabinet, Callaghan stated that '[t]he conduct of the troops had been exemplary, but they were not equipped or trained to do a long-term policing job … This made it all the more urgent to press on with the reorganisation of the regular police forces.'[43] In the meantime, the troops were supposed to act 'firm and cool and fair',[44] avoiding anything that could compromise their perceived position as non-partisan outsiders to an inter-communal conflict. In other words, they were to act as peacekeepers who helped cooling down a situation of civil disorder that had temporarily got out of control. Accordingly, one soldier remembers that '[w]e were told to regard our role as the "Midas" touch – minimum force, impartiality, discipline, alertness and security'.[45] In practice, 'minimum force' often translated into 'minimum action', and indeed the newly appointed (English) head of the RUC, Arthur Young, described his approach as 'softly, softly'.[46] This was particularly true when it was thought that the use of force would cause disruption, or that it would make the security forces unpopular with one or the other community. Protestant marches as well as paramilitary funerals were allowed to go ahead, and the troops failed to establish a presence in the so-called 'No Go' areas of Derry-City and West-Belfast where the security forces only operated sporadically and the IRA was therefore free to organise.

The disastrous consequences of London's determination to ensure a 'swift exit' become obvious if we examine the government's response to the emergence of the IRA. By the end of October 1969, violence on the streets had almost completely died down. Callaghan noted, accordingly, that the atmosphere in the Home Office became 'much more relaxed'.[47] It looked as if time had come to begin scaling down the military presence, and in late January 1970, three of the eight major Army units that had originally been sent to Northern Ireland were withdrawn.[48] In an early chronology of the conflict, an American journalist observed:

> The Labor government appeared to some to proceed on the assumption that its problems in Ulster were solved, or nearly so... When Oliver Wright, Harold Wilson's representative in Northern Ireland, ended his tour of duty there in March, he announced at a press conference: 'Cheer up. Things are better than you think'.[49]

However, from early 1970, the conflict started to change. In the hitherto peaceful Catholic areas of Derry-City and Belfast, riots became a feature of everyday life, and in contrast to the months before, the rioters would turn against the army as soon as the soldiers arrived on the scene. The Provisional IRA had only split from the Official IRA in January, and it clearly needed time to recruit and organise. Nevertheless, it was obvious that Provisionals intended to start a military campaign since they had broken from the Officials because they felt that the Official IRA had neglected military means in favour of parliamentary politics. The strategy of the Provisional IRA (henceforth referred to as IRA) entailed the gradual escalation in the use of the military instrument, namely, to establish itself as a defensive force in the Catholic areas, then to retaliate to individual acts of violence and finally to launch an offensive against the 'British forces of occupation'.[50] It was therefore in the IRA's interest to maintain some tension, and to re-direct the anger of the Catholic youths towards the British troops. In strategic terms, the IRA provided the co-ordinating role Schelling considers essential in the successful formation of riots.[51] Accordingly, in mid-1970, the president of Provisional *Sinn Fein* was quoted as saying that 'his organization is not trying to foment violence; they are trying to control it, so that when it occurs it will not be wholly useless'.[52]

The British government, on the other hand, preferred to rationalise the renewed outbreak of violence as a series of isolated incidents with few (if any) political implications – a combination of excessive drinking, long evenings, boredom and 'a taste of excitement' on behalf of the Catholic youths.[53] In early April, when some protestors confronted the troops in a three-day-long riot on the Ballymurphy estate in West-Belfast, the significance of this event was simply shrugged off. In parliament, Callaghan stated:

> As to sinister elements, I have seen what has been said about this, but I know of no new factions in Northern Ireland that did not exist before; that is the IRA, who talk a great deal in many voices, and the Ulster Volunteer Force ... [T]here is no new sinister conspiracy of which I am aware ....[54]

London conceptualised the renewed violence as a mere bump on the road towards eventual disengagement, and even though this 'outburst of activity'[55] (Callaghan) implied that the withdrawal of the troops needed to be postponed for some time, it did not raise fundamental questions about the nature of the conflict. In that sense, the decision to impose a 34-hour curfew in the Lower Falls area of West-Belfast in July 1970 represented an aberration rather than an indication of change in Westminster's military strategy. After the end of the curfew, the peace-keeping approach was resumed and the policy of troop reductions was continued, so that by the end of the year, the number of regular forces in Northern Ireland had fallen to the lowest level in more than a year. Only in November, the Commander Land Forces (CLF), recognised that the Army was 'now facing organised terrorism', and that the IRA's campaign would result in a 'prolonged campaign of counterinsurgency'.[56]

Even so, elements within the MoD continued to believe that peace was only months away. Instead of refocusing the military effort, a committee 'to establish the allocation of responsibilities ... in the event of a return to normality' was set up as late as December.[57] It took until February 1971 for Carrington to acknowledge that 'the recent riots represented a new phase in the campaign of violence. The disorder was no longer a merely intercommunal matter; and a situation approaching armed conflict was developing'.[58]

The contradictory dynamics of employing the peace-keeping approach in an insurgency situation were obvious. Peace-keeping dictated that the Army should use every means available to stop riots, just like a police force. In Northern Ireland, this meant that whenever the IRA wanted to engage the state's security forces, the troops were anxious to provide an opportunity. As a consequence, the Army was drawn into a vicious circle of attacks and reprisals that increased the sort of violence the presence of the troops was originally meant to stop. From London's point of view, the threat to shoot petrol bombers, the use of rubber bullets and Stormont's Criminal Justice Act (Northern Ireland) 1970 (which included mandatory sentences for taking part in riots) were meant as deterrents, ensuring that the principle of 'minimum force' could be preserved.[59] In reality, though, those measures sent shockwaves through the Catholic community, and they helped the IRA to implant itself into the Catholic community.[60]

Once the government had accepted that it was faced with an organised insurgency, there seemed to be a shift towards military aims. Maudling, for example, now declared that this was 'no time for large political initiatives'.[61] Even so, the British government recognised that there was no point in employing the military instrument against Catholics in a way that would have rendered the objective of reconciling the minority with Stormont impossible. As Lord Blaniel, who was a minister at the MoD, stated: 'Our success ... will depend on our ability ... to eliminate the hard core of terrorists without at the same time drawing the Army into conflict with a large section of the [Catholic] community.'[62] In that sense, the security forces' campaign was never thought to be unlimited in the sense that *any* means would have justified the end of defeating the IRA. Replying to a suggestion in a *Times* leader that the security forces should 'employ the full apparatus of terror' against the IRA, Maudling stated: 'Do they want us to go around murdering people? ... To talk about using the methods of the terrorists against the terrorists seems to me very strange.'[63]

However, if political imperatives remained implicit, it was obvious that London needed to continue its efforts to maintain Unionist support for the Stormont government. The authority of Unionist leaders had already suffered from London's intervention, and there was considerable grassroots pressure on the Northern Ireland government to adopt a more repressive posture towards the IRA. In other words, if Westminster wanted Stormont and the Unionist Party in its present form to survive (and at that point, it clearly did), it had to provide the Northern Ireland government with opportunities to be 'tough' on the IRA. The fixation on preserving the existing constitutional arrangement, and the need to address the contradictory pressures that resulted from this postulate, made it impossible for Westminster to formulate a coherent military strategy.

One way of escaping the dilemma was for the government to distance itself – politically as well as physically – from the execution of security policy. This tendency could be seen in London's attempts to accelerate the 'swift exit' of British forces. The Ulster Defence Regiment (UDR), a locally recruited regiment of the British Army, had been established in early 1970 as a non-sectarian replacement for the exclusively Protestant Ulster Special Constabulary (USC). At the time of its inception, it was believed that 'the Government will allow the regiment to remain under strength rather than become overwhelmingly Protestant in character'.[64] In 1971, though, Westminster's priority had changed. Ian Gilmour, who was a minister at the MoD, stated that 'we are not bound by the previous government's assurances ... We certainly will not hold back recruitment.'[65] Accordingly, the strength of the UDR almost quadrupled in the following two years, reaching its historical peak of 8476 (mostly part-time) members at the end of 1972 (see Appendix).

Furthermore, London now considered it sufficient to declare the principle of legality as the only guideline in relation to the level of force, and to leave any operational decisions about the execution of the military instrument to the Army.[66] From a British perspective, this approach had the obvious advantage of identifying some common ground between the government, 'moderate' Unionists and 'ordinary' Catholics, all of whom were thought to have little interest in IRA-style 'kangaroo courts, vigilante law and danger'.[67] However, the postulate of legality was considerably vague, and its tactical implications were difficult to determine. The principal piece of legislation under which the security forces operated, the Special Powers Act (NI) 1922 (SPA), and its wide-ranging powers (for instance, stop and search, the imposition of curfews, internment without trial) were not seen as legitimate by the minority. The principle of 'minimum force' had never been translated into simple operating procedures. The so-called 'Yellow Card' outlined instructions for opening fire, but it was subject to many revisions, and thus perceived as too abstract by many soldiers.[68] There was a flood of ambiguous (and sometimes rather bizarre) Army statements, such as the declaration that 'we are not going to shoot at stone-throwers on sight, but the situation could arise in which someone … in a crowd throwing stones … would face the risk of being shot'.[69] In practice, it was therefore largely for the troops on the ground to resolve the dilemma of what level of force was appropriate in a given situation. In many cases, this turned out to be far less than what would have been allowed by the law, yet in others, the IRA succeeded in provoking the troops into using excessive force against the civilian population, thus increasing the alienation of the minority.

London's operational problems were aggravated by the lack of accurate intelligence. It had become almost impossible for the security forces to differentiate between ordinary Catholics, youthful rioters, and members of the IRA. Although the files of the RUC Special Branch contained some information on older Republicans, the massive influx of young Catholics, who had only been politicised by the events of 1969, went largely unnoticed by the security forces. The absence of accurate information resulted in large scale cordon-and-search operations which alienated the population and achieved relatively little in terms of finding the insurgents. Things were made worse by the continued existence of the 'no go' areas in Belfast and Derry-City where the Army would not operate without the approval of so-called community leaders who often turned out to be the commanders of local IRA units.[70] Unsurprisingly, Carrington pointed out that '[t]he Army in Northern Ireland has all the weaponry and manpower it needs', and that it needed more intelligence, not more troops.[71]

The introduction of internment without trial on 9 August 1971 demonstrated the shortcomings of London's strategy. Faulkner, who had succeeded Chichester-Clark as Northern Ireland Prime Minister in March, advanced the idea of internment as soon as he had taken office. London's response to the proposal had nothing to do with the potential military advantages of internment, but was determined solely by whether it would help Faulkner to fend off grassroots pressure and make the survival of the Stormont government more likely. The Cabinet concluded that 'before [Direct Rule] was adopted it might well be right to agree that the Northern Ireland Government should invoke their powers of internment'.[72] In public, the issue was portrayed as 'more a decision of practice than of principle' which depended on the Army's assessment as to whether it would be a positive contribution to the counterinsurgency effort.[73] In reality, though, the Army's objections were simply ignored. The GOC, Lieutenant General Harry Tuzo, was strictly opposed to the idea because he believed internment to be ineffective if it was not introduced in the Republic of Ireland at the same time. The government, on the other hand, determined that 'the decision should not depend solely on the response of the Government of the Republic'.[74] In the end, no efforts were made to approach Dublin, and the plans went ahead regardless. When internment was agreed between Stormont and Westminster, on 5 August, it was treated as a security measure with no political implications. Neither was there any serious attempt to accompany it by a political initiative that would have balanced its negative effects in the eyes of the minority, nor did Westminster consider it necessary to communicate the decision to the Catholics.[75] In fact, it was one week *after* its introduction when the Cabinet acknowledged 'that it was now necessary to take some political initiative'.[76]

Internment marked the complete alienation of the Catholic community from the existing structures of government. Instead of defeating the Republicans, it provided the IRA with an opportunity to escalate its campaign: in the six months before internment, there were 25 deaths; in the following six months, there were 185.[77] As predicted by Tuzo, the leaders of the IRA had avoided arrest by fleeing across the border, and due to poor intelligence, it turned out that many internees had no connections with any paramilitary organisation at all. Out of the 1590 people who had been interned between 9 August and 15 December, only 18 were eventually charged with criminal offences.[78] In addition, the use of 'tough' interrogation techniques by the Army was followed by public outrage on both sides of the Irish Sea, prompting the so-called Compton inquiry as well as an investigation by the European Commission of Human Rights.[79] The controversial methods had been employed in previous (colonial) campaigns, and their use in Northern Ireland could have been avoided if London had required the Army to seek approval for every major tactical decision. While there now seems to be some evidence that Maudling and Carrington had sanctioned the use of certain techniques, including the use of methods 'to deprive [the internees] from obtaining any exact sense of time and location',[80] Maudling's parliamentary statements imply that no extensive previous consultation had taken place.[81] Instead, the government appeared to have stuck to the policy of military absenteeism that had been formulated by Maudling in late July: 'The methods used by the Army in Northern Ireland are the responsibility of the GOC.'[82]

In many accounts of British policy, the tragic events of 30 January 1972, when the Army killed 13 Catholic protesters in Derry-City, are portrayed as a 'watershed' with 'profound repercussions for British policy'.[83] Yet, while there can be little doubt that Bloody Sunday was to heighten the government's scepticism *vis-à-vis* military solutions, the lesson that military might alone was counterproductive in the existing strategic environment had been learned by the British government some time before. Immediately after the failure of internment, the British government recognised that – within the strategic parameters set by its overall strategy and the technical capabilities of the security forces – the IRA could not be defeated. In Tuzo's words, the IRA's military campaign was 'an activity that could be carried on until they choose to desist finally from what they are doing'.[84] Under the given circumstances, the notion of defeating the IRA as a *pre*-condition for political progress, was no longer viable, and Maudling stated – accordingly – that 'even though violence continues, discussion about a political solution should begin now'.[85] He also made it clear that London now viewed the military instrument as a means of bringing about 'an acceptable level' of violence,[86] namely, one which facilitated political progress and was conducive to the new British objective of facilitating a cross-community settlement (see later). Significantly, these ideas were to form the ideological paradigm of British security policy in the decades to come.

Too little, too late? Abandoning the Stormont system

Like London's military approach, its use of the political instrument was initially thought to be subordinate to the wider aim of preserving the constitutional relationship between Great Britain and Northern Ireland. In August 1969, the military intervention raised the question as to what extent the British government should insist on changes to the political system in Northern Ireland. Within the Cabinet, there was no sympathy for the 'Orangemen', and it was clearly felt that the civil disorder had primarily arisen because of the supposed onslaught of Protestant extremists.[87] At the crucial meeting on 19 August, the Cabinet concluded: 'There was a good deal of corroboration for the view that the Catholics had acted largely in self-defence, and there was little evidence to support the view of the Northern Ireland Government that the IRA were mainly responsible.'[88]

In strategic terms, the government's political strategy in 1969 needs to be understood in the context of London's wider aim of preserving the *status quo ante* with devolved structures and a Unionist government at its centre. Despite the Cabinet's goodwill, there were therefore firm limits on what amount of reform could be implemented. Some reform was necessary to make Stormont acceptable to the minority; if reform appeared to question the objective of Westminster's strategy, however, it ran counter to its purpose. It was agreed that 'we must push Chichester-Clark only as far as he wanted to go'.[89] The actual priorities of the government were thus quite different from what it claimed them to be. According to Callaghan: 'I said I wanted to be a catalyst [for peace, friendship and equality] ... At the back of my mind, of course, I still did not want Britain to get more embroiled in Northern Ireland than we had to.'[90]

To the British government, this strategy appeared feasible because Westminster's strategic calculus failed to account for the zero-sum dynamics of politics in a deeply divided society. Despite all its reservations about 'deep-seated passions' and 'atavistic violence', the British government believed that its intervention would make it possible to inject the supposed virtues of British political culture – moderation, fairness, and 'British common sense' – into the province: if the government created political conditions similar to those on the mainland, people in Northern Ireland would act accordingly; if one guaranteed that 'there is in Northern Ireland as in the rest of the United Kingdom, a common standard of citizenship',[91] if one helped to remove mutual fears, and if one facilitated the communication between the two communities, the vast majority of both Protestants and Catholics would become willing to identify common interests and strike compromises for the sake of a peaceful co-existence. Accordingly, the government believed that the sectarian divide would gradually be replaced by what Crossman thought of as 'sensible, conservative, Northern Ireland politics'.[92] London's role was that of a mediator to assist in bringing about a 'new contract'[93] (Callaghan) between the Catholics and Protestants. There was no need for significant changes to the power structure in Northern Ireland, and the possibility of a 'broadly-based government' was therefore ruled out.[94]

London's 1969 agenda of political reforms corresponded neatly with the findings of the Cameron commission, which had been set up to investigate the disturbances of the previous year (although it was published only in September, Callaghan had had access to the final report by mid-August).[95] Its conclusions were that the Catholics felt a sense of continuing injustice due to political and social grievances, particularly in relation to the allocation of housing, jobs and the manipulation of electoral boundaries. The Protestants, on the other hand, had acted out of uncertainty about the constitutional status of the province as part of the United Kingdom.[96] Consequently, the DSD stated that the border was 'not an issue', and it affirmed that 'every citizen of Northern

Ireland is entitled to the same equality of treatment and freedom of discrimination ... irrespective of political views and religion' (thereby making the British government a 'guarantor' of British standards of civil rights).[97] After further meetings between the two governments and the appointment of various working parties, a series of new measures and legal safeguards were announced, for example a law against the incitement of religious hatred, a Commissioner for Complaints and a Ministry for Community Relations. Also, to some extent, the British government had understood the outbreak of civil disturbances as a failure of policing, and the swift implementation of the so-called Hunt recommendations attempted to rectify some of the perceived problems.[98] The RUC was to be made a 'British' police force, that is, unarmed and under the guidance of a civilian panel; the exclusively Protestant police reserve, the USC, was to be disbanded, and a new locally recruited part-time force was to be established under the command of the British Army. This force was to become the UDR.[99]

To demonstrate why London's 1969 political strategy was misconceived, one needs to understand how it was received by the two communities. To the Catholics, the 1969 reform programme appeared to indicate that Westminster had tipped the sectarian balance in favour of them. The leaders of the minority signalled their intention to work the system; some of them even encouraged their fellow Catholics to join the RUC and the newly founded UDR.[100] In October 1969, Callaghan declared proudly that '[t]here is now more working together amongst the leaders of the communities ... [and t]he minority is beginning to work with the State much more than it has done hitherto'.[101] On the other side of the sectarian divide, however, Chichester-Clark had come under fierce attacks from within his party. From a Protestant perspective, Westminster had simply intervened on behalf of the Catholics, and the reform of the security apparatus was seen as little more than taking away the only reliable defence against what was perceived as Irish-Catholic expansionism. Instead of softening attitudes, London's intervention had thus fuelled Protestant uncertainty. Consequently, the Stormont government was not merely under pressure from Westminster to implement the reform programme; it also felt the need to assert its independence if it wanted to retain grassroots support and party unity. In practice, agreed reforms were watered down or delayed when it came to introducing the necessary legislation in the Northern Ireland parliament.

By October 1969, Unionist disunity had become a more significant (and immediate) threat to the strategic objective of the British government than Catholic discontent. Since a more intransigent leader of the Unionist

Party was believed to make the introduction of Direct Rule inevitable, London's attention shifted away from effecting political change towards reassuring the Protestants and strengthening the 'moderates' within the Unionist Party. In marked contrast to his later claim that only the Heath government had stopped to press for reforms (see above), Callaghan himself announced as soon as October 1969 that the Stormont government 'has done its part ... [It] has carried out to the full the agreement in relation to the attempt to remove discrimination'.[102] In Cabinet, he made it very clear that 'the overriding consideration so far as we were concerned must remain the importance of refraining from any action which would weaken the position of the Northern Ireland Prime Minister'.[103]

Instead of producing a momentum towards reconciliation and the creation of a 'moderate' majority, the sectarian dynamics in the province had effectively forced the British government to take sides. After the introduction of the 1969 reform programme – and even before most of the suggested measures were on the statute book – the British government had tied its political authority to that of the Unionist government. When it turned out that Stormont was neither capable nor willing to deliver further reforms, Catholic faith in the ability of the British government to temper Unionist rule was gradually used up. As a result, Westminster allowed a power vacuum to emerge on the Catholic side which was to be filled by whoever appeared to be the best alternative provider of 'good government'. For most Catholics in Northern Ireland, the traditional answer to this question lay in Irish Nationalism, and from early 1970, the IRA was able to mount its military campaign on the seeds that Westminster's political strategy had sown. Most significantly, instead of political change, the most visible sign of London's 1969 intervention – the British Army – came to symbolise the continuation of Unionist rule. As the independent MP for Mid-Ulster, Bernadette Devlin, pointed out in April 1970: 'At the moment ...: the Army is enforcing the status quo in Northern Ireland ... [T]he British Army is a military organisation, and it is not the duty of a military organisation to change the situation of a country politically or socially.'[104]

Callaghan's early comment that 'life was bleak' seems to indicate that he had noticed the growing disillusionment within the Catholic community.[105] However, it is questionable whether he understood the power political implications of his government's political strategy. Callaghan thought that it was possible for the British government to continue to play the role of a mediator, and he dismissed the ever more frequent unrest (predominantly in the Catholic areas of Belfast) as 'hooliganism', or as 'nonsense in the streets'.[106] Since he conceptualised the disorder as essentially apolitical, and since its strategy had imposed firm limits on further reforms, the government's response to the IRA's early activity was to employ the military instrument. Callaghan's flawed policy was followed up by the Conservatives when they took over power in June 1970. Still believing that the British government was a benevolent outsider, Maudling interpreted the shift from inter-communal violence to attacks on British soldiers as a positive development: it indicated the 'lessening of sectarian tensions', and even in February 1971, he sensed 'a definite growth in the common will to find some solution'.[107] The IRA, on the other hand, was portrayed as a 'very small ... but very dangerous group' of extremists that was attempting to put a halt to the London-led reconciliation effort, but which would eventually be defeated by the 'decent' majority.[108] Again, it seemed that while there was nothing wrong with the overall strategy, the security efforts had to be increased in order to make it work.

The failure of London's 1969 strategy manifested itself in two events. First, in July 1971, 'moderate' Nationalism withdrew from the Stormont parliament. The SDLP, whose leaders had been willing to work the Stormont system in 1969, concluded that the existing structures were unreformable, and that British policy had no alternative to offer:

> Having refused to face the logic of the situation, the British government, without the slightest constitutional guarantee, asks us to believe that the chief architects of our injustice-ridden society – the Unionist party – are the people who can govern us towards a solution within the same system ... [All this has led] us to the point of questioning the sincerity and determination of the British government to solve the problem ... In so far as we can detect any definite policy it would appear to be the maintenance of Stormont in its present form carrying out minimum civil rights reforms and involving the Opposition only to a point when the Unionist right-wing would not be alienated ... We now take this stand in order to bring home to those in authority in London the need for political solutions to end the instability which leads to continuing unrest here. Even the GOC points out the need for a political solution. How long must we wait?[109]

In setting up a separate assembly, the SDLP took away whatever had remained of Stormont's legitimacy as a democratic – and truly representative – parliament, making it clear that 'Stormont is, and always has been, the voice of Unionism'.[110] Constitutional Nationalism had thus, for the first time, exercised its political veto on how the province was to be governed. The second turning point was the failure of internment without trial, which demonstrated that the IRA was not an isolated group of extremists, and that the reliance on purely repressive means of addressing the situation had turned out to be counterproductive.[111]

Cabinet sources show that the failure of internment without trial triggered a gradual change of Westminster's strategy. As noted above, London now recognised that the province's *internal* constitution could not be maintained in its existing form. Also, contrary to the British tradition of majority rule, London came to accept the sectarian divide as a *modus operandi* of its political strategy, and it acknowledged that minority participation in government had to be guaranteed if stability was to emerge. As Maudling explained: 'I look forward ... to the time when the political battles of Northern Ireland are fought between Conservative and Labour ... In the meantime, [though,] it will obviously continue for a long while on the present sectarian basis.'[112] Yet, in stark contrast to Heath's claim that the idea of power-sharing was immediately adopted as an alternative to the existing Stormont system, Cabinet papers suggest that there was a fair amount of scepticism *vis-à-vis* the viability of a 'compulsory coalition' government. Following the failure of internment, London's initial idea was to launch a constitutional conference at which both sides were to discuss 'whether it was possible ... to devise further means of giving representatives of the minority ... an active and prominent role in the processes of government and administration'.[113] Presumably, this would have meant the inclusion of one or two Catholics in an otherwise Unionist government – in any case, it was not identical with the notion of a coalition, which was rejected in Cabinet as late as 2 September 1971 because 'the divergence of basic political beliefs deprived a coalition between Unionist and Nationalist interests of any effective meaning'.[114]

Like the 'greening' of London's rhetoric on constitutional questions, the gradual move towards a system of formalised power-sharing appears to have resulted from the Anglo-Irish *rapprochement* (see above). At the Anglo-Irish summit on 6 September, Lynch impressed upon Heath the need to establish a devolved coalition government in which the minority was to obtain a guaranteed share of executive power. Aware of the need to re-engage constitutional Nationalism, Heath replied that 'no suggestion consistent with the existing constitutional status of Northern Ireland would be excluded',[115] yet he failed to make any commitment to power-sharing. Instead, Westminster now started to advance the formula of an 'active, permanent and guaranteed role [for the minority] in the life and public affairs of the Province'.[116] This demand became known as 'active, permanent and guaranteed' – or simply APG.

As a concept, APG remained relatively vague, and it appears as if this had been Westminster's intention. Whilst avoiding any commitment, APG seemed to hold out the promise (or threat) of far-reaching constitutional reforms. Clearly, London hoped that this would compel Faulkner to produce substantial proposals of his own, thus preventing the need to impose a compulsory coalition. According to Kenneth Bloomfield, who was Deputy Secretary to the Northern Ireland Cabinet:

> [APG] was a kind of Damocles' sword hanging over the head of Northern Ireland politicans ... [T]he question at Stormont was: what do they mean? Do they mean Nationalists in government? ... Faulkner was very antipathetic to the idea of a compulsory coalition. He thought this was a fragmentation bomb: at some stage, it would blow to pieces ...[117]

Faulkner's response to APG included the appointment of a Catholic to the Northern Ireland Cabinet, as well as a series of proposals on giving the SDLP a prominent role in an American-style parliamentary committee system. In his memoirs, he stated that there was no possibility of going any further without triggering a Unionist revolt.[118]

Faulkner's initiative failed to persuade the SDLP to return to Stormont, which meant that it represented no tangible advance in terms of re-establishing the legitimacy of the political system. Given the rapid escalation of the IRA's military campaign after internment, as well as the atmosphere of turmoil that followed Bloody Sunday, London recognised that substantive changes to the province's political system were now a matter of urgency. The first document, which openly advocated a formalised system of power-sharing, was Maudling's memorandum to the Cabinet in March 1972:

> [T]he simple fact is there are only three alternatives – a Cabinet with minority representation chosen by the minority; a Cabinet that continues to be totally dominated by the Unionists, which I believe is no longer acceptable to the minority; or no Cabinet at all.[119]

Given London's traditional rejection of permanent Direct Rule – except as a temporary fix – the idea of having 'no Cabinet at all' was not regarded as a viable solution. What remained, therefore, was the concept of 'minority representation chosen by the minority', which – without making any explicit connection – equalled power-sharing.

In Cabinet, Maudling's memorandum was given a mixed reception. Reiterating the argument put forward by scholars like Lijphart (see Chapter 2), Carrington's main objection was that 'in those countries where Ministerial offices had been distributed by statute or by convention among opposing political Parties there had at least been general agreement upon the broad objective of preserving the integrity of the state'.[120] Yet, even though there was no explicit decision prior to the abolition of Stormont, the idea of a 'coalition government' was clearly what Heath, Whitelaw, Maudling and other senior members of the government had come to accept as the only realistic solution.

Prosperity for everyone? Outspending the conflict

Throughout 1968 and early 1969, the Cabinet saw Northern Ireland as a drain on the exchequer. Since the Treasury's yearly subvention to the Northern Ireland government could well have been spent in some parts of the British mainland, Northern Ireland was thought of as little more than a financial nuisance, and there was not much interest in the province's economic conditions. According to Crossman: 'Why should we pay vast sums to a firm in Belfast? What good do we get out of the twelve Ulster M.P.s? What social results do we achieve by pouring into Belfast money which we deny to … the North-East coast?'[121] As a result, the British government initially considered using the economic instrument in a punitive fashion. Simply put, Westminster believed that Belfast should be coerced with financial sanctions if it refused to introduce political reforms.[122] In London's view, this way of employing the economic instrument had the advantage of providing the government with a mechanism to achieve its aims without having to reconsider the constitutional relationship. However, with the 1969 intervention, Westminster's attitude towards the use of the economic instrument changed. The punitive approach was abandoned, and the British government became willing to increase the subvention, help with additional funds for housing and the training of the workforce, and provide the province with generous financial incentives to attract further investment. To some extent, this conversion may be related to the fact that ministers were more aware of economic conditions once Northern Ireland had come to the top of the political agenda. More importantly, though, with British troops on the streets, the government had an interest in improving the conditions in the province quickly.

London's economic strategy was guided by the assumptions of the post-war economic consensus, including the idea that there was a link between internal peace – even happiness – and prosperity. Callaghan believed that 'there are social and economic problems that bestride the bigotry of the religious groups there',[123] and the press reminded the government that sectarian strife elsewhere in the United Kingdom (for instance, in Liverpool and Glasgow) had disappeared 'when the slums were cleared and people rehoused in new suburbs'.[124] In the minds of the British Cabinet, economic initiatives to bring down unemployment and raise the living standards were a means of promoting 'political maturity' and lessen sectarian tensions, and therefore a pre-condition for the achievement of London's wider aims. As Callaghan argued: 'While civil rights and non-discrimination were of cardinal importance, the problem of Northern Ireland was also to a very large extent an economic one.'[125] Even so, and despite its assumption that sectarian tensions were aggravated by poverty, the government conceptualised the economic dimension of the conflict primarily in absolute terms. In his book on Northern Ireland, Callaghan remarked that the economic problems in Northern Ireland were 'not unique and could be found in some regions of most advanced industrial countries, especially those furthest from the political, economic and cultural centres of power'.[126] In parliament, he even argued that any challenge to the economic and social status quo would worsen rather than improve community relations:

> Complaints about employment are heard just as much among the majority ... I saw the hatred of poor Protestants, whose housing and whose lack of employment justify a better deal than they have had and they heap it all on the heads of the Catholics.[127]

It followed that the British government's aim was not to redistribute employment and economic opportunities between the communities, but to increase the prosperity in Northern Ireland *as a whole*. The implementation of this idea was based on London's experience in Scotland, Wales and other so-called Development Areas within the United Kingdom, with increased spending on infrastructure and public services as well as additional grants to attract investment from abroad.[128]

Considering the government's efforts to support the Unionist administration (and, thus, stabilise the constitutional relationship), London's reluctance to address the issue of economic inequality may be understandable. Yet, it needs to be noted that British policies lacked consistence. On the one hand, Westminster had accepted the need to establish a central housing agency which operated on a points scheme, and the so-called Macrory reforms of local government were – amongst other factors – intended to equalise access to public resources, such as education or health care, by taking away the substantial powers of patronage from local councils.[129] On the other hand, in public and private employment, London was content to rely on declarations of goodwill and the work of Ombudsmen whose powers were limited to pursuing individual cases where proof of discrimination was hard to establish. None of these measures contributed to breaking the existing patterns of recruitment and material distribution, which relied on informal mechanisms rather than direct discrimination. Maudling, however, believed that 'the bulk of the grounds for complaint against individual discrimination ... will have been eliminated' once the system of Ombudsmen had been introduced.[130] In Cabinet, he even asserted that 'not ... much more needs doing in this field'.[131]

Most significantly, by failing to replace Stormont as a mechanism to administer the influx of economic resources, the British government probably contributed to the widening of the sectarian divide. The economic strategy of the Unionist government, which focused on the largely Protestant 'growth centres' in the eastern part of the province, reinforced existing employment structures and thus tended to favour Protestants.[132] It was only towards the end of the period that London came to recognise the contradictory dynamics of its policy. In March 1972, Heath stated in Cabinet that it would be 'desirable to construct a new economic programme in which the United Kingdom Government would have a more dominant role ... in order to prevent the mismanagement ... of financial subventions and to anticipate allegations that they were used exclusively for the benefit of the majority community'.[133]

Conclusion

The years 1969–72 were a period of rapid strategic change. In August 1969, when the British government agreed to provide troops 'in aid of the civil power', it had decided that the re-insulation of Northern Ireland from Great Britain would be its principal aim. London's immediate objective was, therefore, to revitalise the Stormont system, which would allow for the restoration of the constitutional *status quo ante* with a Unionist-dominated Home Rule parliament in Belfast. Accordingly, the strategic instrument was employed as follows:

- The constitutional instrument: to reaffirm that 'the border is not an issue'.
- The military instrument: to ensure the 'swift exit' of British troops; from late-1970, to 'defeat' the IRA.

- The political instrument: to make Stormont reform itself along 'British standards of citizenship'.
- The economic instrument: to provide generous funds to improve housing and reduce unemployment.

Westminster's reluctance to intervene more forcefully, and its focus on maintaining the province as a self-governing entity, resulted from London's alienation from Northern Ireland, derived from its perception that British interventions in 'Irish affairs' were destined to fail, that 'Englishmen' would do more harm than good on Irish soil, and that the only way to make sure that the province remained relatively calm was to maintain the Home Rule arrangement which had allowed Westminster to practice amnesia with regard to Northern Ireland for almost five decades. This intention appeared feasible because the British government chose to ignore the nature of zero-sum politics in the province. Westminster assumed its intervention to bring about a 'new contract' between Catholics and Protestants, and that changes in the power structure of Stormont were therefore not needed. As it turned out, London's assumptions about the political culture in the province were not viable, and as early as October 1969, the sectarian dynamics forced the British government to side with the Stormont government. As a result, London created a power vacuum on the Catholic side that provided the foundation on which the IRA's challenge could be effective. The initial failure to recognise the IRA as a challenge, and – from late-1970 – the inability to formulate a coherent military strategy on the basis of having to maintain support for the *ancien régime* on both sides of the sectarian divide, led to the abdication of responsibilites and the 'outsourcing' of important security decisions.

Only with the escalation of the conflict after the withdrawal of constitutional Nationalism from Stormont, as well as the failure of internment in August 1971, did the British government acknowledge that the maintenance of the 'old Stormont' was a strategic straitjacket from which it had to free itself. Stormont had clearly proved to be an inadequate mechanism to minimise London's involvement in Northern Ireland, and it had therefore lost its value to Westminster. Moreover, the British government was compelled to recognise that the rise of Irish Nationalism, and the effectiveness of the IRA's challenge, was related to the lack of Catholic access to political power, and that the sectarian dynamics had to be accepted in order to be overcome. Consequently, the new objective was to push for devolved structures which *guaranteed*

Catholic participation in the government of the province. Accordingly, London's strategy now incorporated the following elements:

- The constitutional instrument: to acknowledge an 'Irish dimension' and establish a close relationship with the Irish government.
- The military instrument: to facilitate political progress.
- The political instrument: to urge 'moderates' on both sides to co-operate in government.
- The economic instrument: to continue the provision of generous subsidies to improve housing and reduce unemployment.

In April 1972, the abolition of Stormont was described as 'the most important positive decision made by a British party leader...since Gladstone went for Home Rule at the end of 1885'.[134] Yet, in strategic terms, it represented no indication of a fundamental shift in British government policy. As in 1969, Irish unity was dependent on the consent of the population of Northern Ireland. What had changed, was London's understanding of the political dynamics in the province, its determination to keep the Anglo-Irish *rapprochement* intact, and the need to pursue political aims and achieve military progress in tandem.

4
No Quick Fix: Execution and Failure of British Strategy, 1972–75

With the abolition of Stormont, the British government had freed itself from a constitutional straitjacket. It was now at liberty to implement the strategy it had decided upon after the failure of internment in August 1971. However, as a *Times* leader warned in March 1972, Direct Rule was 'easier to get into than out of'.[1] Indeed, the following years were marked by London's efforts to 'get out' of Direct Rule, and its repeated failure to do so.

Back to square one – from Sunningdale to Direct Rule

In London's view, the replacement of the Home Rule parliament at Stormont with Direct Rule from Westminster was never thought to be a long-term solution. According to government documents, it was meant to create 'a limited breathing-space' in which the violence was to calm down whilst the British government would attempt to mediate a more equitable constitutional arrangement amongst the political parties from both sides of the sectarian divide.[2] In contrast to the previous period, when the political instrument had been guided by the desire to preserve the constitutional relationship between London and Belfast, the use of the constitutional instrument was now guided by the political imperative of inducing agreement between Unionists and Nationalists.

In order to reassure Unionists, the British government strongly reaffirmed Northern Ireland's status as part of the United Kingdom. It recognised the 'great feeling of shock'[3] and constitutional uncertainty which the abolition of Stormont had caused in the eyes of many Protestants. At the same time, the purpose of committing itself to upholding Northern Ireland's constitutional status was to '[take] the border...out of Northern Ireland politics for a period so that the parties could concentrate on other matters'.[4] Accordingly, the consent principle, which had been re-phrased in favour of Nationalist aspirations in late 1971, was now used to re-emphasise Northern Ireland's present status. As David Howell (an NIO minister in 1972–74) put it: 'We repeated it like a mantra ... We said ten times a day they would remain a part of the United Kingdom as long as they wanted to.'[5] In addition, London reinforced its pledge by announcing a so-called 'Border Poll'. The referendum took place on 8 March 1973 and resulted in a clear majority (57.5 per cent of the electorate) in favour of Northern Ireland's continued membership of the United Kingdom. To some degree, London's approach could therefore be seen as a return to what Maudling had once advocated as 'neutralising' the constitutional issue by making it clear to Unionists and Nationalists alike that there was no possibility of change in the foreseeable future.[6]

Yet, whilst attempting to reassure the Unionists, Westminster's commitment to the Union was balanced by the so-called 'Irish dimension'. As an outcome of the Anglo-Irish *rapprochement* in late 1971, London demanded the creation of common institutions between Northern Ireland and the Republic of Ireland, and it made agreement on the Irish dimension a condition to the successful conclusion of any settlement. On the one hand, the necessity to institutionalise the relationship between North and South derived from the fact that both entities shared the same geographical unit, and that closer co-operation in areas like tourism, agriculture and security was believed to be of mutual benefit. More importantly, though, the British government recognised that 'an element of the minority in Northern Ireland has hitherto seen itself as simply a part of the wider Irish community', and that Irish Nationalist aspirations had to be given an institutionalised point of reference if any settlement was to command widespread acceptance within the minority community.[7] Unlike the prevailing political opinion within the two communities, London believed these considerations to be of practical rather than ideological significance, particularly since it was thought that European integration would gradually 'blur and calm down the differences' between the two countries and lead to increased co-operation in any case.[8] Regarding Unionist sensibilities, the British government hoped that the significance of the Irish dimension would be outweighed by the strong affirmation of Northern Ireland's constitutional status, and that the working of the new institutions would soon show that any fears of being 'sold out to the South' were much ado about nothing.[9]

At the so-called Sunningdale conference in December 1973, London, Dublin and the three parties that were to form the 1974 Executive (SDLP,

Alliance and UUP) negotiated the practical meaning of the Irish dimension. They agreed to the establishment of a Council of Ireland (consisting of a Council of Ministers with equal representation from Belfast and Dublin) as well as a Consultative Assembly with members from both legislatures and a permanent Secretariat. The Council of Ministers was to assume 'executive and harmonising functions' in areas of common interest,[10] but any decision would be subject to the unanimous approval of all its members, including the Unionist representatives from Northern Ireland. Significantly, the Irish government accepted 'that there could be no change in the status of Northern Ireland until a majority of the people of Northern Ireland desired a change', and it agreed that a formal agreement would be registered at the United Nations.[11] Contrary to the subsequent perception by the majority community, these provisions make it very hard to understand how the agreement could be seen as a first step towards the unification of Ireland. According to Faulkner, who had led the Unionist delegation:

> We had for the first time ... achieved recognition by the Republic of our right to self-determination within our existing boundaries ... [and] nothing agreed on at Sunningdale infringed on the powers of the Northern Ireland Assembly by which everything would have to be approved and delegated. Given the overwhelmingly Unionist composition of that body and the unanimity rule in the Council of Ministers we were satisfied that the constitutional integrity of Northern Ireland was secure.[12]

Faulkner's analysis coincided with the view of the British government, whose members were keen to stress that Unionist interests were protected by Dublin's recognition of Northern Ireland and the unanimity rule, which amounted to a Unionist veto in the proposed Council of Ministers.[13]

Despite the agreement parties' pragmatic approach, Sunningdale provided the pretext under which various Loyalist groups succeeded in mobilising the majority community against the power-sharing institutions. From a constitutional perspective, one could argue that the major flaw of the 1974 arrangement lay in London's assumption that the majority community wished the return to devolved government at any price. Whitelaw insisted that people in Northern Ireland 'do not want to be wholly dominated by Westminster', and that Unionists 'yearn for their old administration'.[14] This view, of course, concurred with London's desire to keep Northern Ireland at distance, and it was therefore not further questioned. Consequently, the British government failed to appreciate the underlying motive of the Unionist demand for a 'return to Stormont' which – in the eyes of most Unionists – simply represented a bulwark against the threat of 'Irish expansionism', and thus the best safeguard that the Union with Great Britain would be maintained. The new arrangement could not satisfy this demand for constitutional stability, and it was therefore rejected.

The British government's approach resulted in a significant tactical blunder, which demonstrated London's misapprehension of Unionist constitutional preferences once more. In September 1973, Heath decided to put additional pressure on the Northern Ireland party leaders by announcing that the failure to reach agreement would be followed by the 'full integration' of Northern Ireland with Great Britain. In a television interview, he said:

> If there is no prospect of having an executive – if they fail to form an executive or, having formed one, it then breaks down – then under the [Northern Ireland Constitution] Act we return to direct rule, and I think it would have to be direct rule with proper integration. One cannot go on with a temporary arrangement under direct rule.[15]

In strategic terms, Heath had intended to raise the stakes by communicating a public threat, assuming that both Unionists and Nationalists wanted a swift return to devolution and were equally appalled by the possibility of being governed from Westminster. Unionists, however, perceived Heath's message in an entirely different way. In their view, Heath had provided them with an attractive alternative to the limited version of Stormont they had been offered: with 60 per cent in favour, full integration with Great Britain was the 'most desired' form of government amongst Northern Ireland Protestants according to a BBC/NOP survey.[16] Instead of a new constitutional arrangement that seemed to weaken rather than strengthen the defensive function of Stormont, there was now the additional option of 'full integration'; and even though Unionists were traditionally suspicious of London's ultimate intentions, the prospect of being treated like any part of England, Scotland or Wales appeared to provide more constitutional stability and protect the Union far better than the proposed form of devolution. Accordingly, the (then) deputy leader of the SDLP, John Hume, commented that Heath's statement would 'give outright encouragement to the politicians who wanted to prevent the assembly from working'.[17]

In May 1974, after Loyalist workers had organised a two-week stoppage, the British government suspended the power-sharing institutions and returned to Direct Rule. Public opinion in Great Britain suggested that, in defying an Act of Parliament, the supposedly 'loyal' Unionists had forfeited their right to call themselves British, and indeed, the *Economist* reported 'increasing revulsion in Britain against any continued involvement in Ulster in any guise'.[18] There can be no doubt that several Cabinet members in the Labour government under Wilson (which had come to power in March) shared those sentiments, and it is no surprise that the implications of a total withdrawal were considered before and immediately after the fall of the Executive.[19] It is nevertheless mistaken to assume that this mood translated into British government policy, or that it guided the use of the constitutional instrument in the years 1974–75. In view of the anticipated collapse of the power-sharing arrangement and a renewed campaign of violence by the IRA, Wilson decided to set up a Northern Ireland Cabinet sub-committee in April 1974. The purpose of this committee was to explore constitutional alternatives to Direct Rule. It met until early 1976, and according to Rees's diaries, discussion papers on the available constitutional options were submitted three times: in June 1974, November 1975 and December 1975. In each case, the paper included a series of constitutional alternatives, ranging from full integration with Great Britain to devolution, independence, re-partition and Irish unity.[20] Whenever it was considered, any form of withdrawal was almost immediately refuted, and the reason for doing so was remarkably similar to the conclusion other administrations had arrived at before. In the words of Rees, withdrawal would 'precipitate violence on an even greater scale ... It would spread to Great Britain and also to the Republic of Ireland. Withdrawal would be a short-sighted policy, but above all it would be an irresponsible policy.'[21]

London's evaluation of constitutional options in mid-1974 was a reflection of the perceived 'lessons' from the Loyalist strike, but it also reflected some of the more traditional British ideas on the use of the constitutional instrument. In line with British tradition, Westminster ruled out the notion of 'agreed independence' on the same grounds as any other form of withdrawal, and it went to considerable lengths to make clear that an independent Northern Ireland would be economically unviable. Rees, for example, stated that the 'wild talk' about independence in some Loyalist circles was in fact 'disloyal'.[22] The belief that Northern Ireland – and even its 'loyal' citizens – were different from the rest of Great Britain, though, was stronger than ever, and it found its expression in Rees' idea of 'Ulster nationalism' (see later). It followed that the British government would continue to pursue some form of institutionalised devolution, which avoided independence or Irish unity but distanced the province from the 'British mainland'. In contrast to Whitelaw's efforts, the British government also decided to play down the emphasis on the 'Irish dimension'. Whereas the Heath government had seen the 'link to Dublin' as an essential element of any cross-community settlement, the Irish dimension was now interpreted as being divisive and potentially harmful to the development of a distinct Ulster identity: 'The great weakness with the Sunningdale settlement was that it brought back a Council of Ireland, and the Council of Ireland – not power-sharing – brought down the Sunningdale Agreement.'[23] Instead of promoting 'separate "aspirations" in both Dublin and London', as Sunningdale had allegedly done, the political leaders of the two communities needed to focus on identifying common ground in a so-called Constitutional Convention.[24] Hence, there were no plans for a Council of Ireland or any institutional framework between Northern Ireland and the Republic; and rather than providing a point of reference for Nationalist aspirations, the Irish dimension was simply re-defined as a 'practical relationship which ought to exist between two good neighbours with a common land boundary'.[25] Also, there was no need anymore for the close political co-ordination between London and Dublin that had taken place before the suspension of the devolved institutions. In March 1975, Rees declared: 'I am always pleased to listen to [the Irish government] ... None the less, the final decision is for Her Majesty's Government. [We] have to face the problems in Northern Ireland, and nobody else. That must be clearly understood.'[26]

Despite its clear rejection of both withdrawal and the Council of Ireland, London's use of the strategic instrument after the Loyalist strike was conducive to a sense of constitutional uncertainty which manifested itself in the rise of Loyalist activity. The SDLP politican Paddy Devlin, for example, detected a series of 'withdrawal symptoms', such as the exclusion of the Belfast shipbuilder Harland and Wolff from the British nationalisation scheme, or the closure of some military bases.[27] The Irish foreign minister, Garret FitzGerald, thought that NIO statements about the constitutional status of the province had become more ambiguous;[28] and in May 1975, the Rev William Arlow, a prominent Protestant clergyman, stated that 'the British Government have given a firm commitment to the Provisional IRA that they will withdraw the Army from Northern Ireland'.[29] Under closer examination, it turns out that the alleged 'withdrawal symptoms' had little to do with London's constitutional intentions but rather with its failure to communicate how the use of the political and military instruments related to its constitutional strategy, and – more fundamentally – the incompatibility of its military initiatives with the overall objective of devolution and power-sharing. The re-organisation of the British Army presence resulted from Westminster's 'Normalisation' policy, which postulated an increase in the security role of the police so that Army numbers could be gradually reduced. London's restraint in prescribing the political and constitutional future of the province was due to Westminster's self-imposed 'non-interference' in the work of the Constitutional Convention (see below), as well as the need to keep the IRA ceasefire intact. The exclusion of Harland and Wolff from the British public ownership scheme, on the other hand, indicated that London was still pursuing devolution as its preferred constitutional option, so that 'when ... a satisfactory form of devolved government is arrived at, the Northern Ireland people will have a vested interest in this shipyard'.[30]

When the participants of the Constitutional Convention failed to agree on power-sharing in late 1975, London was forced to reappraise the constitutional options another time. Since two attempts at devolution had failed within two years, and as any form of radical constitutional action was ruled out as a matter of principle, Westminster felt that it had to put its constitutional ambitions on hold. The only remaining option within the parameters of British constitutional strategy was to continue the direct rule of the province from London. The British government, however, had not abandoned the idea of devolution. In fact, it now adopted a more gradualist approach which was to prove influential in the years to come. The possibility of 'full integration' with Great Britain was unanimously rejected at the crucial meeting of the Cabinet sub-committee in December 1975, and 'the preferred option was direct rule in a province "distanced" from the UK, which ... might lead to a new form of "community participation" in government'.[31] Community participation, on the other hand, could pave the way for a 'greater council with administrative functions' and – at some point in the future – result in proper devolution with full legislative powers.[32] In the meantime, attention would turn to improving the security as well as the economic conditions as a means of 'normalising' the overall situation in the province. Inadvertently admitting that London had previously failed to appreciate the causal relationship between constitutional security and improvements in the overall political situation, Rees declared that London's new approach required 'a period of constitutional stability',[33] and Direct Rule was the framework which seemed most appropriate to achieve this end.

Buying time – military objectives and political aims

Like its constitutional strategy, London's military approach in the 1972–75 period was fundamentally different from that of the previous period. In contrast to 1970, when the defeat of the IRA was considered a pre-condition for political progress, London now understood its political and military aims to be crucially interdependent. Lord Windlesham, who was a Minister of State under Whitelaw, described the 'twin objectives' of London's policy as follows:

> British policy rests on the security forces in Northern Ireland countering effectively and impartially, the use of force … by extremists of whatever kind. At the same time the government is working towards a new form of administration in Northern Ireland.[34]

To succeed in making the military instrument more responsive to Westminster's objective, however, required a highly sophisticated understanding of how to employ it. On the one hand, London recognised that a lower level of violence was conducive to constitutional politics, which meant that the security forces' efforts to clamp down on paramilitary activity had to continue. On the other hand, the government now acknowledged that actions by the security forces were perceived as 'political' by the two communities. As a result, the military instrument also needed to facilitate the willingness of the political leaders to conform to Westminster's political agenda, and to talk to the British government as well as to each other.

In the first months after the introduction of Direct Rule, London found it difficult to balance the different imperatives that had been imposed upon the use of the military instrument. Initially, the aim of 'regaining the trust' of the minority community, and the belief that parts of the IRA could be persuaded to abandon violence, led to the scaling down of the security force presence in Catholic areas. According to M. Dewar, Westminster's failure to maintain the military pressure on the insurgents was a missed opportunity, as 'it allowed the IRA to regroup [and] extend their influence'.[35] More importantly, it increased Unionist suspicions about the ultimate aim of the British government and resulted in the rise of Loyalist paramilitary activity, especially after it became public that the British government had engaged in secret talks with the leadership of the IRA (see below). Likewise, short-term political expediency guided the decision to confer 'Special Category' status on paramilitary prisoners. When a prolonged hunger strike in June 1972 threatened to undermine support for the SDLP, Whitelaw was told that its leaders 'could not continue [to talk to the British government] ... unless a concession was made'.[36] By granting Special Category status, Westminster provided the insurgents – who regarded themselves as 'political prisoners' – with some legitimacy for this view.

Westminster's ability to realise the 'twin objectives' of reducing violence and achieving political progress increased with the gradual refinement of military tactics. Although Army demands for the introduction of curfews and identity cards were ruled out by the government as being 'too rigorous for the law-abiding section of the community',[37] London accepted that the renewed emphasis on collecting low-grade intelligence was necessary to enable the security forces to operate a more targeted approach. With the help of better intelligence, internment became more selective, and it thus contributed to the decline in paramilitary activity, which followed Operation Motorman in July 1972 (see below).[38] Significantly, with more information on the minority community in general and paramilitary structures in particular, Whitelaw could release those internees who were no danger any longer, thus enabling the British government to respond to Nationalist leaders, who had made the end of internment a focal point in their talks with the government.[39]

Whilst improving the implementation of internment, London acknowledged that its operation needed to be ended if the government wanted to regain some credibility amongst the minority community. Hence, whilst insisting that there were, amongst the internees, 'a number of very dangerous individuals whose release would present great difficulty',[40] Whitelaw publicly described the tactic as 'a repugnant measure' and 'one of the darkest features in the political landscape'.[41] In a typically British 'compromise', the government introduced some quasi-judicial features which transferred the decision to release an internee to a group of so-called Commissioners who were to examine an individual's case after 28 days.[42] In addition, London created non-jury (so-called Diplock) trials for 'terrorist offences',[43] which reduced 'the need for recourse to internment' whilst making sure that the intimidation of witnesses and juries ceased to prevent the conviction of paramilitaries in the courts of law.[44]

The invasion of the 'no go' areas on 31 July 1972 provides an excellent case study of how far London had proceeded in re-establishing the essential link between the military instrument and its overall political objective by mid-1972. In security terms, these areas were insurgent strongholds which represented 'black spots' with regard to intelligence and allowed the paramilitaries to organise and recruit freely. Furthermore, London felt that the 'no go' areas represented a failure of government which – in the words of Howell – 'couldn't be tolerated'.[45] Yet, until late June, London insisted that the removal of the barricades would be a mistake. In particular, Westminster believed that employing the military instrument was harmful to the prospect of regaining the trust of the Catholic community and persuading its political leaders to participate in negotiations about power-sharing. In a speech to Scottish Conservatives, Whitelaw declared that 'there would be very substantial casualties indeed ... It would not only be morally wrong but would cause a bitterness which would not be redeemed for a long time, if ever.'[46] Even after the breakdown of the IRA's first prolonged ceasefire, between 26 June and 9 July, this assessment did not immediately change. Any military operation to bring down the barricades, London argued, would produce a significant number of civilian casualties, thus making it even more difficult for Catholic politicians to participate in any scheme proposed by the British government. Although Whitelaw had publicly promised 'sterner security measures', most Cabinet members were therefore convinced that there was no choice but to continue 'a policy of political and military restraint' whilst hoping for another IRA ceasefire.[47] The crucial turning point was Bloody Friday on 21 July, when the IRA launched 26 simultaneous bomb attacks in the city centre of Belfast. At the Cabinet level, there was an immediate realisation that the event had fundamentally changed the political and military calculus within which British strategy operated. Whitelaw was keen to stress that the event had 'aroused feelings of extreme revulsion ... in the Roman Catholic community'.[48] It now appeared as if there was a unique chance for the British government to resolve the dilemma, which had prevented the government from moving against the 'no go' areas ever since they appeared. As Whitelaw pointed out: '[T]he present climate of public opinion, while the events of Friday 21 July were still fresh, was opportune for the Government to take action, as was its duty, to show that it could no longer tolerate the existence of barricaded areas to which the security forces had only limited access.'[49] These comments demonstrate that Whitelaw clearly appreciated the potential political significance of any operation to this end. In fact, he made it clear that 'its successful execution could produce substantial political advantages and help to open the way for political discussions'.[50]

'Operation Motorman' focused on Derry-City's Bogside, the largest 'no go' area, but it also included the removal of several Republican and Loyalist barricades in Belfast. With almost 31 000 troops involved

(22 000 Army and 8 500 UDR), it was the largest military operation on Irish soil in the twentieth century, including the Anglo-Irish War of 1919–21.[51] Even so, with the re-establishment of the government's legitimate control in the 'no go' areas as its only purpose, Motorman was a strictly limited military operation. The demonstration of overwhelming military strength in combination with explicit warnings about the nature and timing of the operation served the purpose of reducing casualties. It was done – quite deliberately – in order to 'encourage the more responsible elements to keep the streets clear'.[52] It is clearly mistaken, therefore, to describe Operation Motorman as 'a turning point in British policy ... in favour of stepped-up repression'.[53] It is true, however, that the penetration of the Bogside resulted in better intelligence and contributed to the effectiveness of the security forces in reducing paramilitary activity. In the three weeks before 'Motorman' there were 2595 shooting incidents across Northern Ireland; in the following three weeks there were only 380.[54] More importantly perhaps, in political terms, Operation Motorman strengthened the SDLP's resolve to commit itself to constitutional politics, and it reassured the Unionists that there was to be no 'sell-out'.[55] In that sense, Motorman broke the vicious circle of violence which had made a dialogue between Nationalism and Unionism impossible.

London's reaction to the Loyalist stoppage, which began on 14 May 1974, was guided by a similar pattern of strategic calculations, albeit with a different outcome. In the first days of the strike, the British government had hoped that intimidation and violence on behalf of the strikers would soon provoke a backlash from the civilian population, thus making the use of the military instrument inexpedient. This approach had worked in favour of the government during an earlier Loyalist strike, and the leaders of the Executive seemed to concur with London's view that to 'sit back and wait' was a valid response for the time being.[56] By the end of the first week, though, intimidation had ceased, and the strike was starting to pick up strong support from the majority community. Any negotiations with the organisers of the stoppage had now become a matter of not being seen to surrender to the 'bully boys',[57] so that using the military instrument appeared to be the only option. The potential political gains of acting in this way, however, were less obvious. First, despite public statements of support, Westminster had decided that the breakdown of the Executive was inevitable given the lack of support from the majority community and the reluctance on behalf of the SDLP to compromise on the proposed Council of Ireland. As Rees put it: 'My view was that we had to carry on as if it was going to work, but it wasn't going to work'.[58] Second, the military operation that would have been required to 'put down' the strike was believed to be unlimited. It would not only have involved the continued unblocking of major roads and the restoration of essential services, but also the running of the Northern Ireland civil service,[59] the confrontation with Loyalist paramilitary activity, and the possibility that the IRA exploited the situation in order to create civil disorder on an even greater scale,[60] thus igniting the 'civil war' scenario that the British government had always cited as the main reason why it maintained the constitutional link to Northern Ireland.[61]

As R. Fisk notes, the GOC, Frank King, had warned Rees about the possibility of a 'two-front war' at the height of the stoppage. One officer, writing in the Monday Club magazine, even suggested that the Army had performed a military coup in disobeying an alleged order to move against the strikers.[62] Given London's assessment of the situation, it seems unlikely that the Prime Minister has ever given such an order. The notion of a 'two-front war', on the other hand, contains some truth, even if it can hardly be described as a novel insight. Simply put, it was a new formula for London's traditional belief that the 'civil war scenario' had to be avoided. Furthermore, and perhaps more significantly, British strategic thinking dictated that there could be no 'military solution', as none of the two communities could be forced into accepting a political settlement by military means alone. Whilst many Nationalist leaders – and subsequently even Heath – believed that the strike should have been 'put down',[63] Rees made it very clear that this was not an option for the British government: 'You can't put down a popular rising by killing people. We're not Russia.'[64]

The end of the Loyalist strike saw the beginning of a new phase in British military thinking, which was described as Normalisation. Normalisation needs to be explained with reference to its two main concepts, police primacy and Criminalisation. Regarding the latter, the reliance on special powers helped the paramilitaries in gaining some legitimacy, implicitly recognised the 'warlike' situation of the conflict, and undermined the state's monopoly on the use of force.[65] Criminalisation, therefore, aimed at abolishing the two most obvious anomalies in Northern Ireland criminal law, namely, the use of detention and the assignment of Special Category status to paramilitary prisoners.[66] In addition, Criminalisation also involved a significant modification of governmental rhetoric. Whilst London had always portrayed paramilitary activities in Northern Ireland as 'criminal' in the sense of 'anti-social' and 'anti-constitutional', this approach was now instensified – despite the fact that government representatives were, at the same time, engaging in 'secret negotiations' with the Republican leadership. Accordingly, Westminster's statements began to include allegations of organised crime and pathological behaviour. In a typical example, Rees declared that '[p]eople have deep inside them a desire to kill somebody from the other faith... call it religious, call it what one will but I do not believe that they are politically motivated'.[67]

The aim of 'police primacy' was for the indigenous police force – the RUC – to take over all law enforcement. This had been an ideological tenet of British government policy in Northern Ireland ever since the British government had reluctantly agreed to provide troops in order to quell the civil unrest in August 1969 (see Chapter 3). Indeed, in early 1973, Whitelaw, spoke about his government's aim of 'return[ing] to normality', including the transfer of responsibilities for law and order back to the police and the 'reduction in the Army strength to what it was before the Troubles'.[68] It should have come as no surprise, therefore, that – in September 1974 – Rees outlined plans for an expansion of the local police force, articulating the hope 'that the time will come when circumstance would allow a reduction in troop strength'.[69] Regarding London's motivations for embarking on this policy, there was a strong (and typically British) belief in the police force as the ultimately superior mediator in conflict situations. As Moyle put it, 'it was necessary to civilise the situation to start with. The army were not trained to do policing. They would kick down the doors and send the troops in. It was all very rough.'[70] On the other hand, there was a practical need to relieve the British Army from 'chasing around the backstreets of Belfast', which had always been considered a distraction from performing the ultimately superior duty of defending the Western alliance (see Chapter 2). In contrast to what is widely believed, the concern about public opinion in Great Britain did not seem to be the driving force behind the idea of police primacy. The sight of 'Great British' soldiers being shot in a part of the United Kingdom was undoubtedly painful for many television viewers, but it never translated into sustained public pressure for withdrawal. As Moyle confirms:

> If we had had a National Service Army when the Troubles blew up, we would never have been able to maintain the British Army in Northern Ireland on a security role for as long as we have done. By the time Northern Ireland came along, all British soldiers were regulars, full-time employees, career soldiers. That meant in practice that [although] there was a lot of sympathy when a young lad from

Blackheath [Moyle's constituency in London] would be shot dead...
there was always the argument that he volunteered for that risk.
So there was never quite the same tension, and the desperate need to
get the troops out like in Cyprus in the 1960s.[71]

It makes little sense, therefore, to compare the motivation of the British
government in Northern Ireland to that of the Nixon administration in
Vietnam. In Vietnam, the overriding interest was indeed to protect
American soldiers' lives and to 'get out' quickly whilst trying to avoid
any admission of defeat. Consequently, the most difficult operations
were handed over to the indigenous (South Vietnamese) forces. In contrast, the British Army in Northern Ireland continued its policing role in
'tough' areas like West Belfast or South Armagh. Here, the purpose was
not a 'swift exit', but – on the contrary – to make the engagement more
sustainable in the long-term, even if that meant that the regular troops
continued to be exposed to considerably more danger than policemen.

In the academic literature, the policy of police primacy is often
described as Ulsterisation, which implies that the British government
intended the blind expansion of *any* local security agency.[72] A brief look
at the development of UDR manpower should be sufficient to see that –
contrary to what the exponents of Ulsterisation may expect – the overall strength of the regiment had been decreasing almost every year since
1972 (see Appendix). It is therefore simply inaccurate to speak about an
increase in 'Ulster security forces' when quite clearly one of the two
locally recruited security agencies was in a permanent state of decline.
Most significantly, though, the focus on the idea of Ulsterisation meant
that the most significant trend in British security policy – namely, the
continued professionalisation of the local security forces – has been
overlooked. As Figures 4.1 and 4.2 show, there has been a steady expansion of the full-time element within the locally recruited security forces
since the mid-1970s. Whilst in 1974, only 12.4 per cent of UDR members were full-time members of the regiment, their representation
increased to 18.3 per cent by the end of the following year. In 1980,
more than every third UDR member was a full-time soldier (35.4 per
cent), and in 1991, the balance had swung in favour of the full-timers. A
similar trend can be shown for the RUC. While in 1975, the full-time
element of the RUC (including the full-time RUC Reserve) represented
15.2 per cent of the police force's overall strength, it comprised 85.4 per
cent of the RUC in 1999.

Arguably, the introduction of Normalisation in 1974–75 represented
a missed opportunity to defeat the IRA by military means. The IRA's

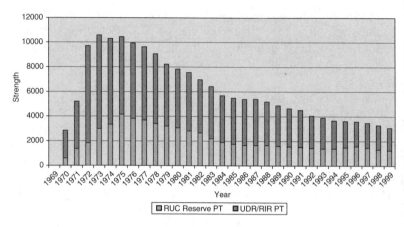

Figure 4.1   Professionalisation: the decline of local part-time forces, 1969–99
Source: see Appendix.

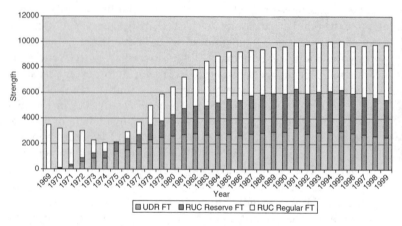

Figure 4.2   Professionalisation: the rise of local full-time forces, 1969–99
Source: see Appendix.

military capabilities had been severely damaged in the wake of
Operation Motorman, and the public outrage after the so-called
Birmingham pub bombings, when the IRA killed 21 people on 21
November 1974, could have provided the pretext under which the Great
British public would have accepted the imposition of draconian security
measures. Yet, apart from extending the period for which a suspect
could be held for questioning, the Prevention of Terrorism Act (1974)
was a largely defensive piece of legislation, which focused mainly on

containing the violence to Northern Ireland by introducing exclusion orders from the British mainland. Again, the government's actions need to be explained with reference to its overall strategy. At the time, London hoped that the 'fluidity' of the political situation after the breakdown of the Sunningdale Executive would offer the opportunity to bring about a political settlement that reached out beyond the moderate core (see below). The initial rationale of the ceasefires in late-1974 and 1975 was, therefore, to encourage the Republican 'doves' by creating conditions 'in which the Provisionals' military organisation ... would find it more difficult to start a campaign again'.[73] This resulted in a decrease in the level of force, and it included the tacit agreement not to pursue the leaders of the IRA.[74]

When it turned out that the IRA could not be persuaded to 'go political', London's motivation in maintaining the ceasefire shifted back towards 'buying time' for the implementation of Normalisation. In June 1975, Rees declared that 'it is a fundamental belief that the best way in which to deal with ... Northern Ireland is by policing, and by people going through the courts. That is what I hope the ceasefire will give me a chance to do.'[75] Accordingly, from mid-1975, Westminster was prepared to excuse even the most obvious violations of the ceasefire, as it allowed the British government to proceed with the phasing out of detention, the building of the new Maze prison, and the restructuring of the RUC. From a military perspective, doing so was undoubtedly a highly effective means of putting the new structures in place, though politically, the lack of compatibility between the political and military strands of London's strategy meant that they contributed to the sense of constitutional uncertainty and were, therefore, harmful to the prospects of returning to devolution. Also, the lower profile of the Army meant that the IRA was free to establish its own system of justice in Republican areas, which undermined state authority and provided the IRA with a seemingly legitimate role.

Struggling for stability – power-sharing and constitutional turmoil

In political terms, the years 1972–73 represent the British tradition in its least diluted form. Most significantly, there was the idea that the British goverment had to mobilise the 'moderate centre' in order to defeat the 'men of violence'. The aim was to empower the 'decent majority' in Northern Ireland who – regardless of their constitutional preference or religious allegiance – was believed to reject the use of violence and wanted a return to constitutional government. Accordingly, Howell summarised his government's intentions for the years 1972 and 1973 as 'build[ing] up, by every means available, a band of moderate opinion drawn from both sides ... [and] to show that it was possible to set up a government again in Northern Ireland which could contain both Catholics and Protestants in fair proportions'.[76] In working towards this objective, London would assume the role of an 'honest broker' with no stake in the political conflict other than 'achiev[ing] a stable peace ... under conditions of equal opportunity for all its citizens'.[77] In June 1972, Whitelaw emphasised that London needed 'to be responsive to any ideas they might themselves form', and that no topics should be excluded from discussion, as 'it may well prove instructive to hear the view of those whose ultimate political aspirations lie in the direction of reunification'.[78]

Despite its emphasis on the so-called 'band of moderates', London also hoped that the IRA could be persuaded to give up violence and participate in constitutional politics. On the one hand, this was seen as a recognition of political realities. In March, the Cabinet had noted that – 'in realistic terms' – the IRA needed to be recognised as a representative of the Catholic community.[79] In April, Whitelaw openly questioned the political influence of the SDLP 'in relation to that of the Irish Republican Army'.[80] On the other hand, the British leadership was encouraged by the well-publicised revelations of a young defector from the Republican movement, Maria McGuire, who had described serious splits within the IRA and *Sinn Fein*,[81] which were interpreted by Westminster as a conflict between 'hawks' and 'doves'. According to the *New Statesman*, Whitelaw started to talk 'in hopefully glowing terms' about the presumed leader of the 'doves', David O'Connell, and the idea of 'politicising the Provos ... [as] an essential part of [the] solution to the Northern Irish problem'.[82] It was people like O'Connell, who Whitelaw meant when he referred to 'the possible emergence of political personalities closely linked with the IRA but sufficiently separate from them to have a possible role in future political discussions'.[83]

A two-week ceasefire enabled London to arrange for a meeting between the Republican leadership and a British government delegation in London on 7 July 1972. Retrospectively, Heath and Whitelaw have played down the encounter as a way of demonstrating Republican intransigence.[84] The idea of a 'token exercise', however, is contradicted by Whitelaw's own statements during Cabinet meetings. Shortly before the IRA called its ceasefire, he asserted:

In many countries (including Ireland in 1921) it had proved necessary to negotiate with terrorist leaders; and suitable channels might be found – whether through the SDLP, the Roman Catholic church or released internees – through which the IRA could be persuaded that an end to violence could be followed by a relaxation of military activity, an end to internment and the restoration of normal life throughout the Province, including the Roman Catholic enclaves.[85]

In typically British fashion, London had apparently believed that once the IRA had been educated about the British position, its leaders would engage in a lengthy process of negotiations, abandon violence and become part of the proposed settlement. Many years later, Heath appeared to confirm this intention: 'When the moment is right, I have no objection to ... telling *Sinn Fein* exactly what the Government's position is and trying to influence them to ... get [the IRA] to pack it all in.'[86]

Arguably, it was naive for London to assume that the IRA – at the height of its military campaign – could be 'educated' or made susceptible to the British notion of negotiation as a means of teasing out a compromise.[87] As P. Bew and H. Patterson put it, in believing that the talks could lead to a negotiated end of the conflict, London was guided by 'a mixture of wishful thinking and an incapacity to understand the dynamics of republicanism as an ideology'.[88] Furthermore, in embarking on the secret talks, Westminster underestimated the degree of constitutional insecurity any attempt at circumventing the Unionists would create within the majority community. It thus aggravated Protestant fears about a 'secret deal' between the British government and the IRA. *The Economist* concluded, accordingly, that there was 'now a good deal of talk of civil war in Ulster'.[89] After the talks had been revealed to the public, Whitelaw needed to promise never to talk to the IRA again, and London's actions in the subsequent weeks appear to indicate that the government had abandoned the idea that the Republicans could be made part of the 'moderate centre'. Even so, in early August 1972, Whitelaw pointed out that he had committed himself 'and no one else ... neither future government, nor even the present Government'.[90]

The process of 'drawing up a band of moderates' started with the so-called Darlington Conference in September 1972, the publication of the Green Paper on 'The Future of Northern Ireland' in the following month, and culminated in the release of the White Paper 'Northern Ireland Constitutional Proposals' (March 1973) which translated the Green Paper principles into a series of suggestions on the shape of the future institutions. On every occasion, the British government restated the consent principle and its commitment to devolution, power-sharing and the Irish dimension. Also, as a lesson from its pre-1972 involvement (as well as because of their divisive nature),[91] London maintained that all public order and security powers were 'reserved' matters, which remained with Westminster at least as long as the emergency continued.[92] Given the British government's relatively clear idea of how the new institutions were supposed to work, the formation of the new executive was therefore not merely a question of whether Unionists and Nationalists would agree with each other, but – perhaps more importantly – if the leaders of the respective parties were prepared to accept the terms which London had pre-determined as an acceptable compromise. Faulkner's UUP, for example, insisted on the immediate return of the security powers, and rejected the notion of 'compulsory power-sharing' as well as the representation of Irish Nationalists in the new executive. The SDLP, on the other hand, demanded a thorough reform of policing and the end of internment without trial, none of which Westminster or the Unionists were prepared to concede. In fact, contrary to Patterson's assertion that 'a reformed police force was on offer',[93] Heath had made it clear that the continued professionalisation of the RUC along British lines – in combination with the SDLP's endorsement – would be sufficient to win back the minority's trust in the security forces, and it was consequently considered unnecessary to upset the majority community on this issue.[94]

The formation of the executive was a remarkable achievement. It was realised by making the constitutional, military and economic instruments responsive to the political imperative of obtaining agreement between the parties, thus enabling London to grant tactical concessions depending on who needed most reassurance at any given point in time. This could be seen, for example, in the case of the Border Poll or with regard to the gradual release of internees (see above). Also, the close co-ordination with Dublin meant that pressure could be brought to bear on the SDLP, which helped in overcoming the party's initial reluctance to negotiate with the British government.[95] Eventually, the SDLP gave way on internment and policing reform while Faulkner's UUP eventually agreed to power-sharing and the retention of security powers by Westminster. The Council of Ireland, with its commitment to 'executive and harmonising' functions represented a rhetorical gain for the Nationalists, although the unanimity rule in the Council of Ministers makes it difficult to see how the desired momentum towards a united Ireland should have developed in practice. In that sense, it was neither the Nationalists nor the Unionists, but London, who emerged as the 'winner' from the negotiation process: with devolution, power-sharing, the Irish dimension, and the acceptance of the consent principle by

Dublin and the SDLP, it had achieved the 'balanced settlement' for which it had strived.

Even so, the 'moderate consensus' turned out to be fragile. Only three days after the Executive had taken office, on 4 January 1974, Faulkner was toppled as leader of the UUP. At the Westminster elections in February, the candidates of the 'anti-Executive' United Ulster Unionist Council (UUUC) gained 11 out of 12 Northern Ireland seats (51.1 per cent of the vote); and three months after the poll, the Protestants joined in with the Loyalist strikers, forcing the British government to suspend the Executive. Arguably, the high degree of Protestant hostility was strongly influenced by the idea that the proposed form of devolution had weakened rather than strengthened the Union. This perception of constitutional insecurity can be explained with reference to some of the core provisions of the agreement, which stripped Stormont of its security powers (namely, the physical capability to defend the Union), demanded the incorporation of people who had openly declared their Nationalist credentials, and included the obligation to share some of the executive powers with the country whose territorial claim Stormont was meant to resist. Equally, though, constitutional insecurity was caused by the structural asymmetry of London's political strategy which postulated neutrality towards the Unionists, yet allowed for 'secret talks' with the IRA as well as the closest possible co-ordination with Dublin. Moreover, the perception was reinforced by mistakes in the micromanagement of the political process, such as Dublin's difficulties in bringing its most substantial concession, the recognition of Northern Ireland, in line with its Constitution; or Westminster's misleading description of the Irish dimension, in March 1973, as 'nothing more than an acknowledgement of the fact that Northern Ireland is affected in many ways by what happens in the Irish Republic and that the reverse is equally true',[96] which stood in marked contrast to the rhetorical monstrosity of the Council of Ireland. Last but not least, despite the significant reduction in violence after Operation Motorman in August 1972, the British government failed to reconstruct the basic connection between stability and physical security against the background of continued paramilitary activity from both sides.[97]

Hence, rather than any singular influence,[98] one may argue that it was the overarching and multifaceted influence of constitutional insecurity, which had made the Protestants believe that the Union was not safe under the proposed arrangement. This perception determined the incentive structure of the majority community, and thus its response. As long as Stormont in its original form was not available, the Unionists would opt for the 'next best' arrangement from the perspective of constitutional security. Given that the new Executive was seen as the prelude to a sell-out, Direct Rule was clearly preferable. By offering the 'full integration' of Northern Ireland with Great Britain, Heath even provided an additional stimulus for the Protestants to oppose the new structures (see above). In doing so, he illustrated London's failure to understand that Unionist attitudes towards any political settlement were not necessarily determined by the extent of self-government, but by the degree of constitutional security it offered.

In the wake of the stoppage, Rees developed the notion of 'Ulster nationalism' as an allegedly new and innovative way of conceptualising the conflict which influenced British policy in the years to come:

> The Protestants began to mistrust British politicians. I just wondered, at the back of my mind, whether two sets of Nationalists – Catholic Nationalists and Protestant Ulster Nationalists – would be able to get together on purposes of government. Whether that could ever have happened, who knows, but they both thought the same way, that is, Ulster is different from the rest. And I was not so sure whether the Catholic Nationalists really wanted a united Ireland, or whether they were more concerned about Ulster than about Ireland as a whole.[99]

Rees believed that the strike had shown how alienated the supposedly 'loyal' Protestants had become from British political culture and institutions, whereas the Catholics 'had learned the hard way from the Ulster Workers' strike, and [they were]…aware that once the British troops were out, there would still be the Loyalists'.[100] In that sense, the British government assumed that the Loyalist strike had had a clearing, almost carthatic, impact on the ideological outlook of the political forces in the province. As Rees noted: 'The situation in Northern Ireland is both more fluid and much less clear-cut than has been the case for a long time. There is a different attitude in all sections of the community.'[101] The collapse of the constitutional arrangement thus offered the opportunity to exploit this 'new awareness'[102] and provide both Protestants and Catholics with the chance to discover a common identity. The so-called Constitutional Convention, which London proposed just five weeks after the end of the strike, was therefore based on the idea that the 'various groups in Northern Ireland…can best find for themselves political relationships which will be acceptable to them'.[103] London would revert to its initial role of a facilitator, which Rees believed it had clearly overstepped in the lead-up to the Executive. Equally, the influence of the Irish government was considered harmful to the prospect of developing the desired 'Ulster' identity. Since the Irish dimension had been watered down, power-sharing was the only substantial pre-condition for a return to devolution. Yet even power-sharing was put in less stringent terms than previously. Orme stated that it was a temporary measure, a 'bridging operation',[104] pending the development of a distinct 'Ulster' identity, which would allow people to overcome the sectarian divisions. Furthermore, it was believed that the 'new awareness' amongst the political forces in Northern Ireland could be used to broaden the political dialogue, encourage constitutional as well as paramilitary groups to talk to each other, and ensure that any new constitutional arrangement would be endorsed by concurring majorities within both communities respectively.

Regarding the paramilitaries, London hoped that the fluidity of the political situation had reignited their desire to engage in political activity. Also, given the Protestant paramilitaries' strong posture during the stoppage, the conversion of the 'men of violence' towards peaceful means, and their possible inclusion in a settlement, was now given more prominence. Accordingly, as early as July 1974, FitzGerald noted 'that Stan Orme seemed to be hoping for IRA agreement to a cease-fire'.[105] When the IRA announced a temporary cessation of its campaign, in December 1974, the government was therefore quick to embrace the opportunity to meet the Republican leadership. The journalist Peter Taylor, who was granted access to Republican sources, quoted the proceedings of one typical meeting as follows:

> [The Republicans] complained that 'the undertaking given regarding the movement of troops out of Ireland has not been fulfilled' ... But [Michael] Oatley and [James] Allan [the British representatives] were more interested in trying to persuade Sinn Fein to take part in the elections for the Constitutional Convention ... They said it was a sign that the government 'no longer wants to dictate events in Ireland and wants Irishmen themselves to "get on with it" '.[106]

The most noticeable sign of London's new approach towards the Republicans, however, were the so-called 'incident centres' in Republican strongholds across the province. They were meant to provide an interface between the IRA and the government, so that any security 'incident' could immediately be explained and the breakdown of the ceasefire prevented; yet they also gave the Republican movement a visible presence and could therefore be seen as an additional inducement to 'go political'. In addition to sponsoring what soon became *Sinn Fein*'s first offices,

Brendan O'Brien maintains that the British government even offered to help with public relations if the Republicans had decided to stand for the elections.[107] Still, London's efforts came to nothing. Once it had become clear that the Republican 'doves' would not 'go political', the government's motivation in maintaining the ceasefire shifted towards the more pragmatic notion of buying time for the long-intended reorganisation of the military presence. Nonetheless, like Whitelaw before him, Rees refused to acknowledge that attempting to include the Republicans in a political settlement had been a mistake: 'If it is considered necessary, it will happen again.'[108]

Whitelaw's and Rees' strategies were equally flawed in that both of them overestimated the degree to which Republicans were prepared to compromise on their ultimate aim. In addition, neither Whitelaw nor Rees appreciated the importance of constitutional stability. Rees, like many observers of the conflict, recognised the devastating impact of the Council of Ireland on Unionist support for the Executive, but he failed to understand the underlying reason. Although he played down one source of constitutional instability, the Irish dimension, he created constitutional insecurity on an even greater scale by talking about 'disengagement' with the IRA (whilst portraying its members as criminals), announcing the withdrawal of troops as part of the Normalisation policy, and failing to give clear constitutional commitments as part of the self-imposed restraint with regard to the Constitutional Convention. He developed the notion of 'Ulster nationalism' as yet another British attempt at circumventing the basic fault line in Northern Ireland society. Contrary to Rees' hopes, though, the Loyalist sense of Britishness was as strong as ever, and the supposed alienation from the British government did not translate into the common identity he sought to project. In short, under the given circumstances of constitutional turmoil, the majority community was not prepared to consider the inclusion of Nationalists in a devolved settlement. Consequently, the Constitutional Convention produced no agreement on power-sharing, and its final report (which recommended a return to the 'old' Stormont system of government with majority rule) was accordingly rejected by Westminster. The lack of remaining options determined the decision to continue with an extended period of Direct Rule.

The end of prosperity – 'Tory socialism' and cautious reforms

Despite the changes in the government's overall strategy, London's commitment to raise the prosperity of the province and achieve economic and social parity with Great Britain was undiminished under Direct Rule. British thinking on the use of the economic instrument continued to be guided by the assumption that there was a direct link between peace and prosperity. As Howell put it:

> The view that Ted Heath gave to me when he appointed me [in 1972] was that if we went into Ireland and organised effectively social improvement, new housing estates, new roads, new transport, clearances of slum areas, and brought in new jobs, attracted new industry from all over Europe and elsewhere, we would uplift the general social structure and living standards, and this would have some immediate ameliorating effect on the violence.[109]

From an ideological perspective, the willingness to engage in resolute state action to 'uplift the social structure' was typically Labour. Yet, even the Conservatives adhered to this belief where Northern Ireland was concerned. As a result, basic Conservative philosophy of non-intervention in British industry was consistently at odds with London's actions in Northern Ireland. Although the Heath government emphasised that the long-term solution for the economic problems in the province lay in additional private investment, London conceded that the state had to assume the role of the private sector as long as unemployment remained high. Accordingly, the government continued with the expansion of the public service sector, both as a means of creating employment and in order to achieve parity with the rest of the United Kingdom.[110]

Neither the Conservative nor the Labour government made use of economic sanctions as a means of coercing good behaviour, even if both administrations regularly stressed the size of Westminster's subvention to Northern Ireland and threatened to withdraw some of the money if the province failed to comply with London's political plans. After the Loyalist strike, for example, Wilson stated that 'it is inconceivable that our people on this side of the water – our constituents – will accept without question ... to meet the cost of these ... politically inspired, self-inflicted wounds'.[111] On the one hand, the public statements about the financial contribution of the British government were aimed at neutralising the idea of an independent Northern Ireland and concentrating the minds of the local political leaders on bringing about power-sharing in a devolved settlement. Heath declared, therefore, that 'the British government would not pay one penny ... to an independent country'.[112] Likewise, the 1974 Green Paper on 'Finance and the economy',[113] which focused heavily on the financial support the province received from the

Treasury, attempted to convey to the Loyalists that independence could not be realised. As Rees admits, 'we were reminding them of the financial contribution as a deliberate policy'.[114]

On the other hand, the verbal emphasis on London's subvention was an exercise in populism, voicing the perceived anger of many people in Great Britain at the 'unreasonableness' of Northern Ireland. Wilson admitted that his television speech at the height of the Loyalist strike, in which he labelled the people of Northern Ireland 'spongers', was primarily meant for an audience on the British mainland: 'The idea I was seeking to get across was that Ulster was always ready to come to auntie for spending money, expressing their thanks by kicking her in the teeth.'[115] His strong rhetorical postures, however, were not followed by any actions. Although an additional grant for Harland and Wolff was put on hold for some days after the strike, the government readily agreed to provide the money as soon as it became clear that the shipyard was threatened with closure. Twelve months later, the company, which saw some of the most vociferous opposition to the 1974 Executive, was promised another massive injection of financial support over the coming five years (£119 m in grants and loans, compared to £31.5 m for the 1971–74 period).[116]

As in the 1969–72 period, London's economic strategy focused on raising the living conditions in the province regardless of sectarian difference. Despite the fact that the measures which had been introduced before the abolition of Stormont had clearly failed to make any impact on employment practices in the province, the level of economic inequality between the two communities was given less attention. By mid-1972, the Commissioner for Complaints had only established a single case of discrimination on sectarian grounds.[117] The most striking example remained Harland & Wolff, where the complete failure to increase the number of Catholic workers was now justified by pointing to the fact that 'there are many thousands of others ... doing subcontract work for Harland and Wolff, and these workers are representative of both communities'.[118] However, the more fundamental flaw with London's approach towards economic inequality lay in the assumption that material differences would disappear once additional investment from abroad had been secured. In spite of financial incentives and several advertisement campaigns, the British government only managed to attract a total of 900 jobs from outside Northern Ireland between 1972 and 1976.[119] As a result of the oil crisis, the ensuing recession, and further decline in manufacturing as well as agriculture, unemployment began to rise from 1973, with 11 per cent reaching a post-war record in early 1976. Consequently, the government's attention needed to shift from creating new jobs towards maintaining the existing level of employment, so that the idea of eliminating relative deprivation by achieving 'prosperity for everyone' became increasingly untenable.

It is notable that the issue of economic inequality was not even yet high on the agenda of the Nationalists. When Unionists, Alliance and the SDLP worked out the political programme of the future Executive, economic and social policy was regarded as the least contentious area.[120] The only actor to articulate the issue of inequality coherently was the Irish government. Yet, in FitzGerald's words, 'there was such an evident reluctance [on behalf of the British government] to embark on a programme [of positive discrimination] ... that I did not take very seriously Willie Whitelaw's offer ... to see what could be done'.[121] To some extent, this unwillingness was due to London's awareness that any serious challenge to the economic and social status quo would provoke an adverse reaction within the majority community, and thus jeopardise the careful political equilibrium the government had to bring about in order to achieve agreement on a political settlement. Howell admits that his government's lack of determination to 'plunge ahead with anti-discrimination measures' was influenced by the amount of 'offence' they would cause amongst Protestants.[122] In a similar vein, Heath principally agreed with FitzGerald that the sectarian imbalance in the civil service had to be corrected, yet he insisted that it needed to be done 'discreetly'.[123] On the other hand, the idea of 'collective rights' was at odds with the British notion of individual opportunity, and Whitelaw accordingly rejected the suggestion that the promotion of Catholics in the civil service should be speeded up. He remarked that 'merit could not be set aside, as efficiency was the criterion for a good civil service'.[124]

London's reluctance *vis-à-vis* the issue of economic inequality was reflected in the restricted nature of Westminster's initiatives. In August 1972, London set up a working party to examine the problem of job discrimination in the private sector. The committee endorsed a 'voluntary' approach to 'affirmative action' (defined by the working party as 'deliberate programmes under which equality of employment opportunity may be achieved'), but it rejected the introduction of quotas or 'benign [that is, positive] discrimination'. It asked for employers and trade unions at every workplace to sign a 'declaration of principle and intent' and demanded the establishment of an agency to investigate individual complaints as well as to conduct research.[125] Moreover, the newly established Standing Advisory Commission on Human Rights (SACHR) would monitor the economic situation in the province and produce annual reports which were to include recommendations on further legislation. In addition, discrimination on religious (or sectarian) grounds was outlawed in the Northern Ireland Constitution Act (1973) and the Fair Employment Act (1976). The number of initiatives, however, could not conceal that London's approach continued to focus on individual cases of discrimination. When it came to the wider issue of economic and social inequality between the two communities, Westminster's proposals remained vague and relied on the goodwill of employers and trade unions (such as the shop stewards at Harland & Wolff, who could hardly be expected to go against their colleagues and insist on hiring more Catholics).

Apart from well-publicised initiatives, the British government implemented a number of measures that could be regarded as evidence of Westminster's 'discreet' approach towards economic inequality. For example, London believed that Catholics often failed to gain access to skilled jobs because their level of education was thought to be lower than the Protestants'. Orme asserted that 'Catholics could not be given skilled jobs for which they had not been properly trained'.[126] The government's emphasis on job training was, therefore, a means of equalising employment opportunities. (By 1973, there were nine times as many job training centres per head of population as in Great Britain.)[127] In a similar vein, Westminster attempted to locate new ventures in predominantly Catholic areas. Howell observed that Catholics and Protestants were living in 'self-contained communities', and that 'a more even distribution of economic activity' between the two communities could be achieved by bringing employment closer to Catholic areas, such as West Belfast or the western counties of Northern Ireland.[128] Significantly, the recognition of Catholic employment needs signalled a move away from the growth-centre strategy of the Stormont administration which prioritised predominantly Protestant towns, such as Lurgan or Portadown. It is doubtful, however, whether these initiatives produced any tangible results, particularly since they depended on the influx of investment and the provision of additional jobs.

Conclusion

The British government regarded the abolition of Stormont in March 1972 as a temporary measure. Westminster's aim remained unchanged: it was to make sure that Northern Ireland would remain 'a place apart', and that the political conflict in the troubled province would cease to impinge upon life and politics on the British mainland. To this end, devolution was still considered the best arrangement, yet London had learned that self-government needed to be supplemented by a cross-community coalition to reflect the sectarian divisions in Northern Ireland society and provide the minority with a permanent share in power. In order to achieve this objective, the strategic instrument was employed as follows:

- The constitutional instrument: to reaffirm the consent principle whilst establishing institutions to express the existence of an Irish dimension.
- The military instrument: to facilitate political progress whilst fighting the paramilitaries.
- The political instrument: to 'draw up a band of moderates' from both communities to form a coalition government.
- The economic instrument: to 'uplift the social structure' by sustaining growth and creating employment.

Crucially, Westminster assumed that the majority community wanted the return to devolution as much as the British government, and that the Protestants were prepared to pay the price in the form of power-sharing and the Council of Ireland in order to get Stormont back. The supposed harmony of interests with regard to devolution, however, was a fatal error of judgement. Whereas for the British government devolution was an end in itself (it guaranteed that Northern Ireland could be re-insulated from Great Britain), the Protestants primarily sought constitutional stability, that is, an arrangement that made the Union safe and prevented the incorporation of the province into a united Ireland. The 'old' Stormont represented a bulwark against Irish expansionism, yet the 'new' Stormont seemed more like the prelude to a sell-out. The feeling of constitutional insecurity was caused by particular features of the proposed arrangement, such as power-sharing and the Irish dimension, but it was further aggravated by the political environment, with structural imbalances towards the Nationalists, grave mistakes in the micromanagement of the political process, and the background of continuing violence.

Even after the breakdown of the Executive in May 1974, Westminster failed to understand that the main lesson from the collapse of the 'old' Stormont, the need to include members of the minority community in the government of the province, could only be realised if the majority was convinced that power-sharing would not entail a threat to the constitutional status of Northern Ireland. Instead, London developed the notion of 'Ulster nationalism' as a new ideological undercurrent for devolution and power-sharing. The strategic instrument was re-arranged as follows:

- The constitutional instrument: to play down the Irish dimension and focus on a devolved settlement within Northern Ireland.
- The military instrument: to 'normalise' the security situation by phasing out emergency arrangements and returning to the primacy of the police in law enforcement.
- The political instrument: to facilitate communication between all political actors, aiming at the re-establishment of a cross-community government.
- The economic instrument: to preserve employment.

'Ulster nationalism' was a pipedream that had resulted from London's misapprehension of the Loyalist strike as an expression of Protestant alienation from Britain. Like the 1974 Executive, the Constitutional Convention failed to agree on power-sharing because its proceedings were accompanied by constitutional turmoil. By now, however, the main source of instability were changes in the use of the military instrument. The military policy of Normalisation aimed at making the British engagement in Northern Ireland more sustainable by re-establishing the security forces' legitimacy and minimising the loss of troops from the mainland. In practice, though, the introduction of Normalisation – with the reduction of British troops, the release of detainees and the need to sustain the IRA ceasefire – appeared to indicate the beginning of a British withdrawal. Only with the failure of the IRA's ceasefire did London begin to realise that whilst the division of society made it necessary to provide the minority with a share in power, the majority needed constitutional security to grant it – an insight which provided the intellectual foundation of London's strategy in the following period.

5
Going it Alone? Direct Rule under Pressure, 1976–82

Recognising its previous failure to create the perception of constitutional security, the British government opted for a continued period of undiminished Direct Rule, accompanied by the strongest affirmation yet of London's will to govern the province. Only six years later, London was compelled to end the experiment. The assumption of absolute British sovereignty over Northern Ireland had become impossible, and Dublin was – again – 'included in'.[1]

Exposed? The Fragility of Direct Rule

After the failure of the Constitutional Convention, the British government had decided to adopt Direct Rule as a more or less permanent form of government (see Chapter 4). Boyce argued that this was a sign of resignation, '[reflecting] the British inability to devise new policies, and their understandable desire to let well enough alone'.[2] Whilst this assessment is true in that London always saw Direct Rule as a 'last resort', it is mistaken to imply that Westminster's policy signified inactivity, the lack of a strategy, or that it indicated the abandonment of the British objective of devolution with power-sharing. In London's view, the new constitutional approach aimed at providing stability for devolution to become more likely at some – yet undefined – point in the future. Roy Mason, Rees's successor as Northern Ireland Secretary, declared that '[i]f progress was to be made, it had to start on the basis of stability. That ... meant reducing the level of terrorism ... [and] somehow reviving the economy of Northern Ireland.'[3] The belief in stability, however, also required that 'the whole issue of constitutional change [was] put on the back burner'.[4]

Given the repeated failure to introduce devolution (see Chapter 4), one could argue that the new approach represented an inherently plausible aberration from traditional British thinking on the use of the constitutional instrument. For the first time, London had acknowledged that the conflict could not be resolved, or contained, in the short term, and that the government had to move beyond the 'institutionalism' of the 1972–75 period in order to create the conditions under which its objectives could be realised. Whereas in 1972 the introduction of Direct Rule was seen as a temporary measure that would enable London to oversee the swift return to devolution, Westminster had now accepted that – for the foreseeable future – it had to exercise its responsibility by governing the province. In practice, however, the idea of 'positive' and 'caring' Direct Rule[5] (Mason) rested on a series of assumptions. First, it presumed that London was capable of delivering tangible improvements in security and the economy. Second, it assumed that Direct Rule was equally acceptable to both communities, and that Protestants as well as Catholics were prepared to acquiesce in London's claim to be an impartial and honest broker. Finally, it postulated that Northern Ireland was a matter for the United Kingdom alone, and that no other actor had a stake in the conflict. In strategic terms, Westminster had therefore presupposed an ideal game situation, namely one in which all other actors strictly adhered to London's assumptions about the nature of the conflict, and one in which other actors' moves would not impact upon the implementation of London's strategy. However, as it turned out, the strategy of the British government was challenged both by adverse circumstances and the interference of actors from within and outside the province, thus rendering its original purpose impossible to achieve.

The military, political and economic pressures that interfered with the implementation of London's strategy are described in the following sections of this chapter. Regarding the assumption that Northern Ireland was a matter for the United Kingdom government alone, the most significant challenge to London's strategy emanated from the government of the Republic of Ireland. Contrary to what one may expect, there had been a high degree of congruence between the two governments prior to the establishment of the 1974 Executive, when both agreed on the objective of devolution, power-sharing and the Irish dimension. In the following years, Westminster's *de facto* abandonment of the Irish dimension and the secret talks with the IRA provoked some misgivings, yet Dublin avoided open conflict as London continued to pursue a power-sharing settlement.[6] However, with the adoption of Direct Rule on a quasi-permanent basis, the Anglo-Irish consensus broke down. As in previous years, Dublin's approach rested on the consent principle, and all the Irish Prime Ministers during the 1976–82 period reaffirmed that the unification of Ireland could only come about 'by agreement and in harmony between the two islands'.[7] Yet, the Irish government also wanted the British government to launch yet another political initiative that would seek to bring about devolution and power-sharing as well as incorporate some form of Irish dimension.

In order to advance its objectives, the Irish government attempted to create a complex bargaining situation. Dublin's potential bargaining power resulted from three sources. First, as its pronouncements carried some weight with the Nationalist minority in Northern Ireland, Dublin was able to undermine London's strategy directly. For instance, the Irish government continued to resist calls for an effective agreement on the extradition of suspects whose actions were 'politically motivated', thus providing them with the legitimacy the British government sought to deny. In an interview on Irish radio, Lynch even considered 'some form of amnesty for IRA men' who were serving sentences in the Republic of Ireland.[8] The fact that Westminster believed it to be 'of absolutely critical importance to Britain that Irish Prime Minister Charles Haughey should not be supporting'[9] the hunger strikes of Republican prisoners (in 1980 and 1981) can be seen as an acknowledgement of Dublin's power to thwart London's strategy.

The second source of Irish bargaining power related to the existence of a land border between the Republic and Northern Ireland, and the significance which London attached to co-operating with the Irish government in security matters. This had been stressed by British politicians as early as 1972, when Heath had insisted in Cabinet that 'there was still scope for more vigorous action against the IRA' by the Irish authorities in the border areas.[10] According to Callaghan, Wilson's successor as Prime Minister, Dublin failed to take 'sufficiently serious the vital need for close border co-operation if the IRA threat was to be contained'.[11] In a similar vein, Thatcher (who followed Callaghan in 1979) thought that '[t]he border ... is of crucial significance to the security problem. Much depends on the willingness and ability of the political leaders of the Republic to co-operate effectively with our intelligence, security forces and courts'.[12] The Irish government, on the other hand, maintained that the British government had exaggerated the problem, and it protested strongly whenever members of the British government accused it of being a 'safe haven' for members of the IRA.[13] Even so, there clearly was an element of discretion when it came to issues like extradition, direct contact between the armed forces of both countries, border crossings, overflights etc., on which Dublin appeared to co-operate only when

London offered political concessions. Raymond Carter, who was a junior minister under Rees and Mason, believed that 'they [the Irish government] always want to extract something extra from the bargaining process'.[14] Thatcher appeared to share this view: '[T]he need for greater security...meant making limited political concession to the South, much as I disliked this kind of bargaining.'[15]

Third, as a means of exerting pressure on London, and in order to limit Republican influence overseas, the Irish government attempted to mobilise elite opinion in the United States of America. The aim was to produce what could be described as a 'soft Nationalist consensus' amongst leading American politicians, that is, condemning the IRA campaign whilst advocating a new political initiative to bring about power-sharing and – in the longer term – a united Ireland by consent.[16] The Irish government's main allies in the United States were four leading Irish-American politicians, the so-called Four Horsemen, whose annual St Patrick's Day statements were close reflections of Irish government policy.[17] In 1977, they persuaded US President Jimmy Carter to adopt a declaration which called for a new political initiative and offered economic aid in return. According to the *Economist*, the draft plan was 'conceived in Dublin and [then]...sent first to the State Department and then to the White House'.[18]

Contrary to A. Guelke's suggestion that the Carter statement had made the conflict in Northern Ireland 'a legitimate concern of American foreign policy',[19] Washington's treatment of the issue in the 1976–82 period remained rather inconsistent. After the Carter statement, the US government refrained from any major interventions for almost two years. In July 1979, the US State Department imposed a ban on handgun sales to the RUC, yet only five weeks later, the Secretary of State, Cyrus Vance, emphasised that Northern Ireland was a domestic matter, and that it was 'not wise' for the US government to interfere with London's handling of the Irish Question.[20] With Ronald Reagan's election victory in 1980, Washington's interest declined almost completely, and FitzGerald's attempts at getting the US government involved in the resolution of the hunger strikes failed, not least because Reagan 'did not show a great deal of close understanding of the problem'.[21] On the American side, there was clearly no inclination to jeopardise Anglo-American relations at the height of the 'second' Cold War.[22] On the British side, there is little evidence that American pressure was perceived as overwhelming, or that it became the one 'key element' in the process of formulating British government policy, as A.J. Wilson claims.[23] In fact, London welcomed the activities of the Four Horsemen in promoting inward investment and

discouraging Irish-Americans from giving money to Republican organisations as 'exceedingly helpful',[24] but it believed that there was 'an
unfortunate tendency [in the USA] to offer advice from [a] rather shaky
base'.[25] Westminster's only direct response to American pressure was,
therefore, to improve public relations, and to pay 'constant attention to
foreign policy aimed at explaining the facts to the misinformed'.[26] Still,
there can be no doubt London regarded the internationalisation of the
conflict as an irritant; it represented another challenge to the assumption that the conflict was a domestic issue, and it added to the destabilising effects of Direct Rule.

How did London cope with the external pressure that had been created by the Irish government? As shown above, the absence of constitutional initiatives was central to London's idea of creating stability.
Whilst reaffirming the objective of devolution and 'partnership' (or
power-sharing) government, Mason declared that any initiative to that
end would be 'very dangerous, especially if it led people to believe that
there was hope and then we plunged them back in the depths of
despair'.[27] On the other hand, the assumption of full responsibility for
the government of Northern Ireland had made the British government
vulnerable: with slow improvements in the security situation, the
increasingly partisan perception of Direct Rule within the Catholic community, and growing difficulties in the economic sector (see below),
London was exposed to the external pressures which had challenged the
idea that the British government was capable of containing the conflict.
As a consequence, there was a process of gradual dilution, resulting in
the admission that the conflict could not be contained as a purely
domestic problem.

The first wave of responses to the external challenge attempted to reconcile the demand for a fresh initiative with the requirement of constitutional stability. They were half-hearted efforts to ease the pressure
from outside, and to extract a more co-operative attitude from the Irish
government. In mid-September 1977, for example, Mason had firmly
ruled out the possibility of another initiative, stating that 'the old differences on the form of devolution still arise...There is at present no
basis for agreement on the need for an interim step'.[28] Only nine weeks
later, however, he told the House of Commons that he intended to enter
into talks with the political parties in the province 'to see whether it
might be feasible to reach agreement on some form of partial devolution
as an interim step', and he sent a letter to the party leaders in which he
outlined the measures that would result in the gradual return to
devolved government.[29] Although there is no 'hard evidence' to account

for Mason's sudden change of mind, the absence of any significant political developments in the period between the two events makes it reasonable to conclude that the reversal was the result of Dublin's
intervention: on 28 September, the British and Irish Prime Ministers had
met at Downing Street, and whilst Lynch pressed for the launch of
another constitutional initiative, Callaghan had tried to persuade Lynch
of the need for more co-operation on border security.[30]

The same logic applied to the so-called Constitutional Conference.
In May 1979, Mason's successor, Humphrey Atkins, had declared that
'[a]s regards political initiatives ... I do not think that it would be right
for me to take any immediate precipitate action'.[31] By October, little had
happened that would have made any initiative more likely to succeed,
yet again, external pressures had become a major factor in the formulation of British government policy. With the handgun sales ban in July,
the US government had carried out its most hostile intervention to date.
According to Thatcher, it was an 'absurd situation' which required
increased efforts on behalf of London to enlighten public opinion across
the Atlantic.[32] Equally important, though, were the events on 27 August,
when the IRA first assassinated Lord Mountbatten in the Republic of
Ireland, and then killed 18 British soldiers in Warrenpoint, Co. Down. In
Thatcher's view, the two incidents highlighted how central border co-
operation was to improving the security situation.[33] The *Daily Telegraph*
suggested that 'Mrs Thatcher could give Mr Lynch a fillip by agreeing
that another round of political talks in Ulster should be tried',[34] and
indeed in October, Atkins invited the local parties to participate in the
Constitutional Conference.

The turn towards the inter-governmental approach of the subsequent
years followed the end of the second hunger strike in 1981. From
London's perspective, the first series of high-profile summits between
the British and Irish Prime Ministers in 1980 and 1981 had implied no
significant change of strategy yet. Whilst the Irish government had
begun to pursue the idea of an inter-governmental accord as early as
spring 1980, the British government continued to maintain the conventional approach, which translated into limiting Dublin's disruptive
potential and extracting concessions on security.[35] Even Haughey, who
had spoken of an 'historic breakthrough' after the Anglo-Irish summit in
Dublin on 8 December 1980, admitted to his Cabinet that '[w]hat's been
going on is nothing'.[36] London's first response to the 1981 hunger strike
was, therefore, entirely consistent with its earlier attempts at containing
external pressures: it launched another constitutional initiative, aiming
at an internal settlement. This time, however, the proposed scheme

(which became known as 'rolling devolution') would appease neither the Irish government nor the SDLP, both of which were terrified at the degree of Catholic support for the hunger strikers and the possible rise of *Sinn Fein* as an electoral force (see below). The resulting momentum towards a re-formulation of London's strategy became overwhelming, and the hitherto uneasy relationship with Dublin was embraced as a framework for a new departure.

'Beating the terrorists?' The contradictions of Normalisation

Whereas most commentators are correct in pointing out Mason's dislike of constitutional experiments, the characterisation of his security strategy is often misleading. Most conventional accounts suggest that the absence of any constitutional or political initiatives meant that the security forces were freed from all constraints. D. Hamill, for example, asserts that there was 'no more nonsense about political progress' once Mason had taken over as Northern Ireland Secretary.[37] In reality, however, the parameters of the British government's military tradition applied in the late-1970s as much as in any other period since the fall of Stormont in 1972. First, Westminster justified its counterinsurgency effort in Northern Ireland with reference to the existence of what it saw as an anti-democratic challenge to the rule of law, and the military instrument could therefore not be executed in a way that would have defeated this purpose. As Mason stated: 'A democracy functions by the will of the people and through the rule of law. It cannot behave like a totalitarian state, nor is it right that it should.'[38] Second, the British government understood that 'tough' security measures would alienate the minority community, help the insurgents to gain popular support, and make a political settlement in the future less likely. As Mason declared, 'The resentment that [blanket reductions in civil rights] would arouse would make the security problem far worse than it is today and prolong it further into the future.'[39] Third, the military policy of Normalisation rested on the assumption that the gradual return to 'normal' law enforcement was conducive to stability. It was irreconcilable with demands for an increased profile of the Army, or any new measures of an overtly repressive nature.

Hence, there continued to be clear limits on what could be done to increase the level of force. For instance, despite the demand from both Army and Unionists, the government decided not to re-introduce internment without trial. Now known as 'selective detention', the measure was believed to violate all three of the principles described above: it contradicted the policy of Normalisation; it would have provoked Catholic resentment; and regardless of the fact that the security forces now knew the identities and whereabouts of many IRA operatives, Mason was keen to stress that ' "known" ... does not constitute guilt in a court of law'.[40] Likewise, even some of Mason's own claims seem to be exaggerated. According to his memoirs, for example, he had '[employed] all the constitutional means at my disposal ... to the limit',[41] including a policy of arrests and re-arrests of paramilitary suspects, which attempted to disrupt illegal activities, harass 'known' members of paramilitary organisations, create opportunities to turn them into informers, and acquire further intelligence.[42] In reality, though, there is little evidence to back this assertion. For Mason's time in office, the British government's figures show a steady decrease in arrests under anti-terrorist legislation: while arrests under the Prevention of Terrorism Act fell from 1066 (1976) to 857 (1979), the corresponding numbers for the Emergency Provisions Act dropped from 8321 (1976) to 2572 (1979) (see Figure 5.1).[43]

The only area in which Mason made a tangible – yet somewhat short-lived – difference concerned the use of undercover units. The deployment of small and highly specialised units followed from the intention to reduce the profile of the Army as part of the Normalisation policy, the desire to cut Army casualties, and the renewed emphasis on improving the security forces' pool of intelligence. Furthermore, the formal introduction of the Special Air Service (SAS) to Northern Ireland in early

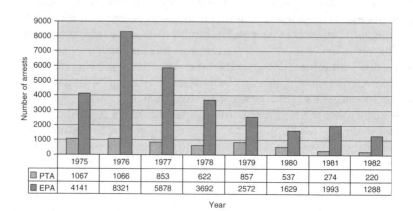

	1975	1976	1977	1978	1979	1980	1981	1982
PTA	1067	1066	853	622	857	537	274	220
EPA	4141	8321	5878	3692	2572	1629	1993	1288

Year

Figure 5.1   Arrests under anti-terrorism legislation, 1975–82

Source: see footnote 43.

1976 – when Mason had been Defence Secretary – served as a deterrent, which is why Prime Minister Wilson took the unprecedented step of announcing its deployment in public. According to Rees, it was 'more presentational and mystique-making than anything else',[44] and the fact that the SAS – with its reputation for ruthlessness and bravery – was soon blamed for every suspicious incident in the province seemed to confirm its value in that regard. Still, the deterrent effect clearly backfired when it turned out that some SAS units were involved in a series of controversial ambushes which involved the accidental – and ultimately avoidable – killing of civilians. Whilst it is not possible to examine every alleged 'shoot-to-kill' incident in detail, it is worth pointing out that the SAS also carried out many arrests, even in circumstances when 'silencing the suspect' could have spared the troops considerable embarrassment.[45] The idea of assassination squads is at odds with the strategic tradition of the British government generally, and it contradicts almost every tactical consideration of the security forces at the time, such as the near obsession with achieving convictions in court and the emphasis on turning arrestees into informers. Nonetheless, by scaling down its frontline role from 1978, the government conceded that the SAS was a military tool that was too imprecise to perform in an environment where the security forces were expected to adhere to the principle of minimum force at all times.

The most significant change in the Mason period was therefore not so much one in the overall level of force, but one of paradigm. As shown in the previous chapter, the belief that the IRA could be politicised had been given up with the failure of *Sinn Fein* to take part in the elections for the Constitutional Convention. The ceasefire was maintained for some time in order to facilitate some of the changes that were necessary to introduce the policy of Normalisation. With neither political nor military incentive left, the British government was free to return to a policy of 'isolating the terrorists'. Arguably, the denial of any sign of political legitimacy was central to the concept of Criminalisation, and only Mason set out to implement it consistently. Still, the constraints of British strategy meant that the most obvious changes in this respect were of a rhetorical nature. Mason repeatedly ruled out the possibility of any form of amnesty, and he announced that there was no realistic chance of him ever talking to, or negotiating with, the representatives of the Republican movement (although even Mason emphasised that he would 'never say never').[46] He deliberately adopted a more belligerent language, which included statements like 'we are squeezing the terrorists like rolling up a toothpaste tube',[47] or the declaration that 'the net will tighten [around]...Ulster's rabble of gangsters and destroyers'.[48]

In addition, the newspapers were filled with security statistics that appeared to illustrate the security forces' success in finding explosives, charging suspects and securing convictions.[49] Mason also put pressure on the media not to provide the IRA with a forum to present their ideas. While this could hardly be described as censorship, L. Curtis is probably correct in pointing out that the 'British way' of exerting subtle pressures on the media was far more effective than Dublin's practice of using censorship powers overtly.[50]

It is debatable how effective Mason's approach was. After he had taken office, the level of violence went down sharply, and the number of annual deaths fell from 297 in 1976 (the second worst year in the history of the conflict) to 81 in 1978. On the Protestant side, the structures of the Loyalist paramilitaries were hit hard by the policy of re-arrests and the increasing penetration with informers;[51] yet more fundamentally, Mason's vigorous statements, his self-declared 'will to win' and the overall strategy of providing stability by making Direct Rule a durable framework of government helped to convince many Protestants that the Union was safe, and that armed resistance to the IRA's attempt at forcing a united Ireland upon the majority community was therefore unnecessary. In the following years, Loyalist paramilitary operations dropped by almost 90 per cent. However, with regard to the activities of the Republican paramilitaries, it is more difficult to pass a clear judgement. Even though Republican violence was halved, the IRA and the Irish National Liberation Army (INLA) demonstrated that they continued to possess the capability to mount highly disruptive attacks, such as with the assassinations of the Tory Northern Ireland spokesman Airey Neave and Lord Mountbatten in 1979. Arguably, the drop in IRA activity was largely due to structural and strategic changes within the Republican movement whose new leadership now asserted that there was 'no quick solution to our British problem', and that the military instrument had to be reorganised to fight a protracted campaign, the so-called Long War.[52] Whether the Long War doctrine was an immediate reaction to Mason's security policies, or whether it had followed from the continued frustration of the IRA's military efforts ever since Operation Motorman, is difficult to say. In any case, Brigadier James Glover, in his 1978 assessment of 'future terrorist trends', conceded that the IRA 'will retain [sufficient] popular support', and he ascertained 'a continued trend towards greater professionalism and selectivity in targeting [sic]'.[53]

The more substantial problems with London's military policy of Normalisation arose from the ideological assumptions on which it rested. Far from merely being 'contradictions of Ulsterisation', as Bew and Patterson chose to describe them,[54] Normalisation highlighted the contradictions of the British military approach in Northern Ireland as a whole. First, the idea of 'police primacy' (as well as the continued reliance on the UDR) ignored the sectarian dynamics in the province. Even though the British government had repeatedly acknowledged that it was desirable to attract more Catholics to serve in the RUC, it clearly decided that the lack of Catholic recruits would represent no obstacle to its expansion. The systematic expansion of the full-time element within RUC and UDR – in other words, the professionalisation of the locally recruited security forces – was recognition of the fact that the conflict in Northern Ireland was not to be resolved easily, and that the government needed to create permanent structures to cope with the security problem. Significantly, it also represented London's response to the allegation that the security forces were far from being impartial and objective in carrying out their duties. Westminster believed that police primacy was an opportunity to reform the local security forces, not least because the new recruits could be trained to follow a more impartial ethos. As early as mid-1975, for example, Moyle announced that the RUC had now become 'a new police force compared with what it used to be'.[55] Although this statement was factually correct, the recruits continued to be almost exclusively Protestant. There was little awareness or understanding that, in a deeply divided society, the acceptance of law enforcement was bound to be perceived in sectarian terms, and that impartiality was not only determined by the objective professionalism of the local security forces but also by their communal composition. From a sectarian perspective, 'police primacy' thus produced a situation where one community was policing the other, and where law enforcement was likely to be seen as a tool in the inter-communal power struggle.[56]

Second, the notion that members of the paramilitaries were ordinary criminals and would be treated accordingly was incredible and inconsistent. The claim that London's presence in Northern Ireland served the purpose of upholding the rule of law was strongly believed by successive British governments, and there can be little doubt that the aspiration to the 'democratic ideal' represented an important ideological restraint on the execution of the military instrument. Still, the tension between the notion of 'normal' law enforcement in a liberal democracy and the requirements of a counterinsurgency campaign allowed for too many inconsistencies to make Westminster's claim believable. The reliance on uncorroborated evidence, extended holding powers, and the continued existence of non-jury courts, for example, proved to be a necessary and largely effective means of reducing the level of paramilitary activity, yet they were widely seen as significant diversions from established norms of justice in a liberal democracy. The restoration of police primacy highlighted the 'normality' of law enforcement in Northern Ireland, yet the need to perform some of the more robust operations that had previously been carried out by the Army clearly contradicted the British ideal of civilian policing.[57] The end of internment without trial was an important step towards re-establishing the primacy of trial in court, yet the resulting pressure to maintain military effectiveness – that is, to produce sufficient evidence to secure convictions – led to instances of police brutality, thus negating the gains in legitimacy which the abolition of internment had generated.[58]

The implementation of Criminalisation turned out to be highly disruptive. Most dramatically, it caused the Hunger Strikes of 1980 and 1981, which followed the withdrawal of Special Category status. Special Category, which had existed since 1972, allowed paramilitary prisoners to claim that they were 'political prisoners', and its removal was consequently the most symbolic means of showing that there was no difference between what the Army called 'ordinary decent criminals' and 'convicted terrorists'. Newly convicted prisoners were deprived of Special Category from March 1976; in March 1980, the status was withdrawn from all inmates who had hitherto enjoyed it. In accordance with the tenets of Criminalisation, Thatcher explained the government's reason for doing so by saying that 'there is no such thing as political murder, political bombing or political violence. There is only criminal murder, criminal bombing and criminal violence. We will not compromise on this. There will be no political status.'[59] Her reluctance to seek an understanding, or to grant some of the prisoners' so-called Five Demands, was based on the assumption that 'what [the hunger strikers] want is not prison reform, but a special different status for some prisoners. This the government cannot concede.'[60] The idea that the principle of Criminalisation was at stake, and that the positions of British government and hunger strikers were therefore irreconcilable, was shared by the hunger strikers themselves, one of whom stated that 'it is only in a continuation of the hunger strike that the pressure needed to break the British criminalization policy can be obtained ... The weapon for the criminalization policy must be removed from the British by achieving political status.'[61]

Whilst Thatcher's stance during the hunger strikes was justified within the limits of the doctrine she wanted to preserve, the government's position on the issue of political status illustrated the ambiguous nature of the doctrine itself. If the question of political status was indeed something that no democratic government could compromise, it is difficult to understand why Special Category had been granted in the first place. The relative ease with which the British government had introduced Special Category in 1972 should have made clear that its subsequent withdrawal was ill-suited to be elevated to the status of principle, not least because it demonstrated that London's principles seemed to be negotiable. Moreover, even on the government's own terms, there was little foundation to support the claim that there was no political dimension to crime. The hunger strikers were arrested, held, questioned and tried under legislation that had been justified with reference to the so-called 'terrorist threat'. Given that – according to the Prevention of Terrorism Act (1974) – terrorism was 'the use of violence for *political* ends' (emphasis added),[62] common sense suggests that there were indeed two different categories of crime: one for ordinary, and another one for 'terrorist' (i.e. political) offences. This differentiation was confirmed by Prior when, in an attempt to calm the mood and thus prevent the repetition of the events, he re-established some of the privileges for paramilitary prisoners after the end of the 1981 Hunger Strike.[63]

Honest broker? The impossibility of an internal settlement

The political impact of the Hunger Strike – and the consequences of security policy under Mason generally – can hardly be understood without reference to the underlying assumptions of London's political strategy. After the breakdown of the 1974 Executive, the British government had decided that the Irish dimension had 'knocked everything', and it was consequently watered down. After the failure of the following initiative, the Constitutional Convention, Westminster blamed the local politicians. According to Rees, the 'level of Irish politicians was very low',[64] and it simply made no sense to 'set exam papers when you know the candidates will fail'.[65] This feeling of contempt translated into a disregard for local political activity of any sort, the existence of which was seen as destructive and destabilising. When Mason set up a local economic council, he made it explicit that he did not want any politicians to be included: 'If, in this province, you decide to bring politicians on … then your economic council, first of all, will be very quickly bloated; and secondly, I don't want political squabbles to spill over.'[66] It followed that, with no input from either Dublin or local politicians, Direct Rule was not only the one remaining alternative, but also a framework which could be used to provide stability and good government

until 'the existing leaders [were] replaced by abler successors more willing to reach a compromise across sectarian barriers', as Mason had
reportedly hoped.[67] In the meantime, the British government would
continue as an honest broker, and Direct Rule was therefore thought to
be equally acceptable to both communities. Citing opinion polls, Rees
believed that there was 'little problem and certainly little opposition' to
Direct Rule because 'the Catholics preferred government from London
to a loyalist government at Stormont, and the loyalists preferred it to a
Stormont government shared with republicans'.[68]

Arguably, it was rather ingenuous for London to expect that the present generation of local politicians would suddenly go away, or – even if
they somehow did – that the next generation of 'abler successors' would
come from nowhere. The more fundamental problem, however, arose
from the central assumption on which the viability of Direct Rule rested.
If, for negative reasons, Direct Rule was workable because it was both
communities' second choice, its acceptability was bound to be affected
by the fact that a significant section of the UUP moved towards full integration with Great Britain as a durable framework and welcomed Direct
Rule as a first step in the right direction.[69] If, for positive reasons, Direct
Rule was politically feasible because Westminster was regarded as an
honest broker, its acceptability was certain to suffer from Labour's loss of
a majority in the House of Commons and the subsequent rumours of a
'parliamentary deal' between Labour and the Ulster Unionists.

Even if London denied it there can be little doubt that there was an
understanding between Labour and the Ulster Unionists. In his memoirs, Callaghan admits that negotiations took place, and he adds that
'cooperation between Michael Foot [then Leader of the House of
Commons] and Jim Molyneaux [then leader of the Ulster Unionist MPs]
proved excellent'.[70] The most tangible result of this 'cooperation' was an
increase in Northern Ireland seats in the House of Commons, which
Unionist MPs had demanded ever since Stormont was abolished in
1972.[71] The largely informal nature of the parliamentary arrangement,
however, makes it difficult to assess what further concessions were
made. M. Holland, for instance, believed that the Unionists succeeded
in stopping the policy of troop reductions.[72] P. Dixon, on the other
hand, argues that Unionist pressure resulted in the delay of Draft Orders
on the legalisation of homosexuality and the introduction of comprehensive education in Northern Ireland.[73] Even so, in one respect,
London was clearly not prepared to give in: despite Unionist demands to
the contrary, the Callaghan government stuck to the principle that any
devolution of powers had to be 'acceptable' to the minority. London's

commitment to this doctrine was first demonstrated in May 1977 when the government defied a Loyalist strike which attempted to bring about the restoration of Stormont.[74] Yet, it equally applied to the Unionist demand for an expansion of local government. Whilst Dixon is right in pointing out that Mason's initiative in 1977–78 (see above) 'closely resembled the proposal for administrative devolution that James Molyneaux had begun to advocate',[75] it was different in one crucial aspect. It demanded that 'political parties representing different shades of opinion must be prepared to make the arrangements work'.[76] Mason stated that even the devolution of additional local government powers, if based on simple majority rule, was unacceptable because 'the minority in the province would reject that sort of approach'.[77] In fact, Mason's deputy, Concannon, reiterated the principle of 'concurring majorities' by declaring that 'any new arrangement must be made acceptable to a majority in both parts of the community. If it is rejected by one or the other, it will not survive'.[78] London's commitment to upholding the Nationalist veto on devolution was particularly remarkable given that, in a 'blatant bid for Unionist support', the Conservative opposition had dropped power-sharing and adopted the Unionist policy of establishing regional councils.[79] This put additional pressure on the Callaghan government, and arguably, Labour could have survived the crucial vote of no confidence in March 1979 if Callaghan had committed himself to Molyneaux's ideas. Ironically, once elected, Thatcher was quick to distance herself from this policy. As Philipp Goodhart (an NIO minister in 1979–81) explained: '[Atkins] realised that it was necessary to proceed with extreme caution, which he did. On the whole, one [therefore] followed pretty much the policy one had inherited.'[80]

Despite Callaghan's principled stance, the parliamentary deal between Labour and the Ulster Unionists had a profound effect on the acceptability of Direct Rule to the minority. Simply, the fact that London's self-declared role as 'honest broker' appeared to be subject to the parliamentary dynamics in the House of Commons implied that Nationalists needed to find a more reliable ally in order to set the balance of power straight. Whereas in 1975, the SDLP seemed willing to play down the Irish dimension in favour of an internal power-sharing settlement, the main Catholic party had convinced itself that its link to Dublin, and the inclusion of the Irish government in any settlement, was essential to ensuring that the minority's interests would be safeguarded. Accordingly, in its 1978 policy document, 'Towards a New Ireland', the SDLP argued that 'the problems of Northern Ireland can only be solved by joint Anglo-Irish action'.[81] The SDLP's turn towards a more Nationalist attitude indicated that Direct Rule had lost any credibility as an acceptable constitutional framework amongst the minority, and that the idea of Westminster as an impartial and honest broker had become untenable. Furthermore, the SDLP's powerful position as the only representative of constitutional Nationalism meant that the party could exercise its veto over any plans to establish devolved structures. In other words, there could be no internal settlement anymore, and any new attempt at bringing about devolution and power-sharing had to include an institutionalised Irish dimension.

It took until 1982 for London to realise the full implications of the shift in Nationalist strategy. In the meantime, the British government undertook three attempts at producing a devolved settlement. With the possible exception of 'rolling devolution' in 1982, all of them sought to ease the (mainly external) pressures Westminster was exposed to as a result of Direct Rule. Structurally, the Mason initiative of 1977–78, the Constitutional Conference in 1980 and 'rolling devolution' followed a similar pattern, and even when compared to the devolutionary initiatives of the previous period, they were exercises in fine-tuning rather than genuine political evolution. In 1974, security powers and electoral arrangements had been excluded from the list of devolved powers, partly because of their divisive potential. The same logic applied to the abandonment of the Irish dimension in the run-up to the 1975 Constitutional Convention. With two failed attempts at achieving a devolved power-sharing settlement, the British government now decided to turn its political approach upside down: instead of handing over a number of pre-determined powers to a Home Rule government upfront, as in the 1972–75 period, any new institutions would have to start with little more than consultative or administrative responsibilities. Subject to agreement between the political parties from both majority and minority, 'real' powers would then be devolved gradually, starting with the least controversial areas and evolving towards full-scale devolution along the lines of the 1974 Executive. In London's view, the notion of 'a progressive transfer over a period of time'[82] had several advantages: it was more flexible and less destabilising, as powers would only be devolved in areas where there was a clear consensus on how the responsibilities would be exercised; and there was an incentive for both sides to find an accommodation, as otherwise there would be no transfer of any powers at all.

With regard to power-sharing, the British government continued to put the requirement of minority participation in less stringent terms than in the run-up to the 1974 Executive. According to Mason, power-sharing was an 'emotive term', and he therefore preferred to make the case for 'partnership and [minority] participation in the administration of Northern Ireland' instead.[83] The White Paper for the Constitutional Conference supplied a whole range of suggestions as to how minority interests could be safeguarded: by minority participation in the executive, through weighed votes and committees, in a so-called 'executive chamber', or by vote of confidence.[84] The 1982 rolling devolution scheme made the support of 70 per cent of the Assembly a requirement for the transfer of powers,[85] and like all his predecessors, Prior declared that 'any arrangement to devolve power would simply not work unless it had widespread acceptance throughout the community'.[86] Hence, even though the attitude towards power-sharing had become more flexible, Westminster's determination to maintain the Nationalist veto on devolution remained firm.

The failure of all three initiatives can be traced back to the shortcomings of Direct Rule, and the strategic changes it had triggered. In 1978, with full integration on top of the Unionist agenda and both Labour and Conservatives competing for Unionist votes in the House of Commons, there was no incentive for the UUP to discuss devolution. In fact, as it was stressed at the time, the Unionists were 'liable to sit tight until Mr Callaghan goes to the country'.[87] In 1980, whilst the UUP refused even to participate in the Constitutional Conference, the SDLP now insisted on a separate round of talks that would deal with the Irish dimension (which had originally been excluded from London's proposals). This, however, proved unacceptable to the DUP, and the Conference consequently ended without achieving any tangible results. The 1982 Assembly, on the other hand, operated until 1986, and even though some observers argue that it turned out to be a valuable forum for consultation, it never achieved its original purpose.[88] The notion that a new political initiative along the lines of the previous attempts at achieving devolution would 'win back support for moderation'[89] backfired spectacularly when the SDLP decided not to take its seats in the 'rolling devolution' Assembly whilst *Sinn Fein* managed to gain 10.1 per cent of the vote. In Prior's words: 'As soon as the SDLP announced that it was not going to take part in the Assembly, it was a dead duck ... One kept it going for a bit, to allow [some Unionist] steam to be blown off, and to show that we were ... committed to [the creation of] a devolved system.'[90]

In addition, the emergence of *Sinn Fein* as an electoral force made it even more difficult for constitutional Nationalism to adopt a moderate position. Hardly anyone – including the IRA leadership – anticipated the extent to which the hunger strikes could galvanise certain sections of the Catholic populace in support of the Republican movement.[91] Regarding London, the ignorance of the sectarian dynamics in a deeply divided society had led to a gross underestimation of the hunger strikers' potential to mobilise the minority community. As Goodhart explained:

> [A]s far as quite a lot of the governmental machine was concerned, *Sinn Fein* was looked upon with the same enthusiasm as one might have looked upon a group of Nazis, and if Rudolf Hess wants to starve himself to death, so be it ... To a degree, Sinn Fein/IRA was regarded as more of a fascist organisation than an ordinary Western democratic organisation. Indeed, those people were regarded as semi-criminal, more criminal than political.[92]

The idea that the fault line in Northern Ireland society was not between the two communities, but rather between the 'men of violence' and the supposedly peaceloving population from both communities, had long dominated British thinking on the use of the political instrument. Yet, the doctrine of Criminalisation had given additional impetus as well as moral and political justification to the notion that the 'terorrists' were at the fringes of the society which, in turn, blinded the British government to the fact that even anti-republican Catholics, such as Mairead Corrigan (who co-founded the peace movement in 1976), saw them as 'men from our community. We know how they have come to be there. And above all we don't want them suffering within the prisons'.[93] It was incomprehensible to the British government that the SDLP withdrew from the by-election for the seat of Fermanagh and South Tyrone in favour of the hunger striker Bobby Sands; and it was equally inconceivable that a majority of Catholics in this constituency neither abstained nor spoiled their votes, but in fact decided to lend active support to an imprisoned 'criminal'. Even if a clear majority of Catholics continued to support constitutional Nationalists, Bobby Sands' victory, as well as *Sinn Fein's* relative success in the Assembly elections, refuted the idea that the 'men of violence' were isolated. Equally, it was a damning indictment of the policy of 'caring' and 'positive' Direct Rule which had left the SDLP with nothing to show. Instead of strengthening the moderates, Direct Rule had in fact proved to many Catholics that constitutional Nationalism was not the way forward, and it forced the SDLP into adopting the more intransigent attitude towards the British government at the time of the Labour–Unionist understanding. In short, the supposedly stabilising impact of Direct Rule had turned out as both destabilising and polarising.

'Bread and circuses'? The limits of economic development

Like London's political strategy, it is difficult to comprehend the wider significance of economic policy in the Mason period without putting it in the context of London's overall strategy. For example, whilst London's commitment to devoting substantial resources to economic development is widely acknowledged, many critics have maintained that – in a 'cynical political calculation'[94] – the British government had decided to substitute political progress for economic largesse. According to J. McGarry and B. O'Leary, for example, Mason's 'bread and circuses' were 'little better than opiates'.[95] This view, however appealing its logic, remains open to challenge. One may argue that it overstates the degree to which the use of the political and economic instruments was co-ordinated in the process of formulating British strategy. Whereas both political activity and economic progress were undoubtedly elements of one calculus, a close reading of the sources suggests that – in London's view – their respective link to the overall objective of stability was autonomous: political activity was seen as destabilising, and it was therefore discouraged; economic progress, on the other hand, was regarded as a positive factor, and it was consequently given more prominence. Thus, from London's perspective, it was perfectly plausible to explain the function of economic policy simply as an outcome of the desire for stability. As Raymond Carter stated:

> You were trying to impose on a chaotic situation some degree of order, some stability, some sense of social cohesiveness ... [w]hat you were trying to do was to make small advances wherever you could. If the building of a sports centre was a contribution, you did it. If building a road would help, if attracting inward investment would help, you did it.[96]

Whilst the critics are therefore wrong to suggest that London 'cynically' aimed at compensating for the lack of political activity by throwing money at the province, the dependence on economic progress was an inevitable – if unintended – result of Westminster's wider strategy. In fact, in a reversal of the critics' argument, one could argue that whereas in earlier periods the political 'opiate' of institutional initiatives had served as a substitute for economic development, this excuse had now become untenable. With no significant political developments – and therefore no one to blame – Westminster had literally exposed itself: whether Direct Rule was indeed seen as 'caring' and 'compassionate' now depended largely on Westminster's ability to come to terms with non-constitutional factors such as security and the economy.

Economic progress, however, hinged on many variables, some of which were beyond Westminster's control. Most fundamentally, London could not easily alter the fact that there was a global recession that accelerated the decline of traditional industries (for instance, textiles and shipbuilding).[97] Even in other sectors of the economy, the recession had forced multinational companies to increase efficiency rather than expand, so that 'in present economic circumstances, the tentacles [i.e. the Northern Ireland branch plants] are likely to be cut off before the main body', as Mason recognised.[98] Accordingly, an assessment by a group of civil servants, the so-called Quigley report, painted a gloomy picture of the province's economic prospects. It warned that any positive development of the Northern Ireland economy rested on a number of factors, such as less violence, a general upturn in the economic cycle, and the retention of Northern Ireland's competitive position. Even if all the conditions were met, Quigley argued, the best the government could hope for was a stabilisation of the unemployment figures.[99] Hence, one could hardly imagine a worse time to stake one's credibility on an upturn in the economy. Yet, by abandoning the idea of immediate political progress, London had done exactly that, and it had therefore made itself and its idea of stability through Direct Rule extremely vulnerable.

The flaws in Westminster's strategy would soon become evident. Despite Quigley's recommendation that 'we must hold onto what we have ... encourage it to increase its efficiency and, where possible, generate its own growth',[100] London's dependence on economic progress implied that the government needed to campaign aggressively for additional inward investment. In times of recession, however, available investment was scarce and the competition between governments fierce. This meant that venturesome (and sometimes fraudulent) investors were not only offered support that would have been difficult to obtain otherwise, but that they were able to shift the financial risk onto the governments that were desperate to secure any additional employment available.[101] These dynamics manifested themselves most clearly in the case of the DeLorean car factory, which resulted in the loss of £85 m in government subsidies between 1978 and 1982 (when the factory was closed down). Despite repeated advice that the demand for sports cars was declining, and that DeLorean's business plan was based on a series of overly optimistic assumptions, the government shouldered the financial risk to the extent that the company's founder,

John DeLorean, 'did not have to put in a penny [himself]'.[102] In his memoirs, Mason blamed DeLorean's failure on the Conservative government's 'lack of political will' and its free-market ideology which contradicted the 'detailed, hands-on supervision' that his government had allegedly exercised.[103] Given that Mason himself had agreed to leaving the government with a small minority of voting shares,[104] this excuse sounds rather unconvincing. In reality, London's reliance on economic progress had simply blinded the government to the fact that DeLorean's project was not viable, and only Prior, who became Northern Ireland Secretary in 1981, would acknowledge that '[o]ne of the tragedies of Northern Ireland is that it attracts so many risky businesses, those which perhaps do not go elsewhere because they can't get the cash'.[105]

London's vigour in promoting inward investment was not matched by an equal degree of enthusiasm in eradicating the relative deprivation between the two communities. Following a recommendation in the Quigley report,[106] the growth centre strategy of the Stormont period (which favoured Protestant areas) was now officially reversed and efforts were made to locate new investment in areas of high unemployment. Equally, improvements in the social infrastructure focused on areas of urban deprivation (especially West Belfast), thus prompting accusations of reverse discrimination by Protestant politicians.[107] Overall, however, the British government continued to shy away from addressing the issue in a way that would have brought about tangible changes to the economic imbalance between Catholics and Protestants. Quigley had warned about the sectarian implications of a declining economy, and even though his description of Northern Ireland as a 'dual economy' did not explicitly refer to the sectarian divide, he had made it sufficiently clear that the global recession would affect those on the margins of the labour market disproportionately.[108] London's total failure to respond to these concerns, or even to formulate a coherent stance on the wider issue, reveals the unease with which the problem was treated. As in the 1972–75 period, it appears that the reaction of the British government was informed by a mixture of ignorance, complacency, the desire not to offend the Protestants and an individualistic concept of social justice which did not allow for sweeping changes along community lines.

The Fair Employment Agency (FEA), which was created by the Fair Employment Act (1976), was of little help. As V. McCormack points out, the agency was underfunded and lacked both the means of carrying out thorough investigations and the powers of forcing employers to change recruiting patterns – or even to reveal the names of companies which had engaged in discrimination. It was, in his words, 'an inadequate piece of legislation being operated by an underfunded and uncertain [agency] opting for education and public relations exercises instead of effective law enforcement'.[109] The mere fact that companies were under no obligation to disclose the religious affiliation of their workforce demonstrates that it was impossible to monitor employment practices effectively. Even staunch opponents of the legislation, like Paisley, wondered how 'this Fair Employment Agency can...act...when there is [no] breakdown on figures'.[110] In an usually frank statement, Atkins therefore admitted that the FEA and the other institutions that dealt with discrimination in employment (such as the Commissioner for Complaints) were 'somewhat cumbersome bodies and rather slow to act'.[111]

It is often implied that the change of government in 1979 fundamentally changed the government's economic policy towards the province. According to B. Rowthorn and N. Wayne, for example, the Conservatives simply abandoned the principle of peace and prosperity.[112] Yet, even if Mason's policy of economic largesse was partially reversed after 1979, the immediate change was not as fundamental as Rowthorn and Wayne imply. Adam Butler, who was a Minister of State under Prior, clearly stated that his government attached 'considerable importance to tackling the economic as well as the political problem, because [there is a] close relationship between the two'.[113] As a result, some areas of public spending escaped the drastic cuts that had been implemented on the British mainland. For example, whilst the government started its retreat from public housing in Great Britain, Prior took pride in increasing the amount of money that was made available for this purpose in Northern Ireland.[114] Equally, the province would keep the most attractive incentive structure for industrial development in the United Kingdom and, arguably, in the whole of Western Europe.[115] The stated objectives of supporting established businesses, encouraging the start of local businesses, and attracting companies from outside were well within the traditional framework of previous governments' economic policy, even if the means of doing so now incorporated some fashionable neo-liberal ideas (for instance, by introducing so-called 'Enterprise Zones' in Belfast and Derry-City).[116] Rowthorn and Wayne are correct in asserting that the expansion of the state sector in the province slowed down from 1979, yet – as their own statistics show – it continued to grow in the first years of Thatcher's reign, most notably in health and education, where differences between Northern Ireland and Great Britain continued to persist.[117] Whilst London demanded that the dependency on government subsidies had to decrease, this trend towards 'greater selectivity and targeting'[118] cannot, in itself, be taken as an indicator of any fundamental change in the attitude of the British government towards the province.

Conclusion

In a reversal of the previous period of British involvement in Northern Ireland, when London had intended to rid itself of the burden of governing the province, the British government now wanted to govern the province but failed to withstand the pressures that would have allowed it to do so.

With the dissolution of the Constitutional Convention, the British government decided that no new constitutional initiatives would be pursued. As a result of the repeated failure to produce a power-sharing settlement, London had concluded that a stable constitutional, political, military and economic environment needed to be achieved prior to launching another political initiative. In other words, while power-sharing with devolution continued to be Westminster's objective, its realisation was now believed to lie in the long rather than the short term. In the meantime, Direct Rule would be embraced as a durable constitutional framework. The strategic instrument was rearranged as follows:

- The constitutional instrument: to emphasise that the 'myth of British withdrawal is dead for ever',[119] and that no devolutionary initiatives would be undertaken.
- The military instrument: to fully implement the policy of Normalisation.
- The political instrument: to discourage local political activity and wait for the current generation of provincial leaders to be replaced by 'abler successors'.
- The economic instrument, to renew the efforts to reduce unemployment and achieve social and economic parity with the rest of the United Kingdom.

In itself, the notion of stability as a pre-condition for constitutional progress was a perfectly coherent response to London's previous experience, and Direct Rule was the obvious constitutional setting under which to carry the new strategy through. Still, despite its apparent appeal to policymakers at the time, Westminster's strategy was fatally flawed. It assumed an almost ideal game situation, that is, one in which London was the only actor to determine the strategic environment. As it turned out, all the assumptions on which the presumed link between

Direct Rule and stability rested were to be undermined. First, the government of the Republic of Ireland consistently – and successfully – frustrated the assumption that Northern Ireland was a domestic matter. Second, as a result of its dwindling majority in the House of Commons, the Labour government compromised its self-declared role of honest broker by forging a parliamentary deal with the Ulster Unionists. Third, Westminster's capability to produce stability through economic development was limited in view of a global recession and the continuation of the conflict. Fourth, the overall security situation improved, yet the self-imposed constraints of Normalisation and London's military tradition meant that the IRA's capacity to disrupt remained considerable. In practice, Westminster's idea of Direct Rule had therefore made the British government vulnerable, and contrary to its original idea, the main effects of the strategy were both destabilising and polarising: external pressures resulted in the need to embark on half-hearted attempts at producing a devolved settlement; the inconsistencies of Criminalisation mobilised the minority against British rule and disproved the idea of a 'moderate centre'; the disdain for local political activity as well as the Labour–Unionist understanding pushed the SDLP towards a more Nationalist position; and the reliance on economic progress in times of recession meant that money had to be wasted on risky or unproductive ventures whilst no tangible improvements to the overall situation could be achieved.

The consequences of the second Hunger Strike in 1981 signified the eventual collapse of London's strategy. Even so, looking at events from a somewhat wider perspective makes clear that it was not one event that explains the re-formulation of British strategy, but that the change in approach had resulted from the deficiencies of London's existing approach as a whole. Regarding the evolution of British strategy, the 1976–82 period showed that the Irish dimension of the conflict was not merely a traditional British instinct – one that could be abandoned if the circumstances did not suit – but that, again, it had become a constitutional and political imperative without which any policy of containment was unworkable. To summarise, in the 1976–82 period, the British government was compelled to acknowledge that the conflict was not a purely domestic matter, even if it had initially declared it to be one. The failure of Direct Rule in the 1976–82 period thus provides the key to explaining the change in attitude towards the government of the Republic of Ireland which dominated the following period of British involvement in the conflict.

6
Sharing the Burden: the Refinement of British Strategy, 1982–88

The Anglo-Irish Agreement (AIA) of 1985 was the central political event of the 1982–88 period. It originated from the political pressures that had made the operation of undiminished Direct Rule in the 1976–82 period impossible. Although it was immediately described as 'the most significant political development since the state of Northern Ireland was created',[1] from a British perspective, it failed to achieve the intended purpose of easing the operation of Direct Rule.

Consensus – the re-emergence of the Irish dimension

At the beginning of the period, the British government had convinced itself that the maintenance of undiminished Direct Rule from London was not a viable framework in which to contain the conflict. As there was little realistic prospect of a devolved cross-community settlement, the British government concluded that the handling of the province could only be eased by exploring the possibility of joint action with the Irish government. Dublin's consistent interventions, and its failure to co-operate cordially with the British government, were regarded as one of the main reasons for why the Direct Rule approach in the 1976–82 period had to be abandoned (see Chapter 5). Consequently, London's aims in the bilateral negotiations were related to the areas in which the actions of the Irish government had been perceived as particularly disruptive.

The most tangible British interest lay in the field of security co-operation, which London believed to be unsatisfactory. As Thatcher emphasised: 'We wanted to bring solutions to these problems, some of which required the Irish to deploy more resources to the border, others of which were really a matter of political will.'[2] Second, the British government expected that Dublin's collaboration would end the minority's reluctance to support the security forces in Northern Ireland and, to a lesser extent, the political system in general. Robert Andrew, who was Permanent Secretary at the NIO, hoped 'that the Agreement would allow moderate Nationalists to support the law and order effort more than hitherto, and that, for example, the SDLP would encourage Catholics to join the RUC'.[3] Third, London aimed at making the Irish government a responsible 'stakeholder' in the management of Northern Ireland, thus ending the 'megaphone diplomacy' between the two governments which had undermined Anglo-Irish relations and produced criticism of the British government from within the British Isles and abroad. Accordingly, Christopher Mallaby, the co-ordinator of Anglo-Irish relations at the Cabinet Office, described his task as follows:

> [W]e were to establish whether it was possible to have an agreement with the Irish Republic which would facilitate the United Kingdom's handling of the Northern Ireland issue without making unacceptable changes... The first question was [therefore]: can we achieve a better relationship between London and Dublin – concerning Northern Ireland but also generally.[4]

Whilst both governments agreed on the need to contain the conflict, and even if none of them questioned the existence of Northern Ireland in principle, there was a fundamental difference in perspective. Whereas London was primarily concerned with settling a number of immediate problems in order to ease the operation of an otherwise acceptable constitutional framework, the Irish government started from the wider assumption that instability and violence would only cease if one managed to overcome the minority's alienation from the institutions of government. Accordingly, FitzGerald believed that the only way of resolving the conflict was 'to act urgently and resolutely together on the political front' in order to find an entirely new constitutional arrangement.[5] In Dublin's view, undiminished British rule – as in Direct Rule – could never achieve this aim. In the absence of power-sharing, the Irish government therefore needed to assume the role of a 'guarantor' by participating in the government of the province through a system of 'joint authority' which would retain British sovereignty over the province but include Dublin as an equal partner in the process of decision-making. It was, in FitzGerald's view, 'simply a method that the British government might choose to adopt in the exercise of its sovereignty in order to regulate affairs of one part of the United Kingdom'.[6] In addition, it was believed that 'joint authority' provided a powerful incentive for the Unionists to agree to power-sharing (see below).

The constitutional tradition of the British government did not contradict 'joint authority'. In practice, however, the British government intended to achieve a 'balanced' outcome, that is, one in which both communities in Northern Ireland would eventually acquiesce. Since Nationalist concerns were represented by the Irish government, the practical limit on what Westminster could concede was determined by what was thought to be acceptable to the majority community. Although London was aware that *any* form of institutionalised co-operation with Dublin would arouse Unionist suspicions (hence 'Thatcher's personal decision not to consult the Unionists until the very last minute when the thing was ready'),[7] the British government needed to avoid a situation in which united Unionist opposition would render the province ungovernable in the same way in which a Loyalist stoppage had forced the British government to abandon the power-sharing Executive in 1974 (see Chapter 4). Westminster assumed this line to be crossed once Dublin was given 'real powers'. As Mallaby explained:

> Any situation where the British government would require the Irish government's agreement to any action or policy would be unacceptable. Where we would have their advice, and where they would have opportunities to lobby us – and indeed reflect the views of the minority in Northern Ireland – that we would be willing to consider.[8]

It followed that whilst any form of joint authority was 'out',[9] the formalisation of a consultative role was believed to be unproblematic. In London's view, consultation did not infringe upon parliamentary sovereignty, nor was it considered a substantial concession. As Prior's successor, Douglas Hurd, explained: 'Giving the Republic a voice in the internal matters of the province did not strike me as a problem, because they already had it. If there was some event … the Irish Foreign Minister, Peter Barry, used to phone me anyway. He didn't need a treaty to do that.'[10]

It could be argued, therefore, that Dublin's intention to seek fundamental political and constitutional change stood against the more limited expectations on the British side. Consequently, even FitzGerald's rhetorical 'trump card' – the growth of *Sinn Fein* and the prospect of a 'British Cuba' – failed to achieve the desired result of impressing upon London the need for substantial changes with regard to Northern Ireland's constitutional status. Thatcher explained that she 'shared his aim of preventing Ireland falling under hostile and tyrannical forces.

But that was not an argument for taking measures which would simply provoke the Unionists and cause unnecessary trouble'.[11] The same logic applied to the possibility of dropping the articles in the Irish Constitution that laid claim to the whole island of Ireland, and which had, therefore, been a longstanding Unionist grievance. Originally, London was keen to secure this concession, yet as FitzGerald linked any change in the Republic's constitution to the attainment of 'joint authority', the British government soon lost interest. According to Hurd: 'A bargain which gave them joint sovereignty – which was a huge concession, and which might have suffered the same fate as the Sunningdale Agreement – in return for a change of the Constitution was not ... a jewel worth paying a big price for.'[12]

From a strategic perspective, the most interesting question is whether the AIA indicated any significant shift in Westminster's attitude towards the constitutional position of the province. As with Sunningdale, the vagueness and deliberate ambiguities of the AIA allowed for a wide range of interpretations.[13] It is useful, therefore, to outline the AIA's content before attempting to analyse its meaning.[14] Without saying precisely what it was, Article 1 affirms that the constitutional status of Northern Ireland can only be changed if a majority of its people are in favour; and that both governments recognise that 'the present wish ... is for no change'. However, if a majority 'clearly wish for and formally consent to the establishment of a united Ireland', the two governments declare that 'they will introduce and support in the respective Parliaments legislation to give effect to that wish'. Article 2 establishes an Inter-Governmental Conference (IGC) – accompanied by a Joint Secretariat – in which the two governments were to deal with political, security and legal matters as well as the promotion of cross-border co-operation. It grants the Republic of Ireland a consultative role. Whilst the British government 'retains responsibility for the decisions and administration of government within its own jurisdiction', it is both government's duty to make 'determined efforts ... to resolve any differences'. Articles 5–10 specify the issues the IGC was to consider, and notes – amongst many others – the protection of both communities' heritage and identity, the use of flags and emblems, the prevention of economic and social discrimination, a Bill of Rights, the increase of Catholics in the RUC, and the idea of mixed courts. Also, Articles 4, 5 and 10 mention the possibility of – and indeed the commitment to – a devolved cross-community settlement. However, in the absence of agreement between the two communities on this matter, the Irish government was expected to act on behalf of the minority within the IGC: 'The Conference shall be a framework within which the Irish government may, where the interests of the minority community are significantly or especially affected, put forward views on proposals for major legislation and on major policy issues' (Article 5).

In an effort to 'sell' the agreement to the majority community, Thatcher asserted that the AIA 'confirms the status of Northern Ireland as part of the United Kingdom and recognises the legitimacy of the Unionist position', but also that it was 'the first time in a formal international agreement that the Republic has recognised this position ... and has recognised that it cannot be changed except with the consent of the majority'.[15] However, all the points raised by Thatcher were open to challenge. Regarding the issue of status, the Irish government had recognised Northern Ireland's international status on numerous occasions prior to the AIA. In 1925, London and Dublin had registered the results of the so-called Boundary Commission at the League of Nations. In 1975, the Irish and British governments – as participants of the Conference on Security and Co-operation in Europe – agreed to 'regard as inviolable all one another's frontiers as well as the frontiers of all States in Europe'. In addition, the Conference's Final Act stated that the signatories 'will also refrain from any demand for, or act of, seizure and usurpation of part or all of the territory of any participating State'.[16] Given that the (then) British Prime Minister Wilson signed on behalf of the 'United Kingdom of Great Britain and Northern Ireland', the 1975 declaration represented a much stronger recognition by Dublin than the AIA, which failed to spell out precisely what the constitutional position of Northern Ireland was.[17] Further, even if it was correct to maintain that the Irish government had, for the first time, accepted the consent principle in international law, this provision was unlikely to be seen as anything but a minor concession. Dublin's commitment to the consent principle had been included in the Sunningdale Agreement, and it would have become part of a binding international treaty as early as 1974 if the Executive had survived. In fact, ever since the fall of Stormont in 1972, there had never been any doubt that the Irish government accepted the consent principle, and it was consequently reaffirmed by Irish as well as British ministers on almost every bilateral occasion. The addition that 'the present wish ... is for no change' was new, yet it is hard to see how it represented anything but a statement of the obvious. There was therefore no reason for Unionists to think that they had made a 'big gain', as London argued.[18] On the contrary, the AIA's deliberate vagueness with regard to Northern Ireland's status fuelled the majority's constitutional insecurity, and the Irish government's continued refusal to remove the territorial claim from the Republic's constitution appeared to underline the ambiguity of Dublin's commitments.

Was there any change in London's position? Unionists were outraged in view of the fact that the British government had agreed to facilitate, and indeed support, the creation of a united Ireland once there was a majority of the people of Northern Ireland in favour. According to E. Haslett, it shifted 'the centre of gravity of Northern Ireland affairs from a United Kingdom to an all-Ireland setting... and puts in motion the process by which that aspiration [that is, a united Ireland] is to be realised'.[19] Nationalists, on the other hand, started to contend that '[t]he British government is neutral in that it is no longer pro-Union'.[20] From London's perspective, the fierce reaction within Northern Ireland came as a surprise, and even an experienced politician like Thatcher's Foreign Secretary Geoffrey Howe now admits that 'the emotional strength [of Unionist opposition] shook me'.[21] The British government maintained that there was no reason for Unionists to worry since London's formal stance on the constitutional future of Northern Ireland had remained unchanged – and indeed, whilst the explicit reference to support for a united Ireland, and its inclusion in an international treaty, had been the most forceful expression of British neutrality to date, the continued commitment to the consent principle meant that the Union was essentially guaranteed. In fact, the principle of consent – so cherished by successive British governments – implied the notion of neutrality, which is why it could be used to suggest that there was no constitutional change imminent (to reassure Unionists), or to emphasise the possibility of a united Ireland through constitutional means (to placate Nationalists).

The AIA's only tangible constitutional implication was that it effectively ruled out the option of 'full integration'. In May 1980, Thatcher had stated that '[t]he future of the constitutional affairs of Northern Ireland is a matter for the people of Northern Ireland, this government and this parliament and no one else'.[22] Five years later, this stance had become impossible, and accordingly, Hurd was the first Northern Ireland Secretary under Thatcher to declare that '[t]he Irish government have a legitimate interest in what goes on in Northern Ireland, especially in those matters which affect the minority community'.[23] Even if the 'legitimate interest' of the Irish government translated into little more than a consultative role, its recognition formally closed the door on the option of treating Northern Ireland like any part of Great Britain.

Considering its intention of negotiating a constitutionally balanced package, London clearly failed. The idea that some vague and practically insignificant gestures in support of the consent principle would make up for the formal inclusion of Dublin in the governance of Northern Ireland illustrated how the British government continued to misapprehend the concerns of the Unionist community, the political representatives of which were far more worried about a gradual drift into joint authority than a sudden transfer of full sovereignty.[24] As an instrument of producing acceptable constitutional change, the AIA had therefore been a serious miscalculation which illustrated the continued psychological and political alienation between the British government and its supposedly natural constituency in Northern Ireland. However, in contrast to the strong reactions from the majority in Northern Ireland, Westminster's view was that nothing substantial had changed – and indeed, the AIA was possibly the purest and most comprehensive combination of traditional strategic themes, such as British neutrality, the idea that Northern Ireland was somehow different from the rest of the United Kingdom, and the desire to distance the province from the British mainland.

Holding the ring – the limits of counterinsurgency

Contrary to the popular image of the 'Iron Lady', the Thatcher period saw no significant increase in the security forces' level of force. As in earlier periods, it seemed that the self-imposed restraints of constitutionality, acceptability and normality implied that, instead of being given any new tools, the security forces needed to gain efficiency within the existing framework. Prior, for instance, comments that 'without putting the whole country on a war footing, there wasn't much else' that could have been done.[25] In a similar vein, Hurd ruled out the three most popular demands for increasing the level of force – internment, shoot-to-kill and cross-border 'hot' pursuit – as politically unacceptable, counterproductive and unrealistic.[26]

The example of Thatcher shows that even when there was an overwhelming political desire, the existing political and constitutional parameters limited the military options that could be pursued. Whilst Thatcher approved of the traditional strategic doctrine that there could be no 'military solution', and that it was 'impossible to separate entirely the security policy … from the wider political approach',[27] she nevertheless adopted an explicitly hawkish attitude towards the IRA.[28] In late 1987, she initiated a review of security policy, declaring her determination that 'nothing should be ruled out'.[29] Accordingly, the list of measures that were considered by the government included: more house searches in Nationalist areas, ending the 'right to silence', banning *Sinn Fein*, the introduction of internment, identity cards, increasing the number of soldiers, replacing the policy of police primacy, relaxing the rules on opening fire, and so on.[30] When the review was concluded, in spring 1988, most of the items had disappeared from the list, and those that were put into practice – such as cutting the remission for 'terrorist prisoners', or enabling the authorities to seize bank accounts – were of a symbolic nature, or phenomena dealt with at the margins. Consequently, even Thatcher concluded that the security forces' resources 'were adequate to contain, but not as yet to defeat the IRA'.[31]

Whilst Thatcher's attitude shows that there was a perception of military stalemate on the part of London, this was by no means a novel development. The main dilemma in devising the British government's military strategy in Northern Ireland was – and had always been – how to reconcile the domestic notion of the rule of law with the need to conduct an effective counterinsurgency campaign. In previous periods of British military involvement, some of the attempts to resolve this dilemma included the introduction of internment, the abolition of juries for scheduled offences and the reliance on uncorroborated evidence, mainly in the form of confessions. With the exception of internment, the British government believed that, on balance, those aberrations from 'normal' law enforcement were acceptable under the existing circumstances, provided that the measures were employed with caution and appropriate safeguards were in place (e.g. a rigorous appeals procedure). In the 1982–88 period, two more attempts at resolving the dilemma were made, both of which demonstrated that – from a military point of view – the 'war' was winnable if not for the self-imposed limits on what was acceptable as a means of restoring the rule of law in Northern Ireland.

The first attempt to make the counterinsurgency campaign more effective was the systematic use of accomplice evidence. There is no evidence that the emergence of the so-called supergrasses was part of a deliberate policy. Nick Scott, who was Prior's junior minister in charge of security, stated that there was no governmental directive to that effect, but that the practice had originated in an operational decision by the RUC.[32] Nonetheless, Westminster had no objections as there was 'no reason to reject in principle evidence simply because it comes from an accomplice', and the idea was consequently embraced by the British government.[33] By 1983, the supergrass system had become the most significant means of reducing paramilitary activity, having 'broken up the Ulster Volunteer Force command structure in Belfast and virtually eliminated the Provisional IRA in Northern Belfast'.[34] Yet, despite its apparent effectiveness, the supergrass system came to an end in 1986.

It was criticised for producing unsafe verdicts, undermining the integrity of the justice system and thus furthering the minority's alienation from the institutions of government.[35] In defending it, London pointed to England where accomplice eivdence had been a well-established practice. However, as M. Cunningham points out, there were considerable differences with the British mainland: in Northern Ireland, there was no jury; in most cases, accomplice evidence was uncorroborated; and supergrasses were offered substantial inducements, such as complete immunity from prosecution and the facilitation of resettlement abroad.[36] As a result, many of those who had originally been convicted were acquitted on appeal, and the system gradually imploded.

The second attempt at refining the military campaign became known as shoot-to-kill. There were several occasions on which the security forces clearly exceeded the level of force that would have been necessary to make arrests, the most prominent of which was a series of incidents during which six unarmed Catholic men (five of whom had paramilitary connections) were shot dead by an RUC undercover unit. It is unlikely, however, that London initiated, or explicitly agreed to, a policy of planned assassinations. At government level, 'shoot-to-kill' was repeatedly rejected for moral as well as practical reasons. Prior, for instance, declared that '[w]e must not fall into the trap of acting in any way which at any time would be against the law ... which we are proud to uphold in the whole of the United Kingdom'.[37] Furthermore, he believed that 'shoot to kill' would have been counterproductive: '[W]e knew that everytime the security forces did kill someone, there was going to be a further outbreak of terrorism from somewhere [else].'[38] At the same time, though, there was little surprise at the occurrence of the shootings, and equally, there was no doubt that the security forces had acted inappropriately. Their actions were regarded as an inevitable, and ultimately unavoidable, reaction to the justice system's inability to achieve convictions in court. Referring to the incidents in 1982, Gowrie was 'certain that ministers were covering for excessive, though understandable, reactions by the police'.[39] Indeed, whilst no one at Westminster would have considered to make 'shoot to kill' an official government policy, there was a degree of understanding, if not sympathy, for the security forces which – according to Hurd – 'were expected to play by rules which the IRA would have never dreamt about'.[40] As Richard Needham, who was an NIO minister in the years 1985–92, put it: 'We knew who was guilty. But when the administration of justice breaks down, the police either sit in their barracks and play cards, or they take the law into their own hands.'[41]

As long as it remained the exception rather than the rule, 'shoot-to-kill' never raised the issue of political control. In fact, Prior was happy to refer to the security forces' operational independence, declaring that he did not 'dictate security to the security forces'.[42] After leaving office, he revealed that government ministers never 'asked specifically to be told when the SAS were going to be used'.[43] As a consequence, police and army had considerable leeway – and, arguably, the government's tacit agreement – in initiating operations that were likely to violate the principle of minimum force. This was particularly true when the security forces managed to produce 'clean kills', that is, shootings that *appeared* to be justified under the given circumstances, and that would consequently not provoke any hostile reaction either from the minority in Northern Ireland or from public opinion generally.[44]

The security forces' ability to avoid civilian casualties was a significant factor, which enabled the government to largely avoid the issue. In contrast to the late 1970s, when the SAS's presence needed to be scaled down after a number of controversial ambushes (see Chapter 5), there were no efforts to inhibit the SAS's increased activity from 1987.[45] From a strategic point of view, the security forces' increased sophistication at employing 'contact' intelligence in order to 'take out' experienced IRA units on active service served as an effective deterrent. According to one minister: 'If you really want to bring about a change in terrorist behaviour, you have to create a climate whereby they are frightened to commit crime because they fear either apprehension ... or being caught in a cross-fire situation whereby they get killed.'[46] Hence, in addition to the immediate value of eliminating a number of accomplished IRA operators, the capability to carry through 'clean kills' communicated the superiority of British military capabilities. In this way, the tactic may have added to the IRA's perception of military stalemate, and its consequent realisation that a 'military solution' to the conflict had become impossible.[47]

Regarding the most important political development in the 1982–88 period, the conclusion of the AIA, the implications for British security policy turned out to be negligible. From Westminster's perspective, one of the main reasons for entering into negotiations about the AIA had been to convince the Irish government that its military activities needed to be co-ordinated with, and integrated into, the British counterinsurgency effort, so that the vulnerabilities of having an open land border (which handicapped the security forces but not the paramilitaries) and two separate jurisdictions would be neutralised. As it turned out, increased security co-operation was the least significant outcome of the

Anglo-Irish process. While some of London's more ambitious aims – such as a joint security zone around the border – had to be abandoned relatively early,[48] the British government hoped that the AIA would strengthen Dublin's resolve to counter Republican activity, increase its efforts to monitor movements at the border, and facilitate the co-operation between the security forces of both countries. Accordingly, Thatcher anticipated progress 'in such matters as threat assessment, ... technical co-operation, training of personnel and operational resources, ... [and the] fuller and faster exchange of information, especially pre-emptive intelligence which helps to prevent acts of terrorism'.[49] With the possible exception of improvements in the communication between the two police forces, however, the majority of Westminster's expectations could never be realised.[50] One explanation for this can be found in London's failure to act upon its commitment to reform the Northern Ireland justice system, the review of which Thatcher had allegedly promised to FitzGerald as a *quid pro quo* for the facilitation of extradition and border security.[51] Yet, Dublin's lack of vigour *vis-à-vis* security co-operation also related to the difficulty of mobilising sufficient support from the Irish public when there was no emergency in one's own jurisdiction. When the British government recognised that the absence of a similar threat had produced 'a different attitude' towards security in the Republic,[52] London eventually abandoned its hopes and concluded that it was unrealistic to expect that 'simply by signing an agreement ... a magic wand would be provided whereby terrorists would pack up their tents and walk away'.[53]

Like the Irish government's reluctance *vis-à-vis* border security, London was slow to accept the logic of Dublin's arguments when it came to the implementation of the measures the Irish government had insisted on as a means of ending the minority's alienation from the institutions of law and order. Many of Dublin's proposals were ruled out by London because they interfered with British sovereignty (mixed courts, the joint policing of Nationalist areas),[54] or – more straightforwardly – because they were seen as unacceptable to the majority (a radical shake-up of the RUC, the abolition of the UDR).[55] When Irish proposals were implemented at all (a Code of Conduct for the RUC, improvements in the security forces' complaints system), London resisted the open symbolism which Dublin thought necessary in order to convince the minority that the AIA was the beginning of a new era. Moreover, contrary to FitzGerald's claim that Ulsterisation had now 'reached a plateau',[56] the AIA failed to have any significant impact on the balance between external and local security forces. In fact, Ulsterisation had reached a 'plateau' of between 14000 and 15000 men as early as 1978, and increases in the strength of the police force had – by and large – been cancelled out by the gradual (yet consistent) scaling down of the UDR (see Figure 6.1). (Contrary to what McGarry and O'Leary argue, the slight proportional decrease of 'Ulster security forces' after 1985 could be explained with the unexpected upsurge of Unionist unrest, which necessitated the rapid deployment of increasing numbers of British Army after 1985.)[57] With some modifications of the regiment's training and vetting procedures, the only tangible change in British security policy resulting from the AIA concerned the UDR,[58] yet it would be far-fetched to argue that the traditional emphasis on professionalisation was an adequate substitute for the more radical demands which had been advanced by the Irish side.

The AIA's actual provisions aside, it is frequently argued that the emergence of the Agreement exemplified a newfound willingness to defy the political will of the majority community. Some Nationalist authors even draw favourable comparisons between London's performance in 1985 and its failure to bring down the Loyalist stoppage in 1974 (see Chapter 4).[59] Yet, despite some similarities between the two events, the analogy fails to stand up to scrutiny. As in 1974, the British government could not see how the AIA had broken the traditional principle that any new system of government needed to be acceptable to both sides. London regarded the AIA as a mere modification of Direct Rule – with all 'decisions north of the border [remaining] a matter for the United Kingdom'[60] – and

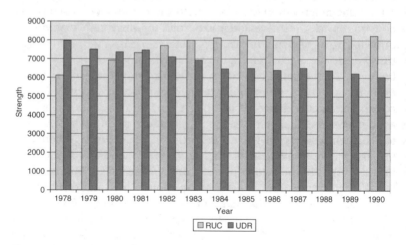

Figure 6.1   Local security forces, 1978–90

Source: see Appendix.

there was no question of 'selling out' the majority community. Rather than because of substantive objections, Unionist resistance was therefore thought to have resulted from the fact that 'they didn't understand it ... [and] because of the way it had been negotiated' (i.e. without any prior consultation of the Unionists).[61] As in 1974, the British government expected that Unionist reluctance would be overcome as soon as the agreement was seen to be working, and once the initial outrage had calmed down. In 1974, however, the majority community also managed to render the province ungovernable within months of the Executive's establishment, and even before the Sunningdale Agreement was translated into a formal treaty. Back then, essential services had effectively broken down, and it was believed that to contain the turmoil would require an unlimited military operation, thus resulting in a civil war. In 1985, this situation never occurred. Although there was a sustained campaign against the AIA – which included marches, symbolic strikes, boycotts and the resignation of all Unionist MPs (prompting by-elections in 15 constituencies) – Unionist resistance to the AIA clearly failed to a level of intensity similar to that of the stoppage in 1974. As Needham explained: '[W]e kept the essential services running, and we did not lose the support of the police, [so] we could continue to govern.'[62]

Exclusion – the ambiguities of marginalisation

The AIA's impact on Anglo-Irish relations was tangible, albeit in a more subtle way than expected. Ruling out the option of 'full integration', the British government conceded that – in the absence of power-sharing – the Irish government had a role to play in the governance of the province. London made it clear that any settlement had to include some form of Irish dimension, and that there could be no return to Mason's attempts at making Direct Rule semi-permanent. In this regard, the British government had followed the agenda of Dublin and the SDLP, both of which had bargained for the formalisation of the Irish dimension and an end to the idea of an internal settlement. Even though London and Dublin continued to be far from the durable accommodation which London had envisaged,[63] one may therefore contend that the AIA provided an institutional foundation from which a lasting accommodation could emerge. Like a marriage, the AIA had welded together the two governments in a contractual framework from which it was difficult to withdraw, and which set limits on the amount of disagreement one could afford. Even Thatcher, who became increasingly critical of the accord once she had left office, maintained that 'it never seemed worth pulling out of the agreement altogether because this would have created problems not only with the Republic but, more importantly, with broad international opinion as well'.[64] In that sense, it literally forced the two governments to work out their differences, and it would – in time – produce 'an instinctive feeling that when things go wrong, [one] immediately gets together and decides what to do about it'.[65]

Even if the AIA's immediate impact on Anglo-Irish relations was slim, the formulation of British political strategy in the 1982–88 period cannot be understood without reference to its origins, conclusion and implementation. Most significantly, many authors maintain that the AIA aimed at facilitating the emergence of the longstanding objective of British government strategy in Northern Ireland, namely, a devolved cross-community settlement. On the Nationalist side, so the argument goes, the AIA would have reconciled the Catholics with the institutions of government, thus strengthening constitutional Nationalism and the role of the SDLP as the voice of the minority, whilst stopping the growth of *Sinn Fein* as an electoral force.[66] On the Unionist side, Dublin's inclusion in the government of the province would have provided an effective incentive for Unionists to agree to power-sharing as devolved powers would be excluded from the scope of the IGC.[67]

To understand the real significance of devolution as a reason for concluding the AIA, it is necessary to dissect the motivational dynamics on both sides. For the Irish government, to support and strengthen constitutional Nationalism was a major stimulus. After the hunger strikes, there was a real fear that *Sinn Fein* would overtake the SDLP as the main Nationalist party in Northern Ireland and make substantial gains south of the border. Consequently, the purpose of the so-called New Ireland Forum in 1983–84, in which the main constitutional Nationalist parties worked out suggestions for a settlement, was to demonstrate that constitutional Nationalism was capable of providing a viable alternative to the armed struggle. FitzGerald's repeated warnings about the dangers of *Sinn Fein's* electoral rise (and the related demand for ending Catholic alienation in Northern Ireland) were genuine, even if Dublin sometimes exaggerated 'the perceived menace' in order to create a renewed sense of urgency on the British side.[68] Equally, it was the declared aim of the Irish government to create 'a powerful encouragement to Unionists to join with Nationalists in a devolved government'.[69] This, Dublin maintained, could be achieved by involving Irish ministers in the government of Northern Ireland, the powers of which would be cut back once a devolved settlement was agreed between the representatives of the two communities.

Whilst enhancing the prospect of devolution was therefore regarded as an important objective on the Irish side, the same could not necessarily be said for London – even if some British negotiators (apparently encouraged by the successful conclusion of the Belfast Agreement) now argue that it had been its purpose all along.[70] On the British side, devolution continued to be the long-term aspiration, yet there was a conviction that its internal *sine qua non* (that is, power-sharing) 'had not worked [and that we] needed to bring in the Irish government to look after the interests of the minority'; in that sense, the AIA was seen as 'almost an alternative to power-sharing'.[71] Consequently, some of Dublin's arguments fell on deaf ears. First, the political advance of the Republican movement had simply not caused the same amount of anxiety in London as it had in Dublin. Although Prior described Sands' election as a 'profound shock' for the British government, he added that its impact was 'not very great in political terms'.[72] Hurd believed that 'to build up the SDLP as an official spokesman of the minority... [was] a motive, but it was a secondary motive'.[73] Furthermore, the notion of providing an incentive for the Unionists to agree to power-sharing was alien to the British government. As shown above, London was sensitive about the extent of Unionist discontent *any* Anglo-Irish agreement would produce, and its attitude towards Dublin's idea of 'encouraging' the Unionists to share power with Nationalists was therefore one of scepticism. As Mallaby explained:

[It] was not an active purpose in our minds, and I think it would have been a risky purpose to give ourselves because it was far from certain that it would have a positive effect. The effect could have been to turn [the Unionists] against any kind of negotiation for a very long time.[74]

Instead of deliberately worsening the status quo for the majority community, the British government set out to produce what was described as a 'balanced package': 'We could not afford to swap the alienation of the minority community for the alienation of the majority. A middle course had to be found.'[75] While Hurd, in an attempt to compensate the Unionists for the involvement of the Irish government, at one point even contemplated the return to an exclusively Unionist administration within Northern Ireland,[76] London's efforts to balance the agreement concentrated on obtaining better security co-operation (which was believed to be in the Unionist interest) and resisting some of Dublin's far-reaching demands, such as the abolition of the UDR.

One more observation appears to reinforce the impression that the British government did not intend the AIA to be an instrument with which to face down Unionist opposition to power-sharing. Considering Dublin's initial demands for 'joint authority' and a thorough reform of the security forces, the British side genuinely believed that they had negotiated a 'fair deal' for the Unionists. London was hardly worried about the formalisation of consultation, and it regarded some of the more controversial commitments in the AIA as 'paper tigers'. For example, only two days after the signing, Hurd's successor, Tom King, made it clear that there would 'never' be mixed courts with judges from both countries – despite a clear reference in the agreement in which both sides agreed to consider this possibility.[77] In short, London assumed that it had achieved the minimalist agreement for which it had strived, and that Unionist fears were therefore unfounded. As a result, most individuals within the British government were surprised by the strong Unionist opposition to the AIA. Whilst it was generally anticipated that Paisley's DUP would come out against the agreement, it was expected that the UUP would eventually acquiesce to it, thus guaranteeing tacit support from the largest Unionist party. As Lord Lyell, who was a junior minister under Hurd and King, stated: 'All the members of the Conservative government, and 90 per cent of Conservative MPs were startled ... They were saying: the Union Jack is there, they get these subsidies. What are they upset about?'[78] Thus, instead of being a shrewd plan to weaken the Unionists' resolve, it appears more likely that – despite its cautious approach when compared to Dublin – the British government simply underestimated the constitutional sensitivities of the majority community, and that it overrated the extent to which the Unionists would trust London as a guardian of their interests.

Whilst it is therefore mistaken to imply that London *intended* the AIA to worsen the Unionists' position, most of the ideas that had been been put forward by the Irish government during the AIA's negotiation were nevertheless co-opted by the British side *after* the AIA had been concluded. Any decrease in electoral support for *Sinn Fein*, for example, was portrayed as a direct consequence of the agreement that '[a]ny intelligent Unionist must take comfort from'.[79] More significantly, the British government started to hold out the prospect of a devolved cross-community settlement as a way of reducing the responsibilities of the IGC. Shocked by the strength of Unionist opposition, Thatcher stated that 'the people of Northern Ireland can get rid of the intergovernmental conference by agreeing to devolved government'.[80] In February 1986, King declared that it was London's 'ambition' to reduce the responsibilities of the IGC and extend the powers of any devolved government 'as widely as we can'.[81] Indeed, to entice the

Unionists to participate in talks about devolution became the principal aim of Westminster's political efforts in the post-Agreement period. In doing so, Thatcher and King not only admitted that London had failed to achieve its objective (to create an inter-governmental framework that would ease the operation of Direct Rule), but they also hinted at a return to the traditional aspiration of devolution and power-sharing. In the post-1985 period, the AIA would therefore assume the function London had originally been reluctant to pursue: it served as an incentive for the political representatives of the majority community to overcome their alleged intransigence and address Nationalist concerns more effectively than hitherto.

Regarding the evolution of political strategy, the second signifi-cant development in the 1982–88 period concerned *Sinn Fein*. At first glance, the 1980s represented the climax of Westminster's efforts to marginalise the Republican movement. Unlike earlier periods of British involvement, the representatives of *Sinn Fein* were now not portrayed as 'doves' or 'moderates', whose conversion towards peaceful politics had to be encouraged, but – on the contrary – as an inextricable part of the Republican strategy of 'the Armalite and the ballot box', according to which the latter sought to legitimise and strengthen the former. Consequently, the British government made no difference between the two: at best, *Sinn Fein* was irrelevant; at worst, it was – like the IRA – 'just an enemy'.[82] The list of measures that were designed to exclude *Sinn Fein* from the political process included the denial of access to ministers, the introduction of a pledge that required local councillors to renounce the use of violence for political purposes, and the 1988 broadcasting ban, which meant that the voices of the representatives of twelve organ-isations – including *Sinn Fein* – could not be broadcast, except during election campaigns and when they spoke on constituency matters.[83]

Even so, the Republican movement's decision to engage in electoral politics created a number of practical difficulties, so that the policy of marginalisation could never be practised as consistently as London hoped it could. For instance, London was compelled to recognise that, whilst being the political wing of the IRA, the representatives of *Sinn Fein* – as local councillors or MPs – made consistent efforts to represent the problems of their constituents. Thus, while Prior hoped 'that nobody will pay any attention to what its members say',[84] he admitted that 'all the elected Sinn Fein representatives have had contact with government officials at local level on a range of constituency matters'.[85] In fact, most members of the government were convinced that 'sooner or later it had to be done' – that is, to talk to *Sinn Fein* – but refused to

break the official convention about ministerial contacts with representatives of the Republican movement.[86] Accordingly, a close reading of
the available sources shows that London's attitude towards *Sinn Fein*
had always been more pragmatic than its rhetorical postures suggested.
As early as 1985, for example, Scott pointed out:

> It would be possible to move from the government's present position in
> one of two directions: either towards the prescription of Sinn Fein ... or
> to give Sinn Fein equality of treatment as elected representatives. For
> the moment we believe that ... to draw as firm a distinction as possible
> between those who advocate constitutional politics and those who
> advocate violence ... is the best way forward. However, I freely accept
> that it is a matter for political judgment, and that judgment could
> change from time to time according to the circumstances that prevail.[87]

Referring to 'changing circumstances', Scott implied that the policy of
exclusion could be reversed if the IRA decided to end its military campaign. As for most of the 1982–88 period, there had been no signs that
the Republican side had any intention of doing so, Westminster saw the
continued marginalisation of *Sinn Fein* as a practical necessity, not least
in order to exert further pressure on the IRA. It is worth pointing out
that – in this respect – London's approach was far more flexible than
that of the Irish government. Granting *Sinn Fein*'s representatives access
to government officials was said to be something that 'would never
happen in Dublin, no matter how many votes [Sinn Fein President Gerry
Adams] won in an election'.[88] In Dublin's view, the policy of exclusion
was the AIA's *raison d'être* – it was a matter of principle, not a temporary
arrangement that 'could change from time to time'.

Towards the end of the 1982–88 period, it became clear that the
Republican leadership was prepared to subject its strategy to a fundamental reassessment. The Republican side's precise motives for doing so
are beyond the scope of this study, but it is possible to point out some of
the dynamics that may have contributed to this change. First, the
Republicans' perception of political and military stalemate was induced
by the security forces' success in containing the IRA, which suggested
that a 'military solution' was impossible. Second, it became obvious that
there was a contradiction between the electoral aspirations of *Sinn Fein*
and the need to maintain the IRA's military campaign. The potentially
harmful effect of military operations on the electoral chances of *Sinn
Fein* – especially when such attacks involved the killing of civilians – was
admitted relatively early,[89] but it was fully realised only in the late

1980s. After the attack on the Remembrance Day ceremony at Enniskillen (Co. Fermanagh) in November 1987, for example, Adams acknowledged that 'our efforts to broaden our base have most certainly been upset in all the areas we have selected for expansion'.[90] Third, the positive reception of the AIA amongst Nationalists furthered the domestic as well as international isolation of the movement. Accordingly, *Sinn Fein* admitted that the agreement was 'good for the SDLP in party terms, helping [SDLP deputy leader] Seamus Mallon to take Newry and Armagh and reducing the Sinn Fein vote'.[91] Finally, London's consistent refusal to make any amendments to the treaty challenged traditional Republican assumptions about the so-called 'Unionist veto' on constitutional change. Both Robert Andrew and Alan Goodison (the British ambassador in Dublin) learned from sources close to the Republican leadership that the AIA had led Adams to consider the possibility that the British government was now prepared to 'stand up to the Unionists', and that a political solution might therefore be possible.[92] Indeed, King now confirms that the British government was fully aware of the shift in Republican thinking:

> It was ... towards the end of my time that we got the first signs that they had second thoughts about the Anglo-Irish Agreement. We had made it clear that this wasn't the prelude to a British withdrawal, that we were entirely robust on the security field, and that Article 1 [of the AIA] meant what it said about continuing to be part of the UK if that was what the population wanted ... [In early 1988,] Hume then launched into opening up those discussions [with Adams] ... I didn't know the details, but I knew that he was talking to them. At that time, the first queries started to come through as to what our position really meant, and I was under no doubt that Father [Alec] Reid and the Clonard [Monastery in West Belfast] were involved in talks with the IRA.[93]

One may conclude, therefore, that London understood the change within the Republican movement's position to be potentially significant. Its political reponse to this development, however, would only become obvious in the following period.

New deal – the advent of fair employment

In the first term of Thatcher's Conservative government, Northern Ireland had largely escaped the consequences of Thatcherite monetarism, including – above all – drastic decreases in public spending and the consequent minimisation of the state's role in the economy (see Chapter 5). Even though it appeared as if, in the following years, some of Thatcher's concepts had eventually found their way across the Irish Sea, traditional influences on the formulation of economic policy in Northern Ireland remained paramount. The principle of 'peace through prosperity' still applied, and even strong supporters of Thatcher's economic policies on the British mainland – such as Rhodes Boyson, an NIO minister in the years 1984–86 – asserted that 'despite the fact that I adhere to my monetarist views... we must face the fact that, unless we can regenate the economy, the transfer of money must continue'.[94]

Still, the uncompromising implementation of monetarism in Great Britain – accompanied by record levels of unemployment and social unrest – raised the question as to why a province which, in Great British eyes, had always been the main financial beneficiary of the Union should now be excluded from the harsher dictates of a national effort. The increasing disparities between Great Britain, where the free market was referred to as the ultimate authority, and Northern Ireland, where subsidies continued to flow regardless, was not missed by the national press, which regularly reported about the province where Thatcherism had 'lost the courage of its own convictions'.[95] Pressure also came from within the British government. Increasingly, ministers found it necessary to explain the need for spending cuts in Great Britain whilst an unlimited amount of British taxpayers' money seemed to be 'wasted' in Northern Ireland. Needham, for example, recalled that '[v]isiting British politicians and civil servants cast envious eyes over the scale and quality of the Housing Executive's efforts'.[96] Hence, rather than guiding the formulation of economic policy in Northern Ireland directly, the principal influence of Thatcherism was an indirect one: it created a consensus which forced the British government to justify its economic policy in Northern Ireland, and it prompted the NIO to increase its efforts to ensure 'value for money' in locating public resources.

Significantly, the need to justify public expenditure, and the consequent realisation that it was neither sufficient nor possible to solve the province's problems through an ever increasing amount of public subsidies, resulted in efforts to make the economic instrument more responsive to the government's overall strategy. Whereas in earlier periods, economic policy was related to the objective only in the most general sense – such as by saying that the creation of employment would contribute to stability and peace (see Chapter 5) – every measure of economic policy was now explained with regard to its anticipated strategic impact. In Republican strongholds, for example, economic policy aimed at undermining the power of the IRA and *Sinn Fein*. The government would therefore try to build up other sources of authority, such as the Catholic clergy or the SDLP. Accordingly, specific measures, such as the creation of regeneration grants and the maintenance of government-sponsored employment schemes, were designed to 'provide the SDLP and their leader with the proof they required to show their people that co-operation with the British government could bring results'.[97] The Republican movement's decision to engage in economic and social agitation, however, created a dilemma. On the one hand, Republican-led co-operatives created jobs and alleviated poverty in some of the areas that had been worst affected by the conflict. On the other hand, supporting those initiatives would have helped the Republicans to strengthen their hold over the population, and it would have generated money for their political as well as military activities. Although it appeared to back up *Sinn Fein's* (misguided) claim that the government had no real interest in creating jobs in Republican areas,[98] London was determined not to support Republican-led ventures, such as the Conway Mill in West Belfast.[99] From a strategic point of view, this decision was entirely sound: if Northern Ireland was excepted from the dictates of economic Thatcherism, it was because economic policy was regarded as a part of its strategic calculus. If it was not, there would have been no justification for why Northern Ireland should be treated differently from similarly deprived areas in the North of England or Scotland.

The most significant development in the 1982–88 period concerned the issue of fair employment. According to London, there was 'a straight line of causation' between the publication of the government's own labour market statistics in 1985 and the introduction of legislation, which resulted in the Fair Employment Act (1989).[100] Whilst this account may be factually correct, it nevertheless concealed the underlying pressures that convinced the government of the need to take action in an area in which it had previously been extremely reluctant to embark upon substantial reforms. Needham's assessment is both honest and revealing:

> There was no doubt that the British government had to introduce legislation to show the world (or rather Irish-America and Dublin) that employment practices were unbiased. The very existence of new legislation showed the power that a combined Dublin–Washington alliance had over a British government. I would need persuading that the Prime Minister [Thatcher] instinctively supported such an interfering law that was alien to her free-market instincts ... Without outside legislative pressures the practices would probably have remained the same in perpetuity.[101]

External pressures originated primarily in the United States, where the Irish National Caucus had conceived the so-called MacBride Principles, which called for an increase of Catholic employees as well as affirmative action programmes.[102] Starting in 1984, the MacBride campaign aimed at making American investment in Northern Ireland conditional upon the adoption of the principles, and it succeeded in convincing a series of US state legislatures and city councils that their respective pension funds should not be invested in the stocks of companies that refused to insist on the implementation of the code. The British government strongly opposed the campaign, arguing that it would lead to disinvestment, and that the principles amounted to 'reverse discrimination', which was illegal under existing British legislation. According to an NIO spokesman, the principles were also 'unnecessary since Northern Ireland has its own Fair Employment Act [of 1976] and agency'.[103]

In contrast to Needham's assertion, the initial reaction of Dublin as well as its leading Irish-American allies in the US Congress was one of scepticism, as the Irish National Caucus was regarded as a Republican front organisation.[104] By 1987, however, the campaign had gained so much momentum amongst Nationalists that the Irish government eventually decided to support it,[105] and reforms of the existing fair employment legislation subsequently became one of the central issues in the IGC.[106] Whereas in 1987, London still believed that it was possible to address the issue by publishing a revised guide with recommendations on how to implement the existing rules, the British government concluded in the following year that new legislation was necessary to fend off the combined pressures of Dublin and Irish-America. Accordingly, both King and Viggers now confirm that Dublin's as well as Irish-American lobbying was crucial in impressing upon the British government the need for stronger legislation.[107]

The Fair Employment Act (1989) represented a significant change in governmental attitudes towards the issue of communal inequality. For the first time, London acknowledged that the material inequality between the two communities was a legitimate grievance that needed to be addressed if political stability was to emerge. The British government also conceded that the perception of disadvantage amongst many members of the Nationalist community had not only resulted from open discrimination and geographical disparities, but from traditions and established practices as well. As King explained:

> [I]n many significant areas there is discrimination – some of it deliberate, some of it inadvertent, some of it merely maintaining past

practices and some of it caused by a shortage of employment and the understandable human determination ... to ensure that a member of the family ... has the chance of a job ... In the circumstances of Northern Ireland, that has the effect of perpetuating employment in one community to the detriment of the other.[108]

London's new understanding of the problem indicated that the government had realised that the question of inequality required a much broader approach than hitherto. Consequently, the monitoring of the religious composition of the workforce, which had been omitted from the 1976 Act, was now considered 'the key to fair employment practice',[109] and the failure to register with the newly created Fair Employment Commission (which replaced the FEA) was made a criminal offence.

Even so, critics pointed to the lack of consistency when it came to the question of how to rectify the under-representation of either community in individual companies. In fact, whilst the 1989 Act compelled employers to consider affirmative action in order to redress existing imbalances, it explicitly prohibited them from taking measures that were exclusive to one particular community.[110] This apparent contradiction illustrated London's difficulties in acting upon the logic of communal rights whilst maintaining the principle of individual merit and trying to avoid an adverse reaction by the majority community. King stated that the effect of 'quotas and reverse discrimination [would be] catastrophic in the climate of Northern Ireland',[111] yet he failed to explain how the goals and timetables (which companies were encouraged – and in some cases required – to design) were to be realised if not through measures that were specifically aimed at increasing the representation of either Catholics or Protestants. Whilst the 1989 Act thus signified a considerable step forward in the evolution of British thinking on the issue of relative deprivation, the inherent contradictions of the legislation made it clear that London had been a reluctant convert to the notion of collective rights.

Conclusion

In political terms, the signing of the Anglo-Irish Agreement was the single most influential event in the 1982–88 period. Concluding this chapter therefore provides an opportunity to summarise London's main intentions *vis-à-vis* the Anglo-Irish process, and to contrast them with the changes that have been triggered by it.

As a consequence of the constraints and pressures that had arisen from undiminished Direct Rule in the 1976–82 period, the British government recognised that governing the province from London offered no satisfactory framework in which to contain the conflict. As there continued to be no realistic prospect of realising the traditional objective of devolution and power-sharing, Westminster concluded that the aim of containing the conflict could only be achieved by seeking an accommodation with Dublin, thus easing the operation of Direct Rule. To negotiate a framework that would expedite cross-border security co-operation, facilitate the minority's support for the institutions of law and order, and make the Irish government a responsible 'stakeholder' in the conflict became London's objective from 1983. London's strategy included the following functions:

- The constitutional instrument: to negotiate a balanced inter-governmental framework by granting Dublin a 'legitimate interest' in the affairs of Northern Ireland but no 'real powers'.
- The military instrument: to gain efficiency at containing paramilitary activity, particularly through improvements in cross-border security co-operation.
- The political instrument: to sideline the local political parties in favour of an inter-governmental accommodation.
- The economic instrument: to ensure 'value for money' within the existing framework of 'peace through prosperity'.

As it turned out, none of London's aims could be realised: after the AIA's conclusion, improvements in cross-border security co-operation were negligible; the minority was no more inclined to support the province's institutions; and instead of reducing the tensions between the two governments, Dublin's public criticism of London appeared to have increased. In addition, Westminster's traditional insensitivity towards the constitutional concerns of the Unionists meant that the accord was strongly rejected by the majority. From a strategic point of view, the AIA had therefore been a failure.

Nevertheless, in this instance, to simply compare intentions and results is far from sufficient. In fact, apart from providing the institutional frame-work from which a durable accommodation between London and Dublin could emerge, the treaty produced a series of unexpected outcomes which turned out to be highly significant in the longer term. On the Unionist side, the perception that the majority's constitutional and political posi-tion had been worsened unacceptably would – in time – become an incentive to re-engage with the other political parties in the province. On the Republican side, the AIA increased the movement's domestic as well as international marginalisation; it added to the impression of political and military stalemate, and thus forced the leadership to review the assumptions on which its strategy was based. Moreover, in a separate (yet related) development, the AIA contributed to the shift from an individualistic towards a collective conception of fair employment, thus helping the British government to recognise some of the realities of a deeply divided society, which it had previously found convenient to ignore.

Whilst it is therefore correct to conclude that London had failed to achieve its objective, it is equally important to note that the AIA provided some of the foundations that enabled London to return to its traditional objective of devolution and power-sharing. In that sense, the Anglo-Irish Agreement was a crucial pre-condition for the emergence – and indeed success – of the peace process, which is the subject of the following chapter.

7
The War is Over? Success and Failure of British Strategy, 1989–98

The conclusion of the Belfast Agreement in 1998 has undoubtedly been the climax of British policy in Northern Ireland. The political continuity of the peace accord was immediately acknowledged, most notably by a Nationalist MP, who described it as 'Sunningdale for slow learners'.[1] Arguably, with the Belfast agreement, the British government has finally achieved its political objective, yet it still remains to be seen whether it can provide the structures – and the political logic – necessary for the fulfilment of London's long-term aspiration, that is, the containment of the Northern Ireland conflict.

Agreeing the Irish dimension? The limits of constitutional change

Regarding the constitutional status of Northern Ireland, London's attitude in the 1989–98 period was one of explicit neutrality based on the principle of consent. Westminster did not act as a 'persuader of unity', who encouraged the Unionists to join a united Ireland. Nor, indeed, was it the British government's intention to rally the Nationalists in support of the Union.[2] However, apart from Westminster's long-established neutrality *vis-à-vis* the constitutional future of Northern Ireland, the British government now also refused to pursue any form of constitutional change for which it had no explicit support from both Unionists and Nationalists. In marked contrast to the AIA, the cornerstone of London's strategy was to produce an *agreed* settlement, and there was obviously no point in trying to impose changes to the constitutional position of Northern Ireland that one or both sides would find unacceptable. This implied, in turn, that the British government was prepared to implement any outcome as long as it had achieved sufficient agreement between the local parties. Mayhew, who became Northern Ireland Secretary in 1992, believed it 'impossible to visualise anything on which they together, freely and without impediment, agree that the British government would wish to stymie'.[3] In this regard, London's use of the constitutional instrument needs to be seen as a function of the political process.

In addition to stressing its neutrality, the British government regarded itself as a guardian of the process, who would facilitate practical options for constitutional change, as well as reject those that were unlikely to secure agreement – put simply, London was 'partisan for progress'.[4] In performing this role, Westminster's actions were guided by several considerations. First, there was a well-balanced set of established demands and principles on which the local parties were not prepared to compromise. On the one hand, the scope for movement in the direction of 'full integration' with the United Kingdom was limited by the Nationalist demand that there could be no 'internal' solution, and the resulting need for an institutionalised Irish dimension which expressed the Nationalist aspirations of the minority. On the other hand, the dynamic for a united Ireland was impeded by the Unionist reluctance to consider any substantial transfer of sovereignty, which also rendered ideas like 'joint sovereignty' or 'joint authority' impractical. Moreover, by acceding to the principle of consent, all the local parties (with the possible exception of *Sinn Fein*) and the two governments had accepted that self-determination was to be exercised by the people of Northern Ireland who would – for the foreseeable future – come out against a united Ireland if any such proposition was put to them. Taken together, this set of imperatives narrowed the scope for agreed constitutional change considerably, and it was therefore 'perfectly logical' in London's view that any search for constitutional change was bound to revolve around the nature, extent and responsibilities of cross-border bodies.[5] This idea seemed to satisfy the demand for an Irish dimension whilst complying with the guarantee that the constitutional status of Northern Ireland would only be changed with the consent of a majority.

Second, in promoting agreement on the future constitutional status of Northern Ireland, London needed to consider the dynamics of the political process as a whole, as well as the possibility of trade-offs between different areas of negotiation. Brooke, who preceded Mayhew as Northern Ireland Secretary, established a set of rules that were to become the founding principles of any political process throughout the 1989–98 period. Most significantly, he determined that any settlement had to include agreement in three so-called Strands (relations within Northern Ireland, within the island of Ireland, and between the two governments), and that 'no agreement on any aspect would be reached unless and until all parties were finally satisfied with the whole'.[6] This structure reflected the desire, amongst members of the British government as well as all the local parties, to achieve a comprehensive solution, and it offered the advantage of 'provid[ing] everybody with the opportunity to see that there was potentially something for them in it'.[7] In turn, it implied that constitutional issues could not be seen in isolation, and that it was possible, for example, to counter-balance far-reaching proposals in the second strand (which would typically deal with the constitutional status of Northern Ireland in relation to the Republic) with concessions in the others. Equally, the drawn-out nature of the political process made it opportune to promote the constitutional ideas or concerns of one side at the expense of another if the former was believed to be in immediate need of public reassurance.

To demonstrate the British government's effectiveness in its role as a facilitator of constitutional change, it seems useful to provide a brief evaluation of London's performance during each of the main political initiatives in the 1989–98 period. At the so-called Brooke/Mayhew talks in 1991–92, the British government assumed an explicitly non-prescriptive role, arguing that it would be wrong to 'prejudge the detailed form that ... arrangements should take'.[8] It was nevertheless clear that Westminster envisaged an outcome, which involved limited constitutional change within the constraints described above. London was therefore greatly encouraged when the Unionist delegations stated their willingness to meet Irish ministers, travelled to Dublin, and – in the case of the UUP – offered the establishment of a so-called Inter-Irish Relations Committee in exchange for the removal of Articles 2 and 3 from the Irish Constitution.[9] Given that the Irish government had repeatedly signalled that Articles 2 and 3 were 'on the table' as part of a comprehensive settlement, the British government was extremely disappointed when its efforts to produce movement on the Nationalist side came to nothing. In fact, Dublin's refusal to commit itself to changing Articles 2 and 3 was regarded as a 'total breach of faith' by the British side.[10]

In 1992–93, the need to preserve the integrity of the political process made it necessary for London to reject a series of proposals that attempted to overturn the implicit consensus on the limited scope for constitutional change. In an attempt to trigger a permanent IRA ceasefire that would enable *Sinn Fein* to participate in political talks, the leaders of the SDLP and *Sinn Fein*, Hume and Adams, produced several drafts of a declaration of principles which needed to be announced by the British and Irish prime ministers. Hume presented the final draft to the Irish government, which – after further modifications – handed it to the British government. The final document referred to the collective right of the 'Irish people' (i.e. all the inhabitants of the island of Ireland) to self-determination; it made the British government a persuader of unity who 'will use all their influence and energy' to overcome Unionist reluctance; and it overturned the idea of consent by stating that consent had to be achieved 'over a period' before the two governments would legislate for Irish unity regardless of opposition from within Northern Ireland.[11] Given that the document fulfilled all its traditional demands, it is easy to understand why such a declaration would have triggered an end to the IRA's military campaign: it negated the principle of consent, the need for agreement, and it asked Westminster to abandon its role as a neutral arbiter. For London, the draft was therefore 'little more than an invitation...to sell out the majority in the North, and the democratic principles we had always defended.[12] Rather than leading to a stable, durable and agreed system of government, London anticipated that the adaptation of the draft would have destroyed the political process, resulted in another sustained period of Unionist political withdrawal, or – even worse – it would have ignited the civil war scenario which London had traditionally referred to as the primary reason for maintaining Northern Ireland as part of the United Kingdom.

The Joint Declaration for Peace (also known as Downing Street Declaration) was announced by Major and the Irish Prime Minister, Albert Reynolds, on 15 December 1993 after several months of bilateral negotiations. It resembled the Hume–Adams drafts, but even if its choice of language was deliberately 'green', its content was fundamentally different from what had originally been proposed by the Nationalist leaders. Indeed, in many ways, it was exactly the opposite: it referred to Irish self-determination, yet restored the constitutional *status quo* by stating that self-determination had to be exercised 'on the basis of consent, freely and concurrently given, North and South'; instead of using its 'influence and energy' to persuade the Unionists of a united Ireland, the British government committed itself to what it had always perceived as its role, namely 'to encourage, facilitate and enable' agreement; and rather than establishing a timeframe for the realisation of a united Ireland, the Irish Prime Minister now declared that 'it would be wrong to attempt to impose a united Ireland, in the absence of the freely given consent of a majority of the people of Northern Ireland'. In addition, the Irish side now firmly pledged to change Article 2 and 3 of its Constitution in the event 'of a balanced constitutional accommodation'.[13] In a tactical masterstroke, London had thus turned Hume–Adams into an initiative which furthered rather than hindered the political process, and it had produced a document which united the whole spectrum of constitutional Nationalism as well as the biggest Unionist party behind its agenda for limited constitutional change on the basis of devolved government in Northern Ireland and the principle of consent.

At the time of the JDP, London also persuaded Dublin to work out joint proposals to show the local parties what a settlement might look like. As Mayhew stated, the idea was 'to try to develop a shared understanding of the sort of overall accommodation that might have the best chance of winning the wide acceptance across the community'.[14] Although the intention was therefore in line with Westminster's role as a facilitator, the actual outcome destroyed some of the momentum that had developed as a result of the JDP. Published in February 1995, 'A New Framework of Agreement' proposed North–South institutions that were established through an Act of Parliament rather than by a future Northern Ireland assembly; and while they were accountable to the assembly, the bodies' responsibilities were to be transferred to a standing Inter-Governmental Conference if the internal arrangements in Northern Ireland broke down.[15] Given that there were no new concessions by the Irish side (Dublin simply reaffirmed the commitment to change Articles 2 and 3), the document was clearly overbalanced towards the Nationalist position. Its 'default mechanism' was, in fact, an invitation for Nationalists to make the Northern Ireland assembly unworkable, thus sidelining the need for Unionist agreement.[16]

Dixon argues that the lack of balance was deliberate, and that its purpose was 'to underpin the *Sinn Fein* leadership's position and entrench [the IRA's] ceasefire'.[17] This argument remains open to challenge. Considering that the ceasefire was not yet thought to be in acute danger, it appears unlikely that the British government would have sacrificed a major initiative for this purpose. It also contradicts the evolution of Westminster's response to the decommissioning deadlock, which entailed direct concessions to the Republicans only from mid-1995. In reality, Westminster was genuinely surprised by Unionist opposition to the proposals. Like London's response in the wake of the AIA, the British government believed that the political representatives of the majority community had misunderstood the content of the document, and that it only needed to 'simmer for a while' before Unionists would acquiesce. in it.[18] Indeed, Michael Ancram – the NIO minister who had drafted much of the document – now confirms that there was little awareness that the document might be received in a hostile manner:

> The paragraph about the default mechanism was literally written in ten minutes because nobody saw that as meaning anything... Our idea was that if the Assembly broke down, and if you had a joint tourism initiative in America, that the two governments would keep that going. We never saw that as this great monster. It was seized on unfortunately by the *Times* newspaper, and they leaked the default mechanism as the sign of a sell-out. I was aboslutely amazed. I knew that document, I was living with it for eighteen months. That nuance had never struck us.[19]

Rather than a deliberate attempt to overbalance, a more realistic explanation is that the proposals were a blunder, resulting from Westminster's traditional insensitivity *vis-à-vis* the Unionist fear of being drawn into an all-Ireland context with no ability to control the process.

During the final phase of the multi-party talks process, from September 1997, the British government returned to its role as an effective facilitator of constitutional agreement. Throughout the 1989–98 period, London made it clear that it was 'not committed to any single outcome and would support any conclusions, achieved by sufficient consensus, that emerged from the discussions'.[20] In contrast to the 1991–92 talks, however, Westminster now advanced detailed suggestions on the constitutional future of Northern Ireland with a view to accelerating the process, but also in order to provide reassurance. For example, 'Propositions on Heads of Agreement', which was issued by the British and Irish governments in January 1998, was designed to allay Unionist doubts about the peace process. It stated that a North–South ministerial council would only operate 'within the mandate of, and accountable to, the Northern Ireland assembly', and that '[a]ll decisions will be by agreement between the two sides'.[21] As soon as the Republicans voiced their anger about the document, the two governments determined that it was time to counterbalance the Unionist bias of 'Heads of Agreement'. As George Mitchell, the American chairman of the talks, explained: '[Since UUP leader] David Trimble had hailed the adoption of the "Heads of Agreement" ... as a victory for Unionism ... the governments were [now] trying to even the score [by coming] up with a document that Gerry Adams could declare as a victory for Nationalism.'[22] Hence, the so-called 'Mitchell draft' once again displayed a Nationalist bias, including a detailed exposition of possible areas for North–South co-operation, and the redesignation of some authority over the North–South bodies to the two governments.[23]

In the final hours of negotiation, the talks participants agreed to a last-minute compromise according to which Unionist gains in the second Strand were traded with Unionist concessions in the first Strand.[24] The constitutional provisions of the final agreement thus turned out to be closer to 'Heads of Agreement'. Indeed, with the North–South ministerial council strictly accountable to the Assembly, the ending of the AIA, changes to the Irish constitution's territorial claim, and the establishment of a so-called Council of the Isles to neutralise Irish North–South co-operation, the agreement can be seen as a 'victory' for the Unionist position.[25] From London's perspective, however, it was not the outcome as such but the fact that agreement could be achieved, which vindicated its performance as a facilitator. In the course of the 1989–98 period, Westminster not only managed to rally the participating parties behind the set of principles it judged to provide the most likely basis for a negotiated solution, but it also succeeded in steering the parties towards an agreed accommodation that was well within the framework for limited constitutional change it had assumed to be realistic. Most importantly, with the restoration of devolved government on an agreed basis, London had achieved the core objective of British constitutional strategy ever since the fall of Stormont in 1972. From a purely constitutional perspective, Westminster had thus created the circumstances in which it became possible to realise the traditional aim of keeping the province at maximum distance from the British mainland without implying the so-called 'civil war scenario', which was believed would have been triggered by any open transfer of formal sovereignty.

Bargaining for peace? The response to the Republican stalemate

In contrast to London's relative clarity about constitutional matters, ministerial statements gave rise to debates about whether or not London had adopted a new approach *vis-à-vis* the military containment of the conflict. In November 1989, for example, Brooke declared that he could 'not envisage a military defeat' of the IRA.[26] Almost four years later, NIO security minister John Wheeler maintained that the IRA was 'already defeated'.[27] Both statements were received with some amazement at the time, yet from a strategic point of view, none of them indicated any new approach or attitude, nor indeed did they contradict each other. Brooke's assertion summed up the central tenet of the British military tradition in Northern Ireland, which was that – given the constraints of acceptability, constitutionality and normality, which structured the strategic environment in Northern Ireland – there could be no 'military solution'.[28] As shown in previous chapters, even supposed hardliners like Thatcher or Mason accepted the impossibility of defeating the IRA by military means alone, and in rejecting most of the measures that could have delivered a 'military defeat', they acted accordingly. Wheeler's comment was equally unspectacular. Put simply, he expressed the determination of the British government 'not to let them win', and that to deny the IRA a victory would, in the long term, equal its defeat.[29] Arguably, the two statements simply illustrated the perception of military stalemate which had been prevalent amongst members of the British government ever since the first half of the 1970s. The crucial difference was that there was now a similar perception growing amongst Republicans. The real issue was therefore not whether anything had changed on the British side, but rather how London would respond to the changes that occurred on the Republican side.

To understand the way in which the British government determined its military response to the Republican stalemate, one has to explain the constraints within which London operated. In the 1989–98 period, the formulation of military strategy was guided by three influences, the first two of which demonstrated that there were limits to the extent to which the military instrument could be utilised as a tool for bargaining. First, there was the so-called 'level of threat', which had always been the primary determinant of the security forces' response. Brooke made it clear that the military presence was 'made necessary by violence, will be maintained as long as there is violence, but will certainly be reduced when violence comes to an end'.[30] In London's view, there was no point in keeping the 'troops on patrol just for the sake of it',[31] yet as long as armed paramilitaries challenged the authority of the state as well as threaten the lives of British citizens, it was seen as the ultimate responsibility – and indeed, duty – of the British government to respond to that challenge. Republicans have always found it hard to accept this point, partly because Republican ideology only allowed for the British government to be seen as an imperial oppressor.[32] To rationalise the continued British military presence, Republicans have recently started to argue that – despite the genuine desire by some British politicians to resolve the conflict – the security forces (the so-called 'securocrats') had a vested interest in resisting any form of change.[33] There is no hard evidence for this claim, and indeed, it is not taken very seriously by those who knew the securocrats best. For example, in stark contrast to the Republican hypothesis, Adam Ingram (the NIO's security minister from

1997) thinks that the security forces were a 'great motor for change':

> The senior people in the civil service, and the senior people in the RUC, all came from Northern Ireland. They wanted a future. All of them were products of the Troubles, all of them wanted their children, grandchildren and future generations not to have the same problems ... The real heroes in all of this are [therefore] those people who were identified and vilified as securocrats.[34]

The second influence related to the mechanics of politics in a liberal democracy. Simply, faced with a continuing (and, at some points, escalating) military campaign, no government could afford to scale down its military response unilaterally. While the British government understood that the IRA needed to show that it had not surrendered, it was also a matter of explaining reductions in the level of force to Parliament and the British public, both of whom London needed to justify its actions to, particularly when attacks took place on the British mainland.[35] It comes as no surprise, therefore, that Westminster repeatedly used its secret backchannel to the Republicans in order to impress upon them that 'events on the ground are crucial'.[36]

Third, the formulation of Westminster's military response was guided by its political objective. London's objective was to restore devolved government on the basis of an agreed settlement, and it had always been implicit that Republicans could be part of such a settlement if the IRA ceased its military campaign. It was recognised, therefore, that a permanent ceasefire would only represent the beginning of a process which could lead to an inclusive settlement. For this to succeed, it was not only important that violence be stopped but also that it was seen to have ended without compromising the core principles on which all the other participants agreed, that is, the need for a balanced accommodation on the basis of the three strands, as well as the principles of consent and non-violence. If, on the contrary, London was seen to have surrendered – or struck a 'secret deal' with the Republicans – the majority community would have lost the confidence to participate in the process, or indeed they would have resorted to violent methods themselves in order to make their opposition felt. On the other hand, increasing the level of force beyond what was seen as justified as a response to the level of threat would have lost London the support of the SDLP and the Irish government, both of whom strongly believed that any agreed settlement had to include *Sinn Fein*. As a result, whilst being careful not to go 'over the top', some military pressure had to be maintained if London wanted a possible cessation of violence to be followed by a viable peace process. Moreover, since it was believed that it was the perception of military stalemate which had caused the Republicans to rethink their position, it was crucial that this remained a pretext under which supposed 'politicos' like Adams could persuade their followers that there was no possibility of a military solution (see below).

Given this strategic environment, London's military response can be seen as entirely proportionate. In the first phase (i.e. before the IRA had announced an indefinite ceasefire), there was little that *could*, and indeed little that London *wanted* to do in terms of scaling down the security effort. Equally, the British government resisted calls for an increase in the level of force at a time when only 6 per cent of IRA operations actually went ahead. The RUC estimated that, by the early 1990s, 70 per cent of all planned IRA operations in the province needed to be aborted for fear of detection, whilst of the remaining 30 per cent, another 80 per cent were prevented or interdicted by the security forces.[37] In that sense, the IRA's switch back to operations in England was a sign of weakness, and it was interpreted as such by Westminster.[38] Despite the view by some within the security forces that it was possible to 'finish off the IRA' by military means alone,[39] the British government had convinced itself that the rise in paramilitary activity on the British mainland represented the prelude to a political settlement, and that it would be counterproductive to attempt a military solution. As Major put it: '[A]n offer of peace needed to be accompanied by violence, to show their volunteers that they were not surrendering.'[40] Accordingly, the British government rejected demands for the reintroduction of internment as well as a list of proposals by the Chief Constable of the RUC, Hugh Annesley, that called for further limitations on the right to silence and the resurrection of the supergrass system.[41]

Throughout the ceasefire period, British intelligence showed that the IRA's military machine was far from being stood down. In fact, whilst the ceasefire was relatively secure, targeting, training and acquisition continued as usual.[42] London's immediate response to the declaration of the ceasefire, on 31 August 1994, was therefore understandably cautious, and Mayhew emphasised that '[n]othing has been reduced or discontinued that cannot be very quickly put back should the situation be seen to require it once again'.[43] Given that Hume had told Major that 'if there was a cessation for three months, the IRA would not be able to start up violence again',[44] Westminster's aim was to create a 'feelgood factor' amongst Nationalist, which made it more difficult for the IRA to return to war. The British government avoided anything that could be interpreted as part of a 'secret deal', but introduced measures which benefited the minority community as a whole, for example, the opening of border roads, reductions in military patrols, helicopter activity, vehicle checkpoints as well as symbolic changes in weapons and headgear.[45] Only from mid-1995, when the peace process had got stuck over the question of prior decommissioning, did the British government start to target political concessions more directly towards the IRA, partly as a means of stabilising the position of those within the Republican movement who continued to be in favour of the ceasefire, but also to demonstrate flexibility on questions that were believed to be of crucial importance to the IRA. Those included, amongst others, the lifting of exclusion orders from the British mainland and the restoration of pre-1987 remission rates for paramilitary prisoners. Even so, the actual release of prisoners was judged to be part of an agreed settlement, and needed to be withheld as an incentive for the IRA to further engage with the other parties.

London's response to the breakdown of the ceasefire, in February 1996, illustrated that the British government continued to believe in the possibility of an inclusive settlement. Although the increased level of threat made it necessary to restore much of the military activity 'on the ground', many concessions (e.g. relaxations in prison arrangements) were retained. Most importantly, London resisted widespread calls for an all-out security offensive, including the introduction of internment, which many commentators regarded as a plausible conclusion from the IRA's failure to commit itself to exclusively peaceful means.[46] Likewise, Westminster's military response to the launch of the second 'permanent' ceasefire, in July 1997, followed the pattern of 1994, except for a renewed sense of urgency and increased flexibility on the question of prisoner transfers, which addressed one of the issues that London had failed to deal with during the first ceasefire.[47]

Another reason for London's considered approach in formulating its military strategy was the Republican movement's deliberate switch from anti-state to inter-sectarian violence, which manifested itself most virulently in the annual confrontation over the Orange Order parade in Drumcree. In London's view, there was little doubt that the controversy had been orchestrated by *Sinn Fein*, even if Ingram now concedes that the Republicans had managed to turn the issue into a genuine Nationalist grievance: '*Sinn Fein* were not wholly in control of this, but if it was ever going to change direction...they would have taken control'.[48] For London, the situation in Drumcree recreated the traditional dilemma of how to keep law and order in a society in which the rule of law was actively resisted by a significant proportion of the population.

Westminster's response, however, was not solely determined by the fact that Unionists could mobilise a greater number of people,[49] but rather by considerations of geographical concentration and intensity. In 1996, the reversal of Annesley's original decision not to let the Orangemen march the Garvaghy Road resulted from intelligence reports, which suggested that up to 50 000 Protestants would have converged in Drumcree, resulting in the loss of many of the residents' lives and, possibly, triggering a civil war like situation.[50] Under these circumstances, Annesley believed the Catholic 'spill-over' (in terms of riots and general unrest) to be easier to handle, not because it involved fewer people but because it was likely to be less concentrated. Whereas a similar conclusion was reached in the following year,[51] the judgement changed in 1998. By then, the majority community had become divided over the issue, and the security forces believed that the Protestant 'spill-over' was easier to contain than united Catholic opposition.[52] There can be no doubt, however, that London was unhappy about having to make decisions that would pitch one or the other community against it, and thus undermine its role as an 'honest broker'. In a typical response, Westminster therefore created an independent commission which was (eventually) given the right to determine whether or not a specific parade should go ahead.

Apart from understanding the formulation of London's immediate military response to events in the 1989–98 period, it is important to examine the evolution of some traditional concepts of British military strategy. The reliance on locally recruited security forces came under intense scrutiny from 1989, following the discovery that senstitive files had been passed on to Loyalist paramilitaries by members of the UDR. The consequent inquiry (conducted by John Stevens) found that there had been intense pressure on individual members of the regiment from within local communities, and whilst 'collusion' was neither widespread nor systematic, 59 UDR officers were charged as a result.[53] For Westminster, the problem was not merely that 'collusion' took place (indeed, it occurred on the Irish side too),[54] but that the unbalanced composition of the security forces implied that only one of the two communities was affected, thus undermining the perceived impartiality of the security forces and damaging Westminster's credibility as a neutral arbiter. At a time when Brooke had just started to mediate an agreed settlement, it was – in the words of NIO security minister John Cope – 'extremely important that there should not be [any further incidents of collusion]'.[55]

Nevertheless, there was little change regarding the overall balance between local and external security forces. Contrary to FitzGerald's claim that the AIA had halted the expansion of the local security forces (see Chapter 6), the UDR's full-time element reached an historic peak in 1991. Also, in the same year, the RUC was given permission to recruit another 400 full-time regulars.[56] Once more, London's only tangible reaction to problems within the locally recruited security forces was to re-emphasise the commitment to the principle of professionalisation. Within this limited framework of reform, the fusion of the UDR with the Royal Irish Rangers in 1992, and the further decline of the part-time element within the newly created Royal Irish Regiment (RIR), was an imaginative response, removing an offensive symbol to Nationalists whilst representing continuity in the eyes of the majority. As Peter Bottomley (who was a junior minister under Brooke) put it:

> Evolving the UDR into the [RIR] allowed the semi-professional people in the UDR to feel this continuity, and it also allowed the UDR to become a part of history. I think that the adaptation was clever and wise and timely. The UDR was not abolished, but after a time, it did not exist anymore.[57]

Still, any fundamental reform of the local security forces' make-up was postponed indefinitely, partly because the British government feared that the majority community would be offended, but also as a consequence of London's traditional indifference *vis-à-vis* the fact that law enforcement in a deeply divided society was bound to be perceived in sectarian terms. For example, like the 1969 Hunt Report, the 1996 White Paper 'Foundations for Policing' emphasised that officers were under a legal obligation to exercise their duties impartially, but – yet again – it failed to introduce any substantial reforms that would have reflected the special needs of policing in a deeply divided society.[58] It was only after the conclusion of the Belfast Agreement that some fundamental reforms – for example, changes to the RUC's name, oath of office, symbols and a balanced recruitment policy – were eventually implemented.[59]

Regarding the policy of Criminalisation, the early release of paramilitary prisoners – as agreed in the Belfast Agreement – appeared to be the logical conclusion of the peace process: not only was it a practical necessity without which any inclusive settlement would have been impossible. Given that prisoners' licences can be revoked if either they or their organisations engaged in acts of violence, it also seemed to provide a powerful incentive for the paramilitaries not to return to war.[60] Even so, London's belief that early release was somehow 'inevitable', and that all its critics were either intransigent 'nay-sayers' or people who had no insight into the intractabilities of conflict resolution,[61] continues to stifle any real debate about the issue. Most importantly, it has concealed the fact that the decision to grant early release represented a sharp discontinuity in the evolution of British military strategy. For decades, British ministers had reiterated that there was no such thing as 'political crime' under United Kingdom law, and that – consequently – there could be no 'political prisoners'. This point of principle was maintained throughout most of the 1989–98 period. Michael Mates, who was the NIO's security minister in 1992–93, asserted that he believed 'terrorist organisations [to be] criminal conspiracies, representing perhaps the most dangerous threat to the fabric of any democratic society';[62] and Mayhew made it clear that '[t]here will be no amnesty. There are no political prisoners in the United Kingdom'.[63]

Considering the clarity with which the idea of 'political prisoners' was rejected, one would have expected the British government to resist the idea of negotiating about the issue, let alone making it part of a political settlement. After all, if there was no political dimension to crime, how could it be the subject of political bargaining? In reality, though, London had consciously dropped the principle, and decided to turn it into a bargaining chip with which to achieve the removal of the IRA's weaponry. The first explicit recognition of the issue as something that was to be bargained away dates from 1994, when the British government, in its exploratory talks with *Sinn Fein*, started to hold out the early release of prisoners as a *quid pro quo* for the decommissioning of illegal weapons. Quentin Thomas, who was the NIO's Deputy Permanent Secretary, confirms that the two issues were thought to be linked under the heading 'the practical consequences of the ending of violence'.[64] Accordingly, Mates now admits that 'we knew that any deal would have to involve prisoners and decommissioning'.[65] When it came to the final hours of negotiation, however, no 'deal' along these lines was done. As the memoirs of Marjorie Mowlam, who succeeded Mayhew in 1997, show, the British government agreed to the early release of prisoners not in return for the IRA's arsenal of weapons, but in the hope that the Republicans could be persuaded to agree to the other parties' constitutional proposals. Indeed, Mowlam makes it very clear that there had not even been an attempt to link the two issues.[66] In the end, London thus gave away what had once been a sacred principle without having addressed the issue of decommissioning at all.

The implications of this decision are difficult to anticipate. On the one hand, one might argue that the idea of Criminalisation had always been flawed, and that it was therefore time to abandon an outdated policy (see Chapter 5). On the other hand, the sheer scale of the measure makes it difficult to see how – in Mayhew's own words – it can 'be very quickly put back should the situation be seen to require it once again' (see above). Indeed, it is almost impossible to imagine – both logistically and politically – how Criminalisation could be reintroduced. In assuming that the current strategy of the Republican movement is irreversible, London's decision to abandon the principle therefore represents a considerable leap of faith. From a principled perspective, it could be regarded as a potentially disastrous political fix, undermining the rule of law by conceding that paramilitary prisoners had always been little more than political hostages to be bargained away at the earliest sign of a political deal. From a practical perspective, the failure to achieve a direct linkage between early release and decommissioning in the Belfast Agreement underlines the structural asymmetry of post-agreement politics. In fact, with prisoner release now complete, the Republicans have no reason to make their commitment to exclusively peaceful means permanent, or indeed to proceed with the removal of their arsenal, except when there are even more concessions on offer.

Reaching agreement? The making of an inclusive settlement

The public focus on issues like prisoner release and decommissioning had not always been obvious. In fact, in the first years of the 1989–98 period, London was not yet primarily concerned with the inclusion of *Sinn Fein* in a political settlement, but rather with how to revive the talks process between the constitutional parties. Westminster's interest in political talks had arisen from the majority community's continued rejection of the AIA, and the consequent belief that 'any agreement which alienated one part of the community could not be regarded as the final point'.[67] As a result, it became London's declared objective to work towards a comprehensive and agreed solution, which was most likely to the take the form of devolution and power-sharing, as well as including some element of North–South co-operation. In this regard, the British government saw its own role as that of a facilitator who would advance realistic options, and implement any package on which the local parties could agree (see above).

To focus on the talks process, however, did not exclude the possibility of inclusion. On the contrary, the two concepts were seen as complementary. First, if the end of the IRA's campaign was to be followed by a viable peace process, there was no alternative but to include *Sinn Fein* in a process of multilateral negotiations based on the principle of consent.

In London's view, the aim was political stability, and there was consequently no point in pursuing the inclusion of the Republican movement if it destroyed the chances of securing an agreed settlement. As Major explained: '[A] settlement which did not enjoy genuine consent would have stood no chance of working ... [W]e would have replaced one problem with a far bigger one.'[68] Equally, London believed that the talks process produced a political dynamic which attracted the Republicans into the political process, thus compelling them to take a decision in favour of abandoning their military campaign. According to Thomas: '[I]f there was a vibrant political process going on and *Sinn Fein* were outside it, it was hoped that this would bring pressure to bear on them because they would be missing what would be an important event.'[69]

In the literature on the peace process, it is often maintained that British policy had to undergo a radical shift in order to accommodate the possibility of an inclusive settlement, and that Westminster's reluctance could only be overcome through sustained lobbying from Dublin and other actors on the Nationalist side.[70] J. Ruane and J. Todd, for example, conclude that 'the British government had entered the peace process [only] in response to Nationalist pressure and persuasion'.[71] This view results from an insufficient understanding of British strategy. From an ideological perspective, there had never been any aversion to the idea of an inclusive settlement. In 1972 as well as in 1974–75, Westminster had pursued the idea of an inclusive settlement in direct talks with the IRA and *Sinn Fein*, and even during Thatcher's term in office, there were clear indications that London was prepared to contemplate an inclusive settlement if the Republicans were ready to abandon their military campaign. It was, in fact, one year before Thatcher's resignation when Brooke indicated that talks with *Sinn Fein* were possible once the IRA had ended its campaign of violence.[72] In November 1990, he then held a speech in which he explained the traditional British position of constitutional neutrality to Republicans, stating that '[t]he British government has no selfish or strategic or economic interest in Northern Ireland'.[73] Two years later, Mayhew publicly reaffirmed this message, stressing that the outcome of constitutional talks was not predetermined, and that *Sinn Fein* could participate in negotiations if the Republicans had sufficiently demonstrated that their commitment to exclusively democratic means was 'real'.[74]

Hence, whilst it is – quite simply – wrong to imply that Westminster needed to change its traditional outlook in order to provide for the inclusion of *Sinn Fein*, it is equally mistaken to overestimate the extent to which the possibility of an inclusive settlement featured in the minds of British ministers. Some authors, for example, maintain that Brooke's speeches and the alleged opening of a secret 'backchannel' to the Republicans in 1990 marked the beginning of a new departure in British policy.[75] Yet, although it is true that Brooke's as well as Mayhew's statements were calculated attempts to support and stimulate the Republican debate about the movement's future strategy, it would be far-fetched to argue that two speeches over a period of almost two years amounted to an initiative. The 'secret backchannel', on the other hand, had existed for many years, and even King now admits that there were 'intelligence people manoeuvring around at the margins' in the late 1980s.[76] Likewise, Brooke – who, in earlier interviews, stated that he had launched the 'backchannel' in October 1990 – now makes it clear that there was nothing particularly novel about the discussions between the leadership of the Republican movement and representatives of the Secret Service:

> *Brooke:* I was not actually asked for my authority until the February of the following year [1991]. That is logical, because what triggered the request to me was a change in personnel. The person that had previously conducted the exchanges was retiring from the Secret Service. Therefore, they had to have cover, they had to have authority for someone else to be introduced into the process.
>
> *Author: There was no conscious decision to open a line of contact to the IRA?*
>
> *Brooke:* No. It was a continuation of the same process.[77]

Throughout the conflict, the purpose of the 'backchannel' had been to provide an 'opportunity to carry on conversation'[78] as well as to pass on messages between the two sides at times of crisis (e.g. during the Hunger Strikes in the early 1980s), yet it had never been a vehicle through which any peace process was conducted. If at any point at all, the 'backchannel' assumed real significance in February 1993, when the British government received a message according to which '[t]he conflict is over but we need your advice on how to bring it to a close'.[79] Whilst it is unlikely that the Republican leadership would have phrased a message in this way, London nevertheless believed it to be genuine.[80] The communication was thought to be highly significant and triggered the personal involvement of Major and a selected group of senior Cabinet members. Mayhew was aware that London's conduct during the 1974–75 ceasefire had been 'designed to "trap" Sinn Fein and ... had thus done enormous damage' to the government's credibility, which is why he now wanted to make sure that the messages were accurate reflections of the British position.[81] This would also provide a plausible explanation as to why London's communications suddenly changed from the casual, suggestive and sometimes speculative style of a Secret Service agent towards the Cabinet's careful exposition of British government policy.[82]

In contrast to the traditional view, one may argue that the only significant change of policy in the years 1989–92 occurred not on the British but on the Irish side. As shown in the previous chapter, one of Dublin's principal aims in pursuing the AIA was to marginalise *Sinn Fein*. Eamon Delaney, who was a civil servant at the Irish Department of Foreign Affairs, described at length Dublin's 'paranoid caution' about being associated with *Sinn Fein*, stating that 'so distant were Sinn Fein kept, that if people called us looking for their address, we'd say: "It's in the phone book"'.[83] It was only in the years 1991–92 that Dublin fully recognised the Republican desire to end its political and military isolation. Despite occasional contacts between *Fianna Fail* and *Sinn Fein* in the late 1980s,[84] the formal opening of a 'backchannel' to the Republican leadership in 1992 was seen by Albert Reynolds as 'a total shift in direction, a total shift in policy'.[85] As a consequence, the same degree of enthusiasm with which the Irish government had once pursued the policy of marginalisation was now put into integrating *Sinn Fein* into the political process. Yet, even if this 'pan-Nationalist' approach had its merits in terms of generating some political confidence amongst the Republicans, Dublin spent little time thinking about how to construct a viable peace process. The ultimate priority for Dublin was to trigger a cessation of Republican violence, which appeared to equal peace and thus represented the final point of any peace process. In Reynold's words: 'Peace can't wait. The killing must be stopped. Time is not on our side.'[86]

Many authors have overstated the extent to which Anglo-Irish relations had become harmonious after the conclusion of the AIA. For instance, Dixon asserts that both governments worked on the same 'project', and that most of the alleged conflicts between the British and Irish governments were orchestrated in order to generate confidence amongst their respective constituencies.[87] This view, however, is not shared by the British ministers and civil servants who have been interviewed for this study, all of whom emphasise that 'it wasn't a choreography to which we were willing partners at all'.[88] Indeed, Major's Cabinet Secretary, Robin Butler, stresses that 'disagreements were genuine when they occurred'.[89] At the Brooke/Mayhew talks, for example, the Irish government's reluctance to embrace the Unionist advances was regarded with amazement by the British side. Westminster's priority was to establish a robust framework for a negotiated settlement, an important (and desired) side effect of which could have been the inclusion of *Sinn Fein*. Dublin and the SDLP, on the other hand, had decided that an inclusive settlement was 'the only game in town', and that the talks process undermined the chances of achieving this objective. Delaney confirms that it was Dublin which had decided to let the British initiative fail, recalling that 'half-way through [the 1992 talks] the Irish government realised that...the Provos would have to be "stitched into a settlement"'.[90]

Given the SDLP's and the Irish government's veto, the British government's indirect approach of integrating *Sinn Fein* into the political process had thus become untenable. Equally, adopting the 'pan-Nationalist' approach of halting the talks process until its terms were acceptable from a Republican point of view would have chances for a settlement that included the Unionists. According to Gary McMichael of the Loyalist Ulster Democratic Party:

> [N]either Reynolds nor Hume recognized that their objective...was isolating Unionism because it was seen as a narrow Nationalist agenda...Sinn Féin was not concerned at all whether Unionism was alienated, because it did not accept that a peace settlement was based on the need for Unionist support. But Reynolds' and Hume's blind fixation with bringing Sinn Féin on board almost ruined the opportunities that were to be created farther down the line.[91]

As the self-declared 'guardian of the process', it was up to the British government to formulate a new approach that reflected the need to build the foundations for an agreed settlement whilst accommodating the Nationalist urge to integrate *Sinn Fein*.

The JDP represented the successful conclusion of this task, and its significance can hardly be overemphasised. After months of 'hard bargaining' with Dublin, London had effectively managed to turn the Hume–Adams proposals into a declaration which united the whole spectrum of constitutional Nationalism as well as the UUP behind the British agenda for inclusion on the basis of consent and non-violence (see above).[92] While the overall tone of the document was undoubtedly 'green', thus allowing the Nationalist side to claim ownership of the process, the British government had avoided any concessions regarding its own role or the principle of consent. As a means of reassuring the Unionists, London now also pledged to hold a referendum on the outcome of any talks, so that the Ulster Unionists were at liberty to argue that 'the final version...contains no single cog or wheel of mechanism which can be used to the disadvantage of the greater number of people in Northern Ireland'.[93] The Republicans, on the other hand, realised that there was little in the JDP which represented a tangible advance from their point of view. Adams stated, quite correctly, that 'the British [have] merely conceded the wording of certain irresistible concepts, and then, by qualification, rendered them meaningless'.[94] However, with the Irish government and the SDLP now satisfied that the Republicans had been offered a fair deal, the veto of the constitutional Nationalists had been neutralised, and London's indirect approach of promoting political talks in order to put pressure on the Republicans could eventually be made effective. Ironically, it was Reynolds who became the main executor of the British approach. In early 1994, Reynolds recommitted his government to the idea of constitutional talks,[95] and by mid-August, he had sent a message to the IRA, warning that the Irish government would resume their participation in the talks process if the IRA failed to deliver an indefinite cessation of violence. He told his press officer: 'If they dont do this right, they can shag off...I'll walk away. I'll go off down that three-strand talks...road with John Major.'[96]

Once the IRA had declared its ceasefire, on 31 August 1994, the issue of illegally held weapons assumed central importance. According to Nationalist commentators, the demand for the full decommissioning of the IRA's arsenal represented an arbitrary hurdle which had surfaced as a result of Major's dwindling majority in the House of Commons.[97] Whilst London's credibility as an honest broker was certain to suffer from these accusations whether they were true or not, circumstantial evidence suggests that Major's dependence on the votes of the nine Ulster Unionist MPs has been overstated. Although some of London's actions could indeed be interpreted as bids for Unionist support (e.g. the granting of the Unionists' longstanding demand for a Northern Ireland Select Committee), there were at least as many instances when the government acted in a way that was likely to upset the Unionists (e.g. by giving in to *Sinn Fein*'s request for clarification of the JDP).[98] Given that Labour abandoned its opposition policy of 'Irish unity by consent' only once Tony Blair had taken over as leader in 1994,[99] the Unionists' bargaining power was very limited indeed. Compared to the late 1970s, when Thatcher (then in opposition) had promised full integration, one may even argue that the Unionists had an overwhelming incentive to keep Major in power as long as possible precisely by not pressuring the government with ultimatums.

The public debate about decommissioning – including the allegations about a parliamentary deal between Major and the Ulster Unionists – has clouded rather than illuminated the circumstances under which it became the main obstacle on the way to an agreed settlement. For example, whilst many Nationalist observers claim that it was imposed by the British government *after* the ceasefire had been called,[100] Bew and Gillespie point out that the Irish Foreign Minister, Dick Spring, referred to 'the handing up of arms' as early as December 1993.[101] Still, not one of the commentators has been struck by the absence of any sustained debate about the issue prior to the ceasefire. Apart from a cluster of casual references at the time of the JDP, the question of what to do with the arsenal of the best equipped private army in Western Europe appeared not to generate much interest, and no explicit references to the removal of illegal weapons can be found in any official document, including the JDP, the letter of clarification sent to *Sinn Fein* in May 1994,[102] and the British government's secret communication with the Republican leadership in previous years. Put simply, the two governments' handling of the question before the ceasefire allowed no other conclusion than that it would be of minor importance, and while Adams acknowledged the existence of the issue as early as January 1994,[103] he must be forgiven for thinking that his movement could simply ignore it in the same way in which the two governments did.

Why had London ignored the issue for such a long time? Two explanations are conceivable, both of which make clear that the British government needs to share some of the blame for mishandling the issue: first, because it failed to be explicit about what was certain to become a significant concern, and second, because it grossly underestimated the historical, tactical and strategic importance with which the Republicans viewed their weaponry.[104] The first possibility is that the issue was genuinely overlooked. British ministers and civil servants have subsequently argued that the JDP – according to which parties needed to 'establish a commitment to exclusively peaceful methods and [show] that they abide by the democratic process' – was understood by both sides to cover the decommissioning of illegal weaponry.[105] If that was the case, one would have expected the civil service to start working out the modalities under which decommissioning was to take place straight away. In reality, though, it took until after the breakdown of the first ceasefire for the legal foundations for the verifiable destruction of illegal weapons to be created,[106] which suggests that London had not expected the issue to assume any real significance, or necessitate any preparation, before it actually did. The second possibility is that London had avoided the question deliberately, assuming that it was better to confront some of the more controversial issues only when the ceasefire was in place and the IRA would find it more difficult to return to war. In his memoirs, Major

emphasised that his government's reference to 'the practical consequences of the ending of violence' meant the issue of decommissioning.[107] As we now know, the same phrase also covered the question of
early release for paramilitary prisoners (see above), which makes it
entirely plausible to conclude that the British government anticipated
a problem-free trade-off between the two issues as soon as British
representatives were able to meet and discuss the details of a deal with
the leadership of *Sinn Fein*.

Once decommissioning had – contrary to British expectations –
become the focal point of the peace process, London found itself in a situation that was almost impossible to balance. On the one hand, the
British government had no interest in an all-out confrontation, knowing that there continued to be an internal debate within the Republican
movement, and that to focus on the question of decommissioning
would undermine the position of people like Adams who were believed
to be genuine 'politicos'. As Thomas explains:

> [W]e would deal with *Sinn Fein* on the basis that they had renounced
> violence. Of course, everyone knew that it was more complicated
> than that... We had a situation of converting a movement that was
> engaged in physical force into a wholly democratic political move-
> ment. Anyone who manages political change knows that it is difficult
> to judge the moment when you take on those within your movement
> who have the strongest views... And the bad thing about decommis-
> sioning was that it kept inviting the *Sinn Fein* leadership to confront
> those within their movement who they did not want to confront for
> perfectly normal political reasons.[108]

On the other hand, the British government needed to create the
necessary confidence for the political representatives of the majority
community to participate in inclusive talks. Westminster had repeatedly
misled the public about its secret contacts with *Sinn Fein*, and it was
therefore no surprise that London's assurances – according to which
there was no 'secret deal' – were regarded with suspicion by the
Unionists.[109] Moreover, the IRA's intention to hold on to its weaponry
was an understandable disincentive for Unionists to engage with a party
which could continue to threaten the use of violence in order to achieve
favourable outcomes. From London's perspective, it was difficult, therefore, to compromise its initial demands without further eroding
Unionist confidence in the process. As Major explained: 'Unless there
is... decommissioning there is unlikely to be confidence among the
other political parties that Sinn Fein is committed permanently to

peace, and we cannot have all-party negotiations unless all parties are prepared to sit down and talk together.'[110]

Given the strategic environment, it comes as no surprise that much of the first ceasefire period was spent on attempts to remove the stumbling block of decommissioning. In the first phase (October 1994 until March 1995), the British government tried to facilitate movement on the Republican side by watering down the original demand for the full decommissioning of the IRA's arsenal. As early as October 1994, Major emphasised that the dismantling of the IRA's 'offensive' capability (e.g. Semtex and detonators) was more important than the removal of supposedly 'defensive' weapons, such as guns.[111] In March 1995, London then postulated that *Sinn Fein* could be admitted to full negotiations as soon as the IRA had performed a token gesture on decommissioning (this demand became known as 'Washington 3'). Given that this was believed to be the outer limit beyond which the Unionists could not be pushed,[112] the second phase (April to September) was marked by attempts to generate Republican confidence through different means. In order to entrench the position of the *Sinn Fein* leadership, London reversed its original policy and enabled the Republican leaders to meet Ancram prior to the start of decommissioning.[113] In addition, and despite the limited extent to which the military instrument could be used as a tool of bargaining, Westminster aimed at demonstrating flexibility on issues that were considered to be of importance to the Republican grassroots. For instance, the government removed several exclusion orders, announced significant relaxations in prison arrangements, and consciously restored the pre-1987 remission rates for paramilitary inmates as a means of 'bring[ing] the prisoner issue into the equation'.[114]

Having accepted that no Republican gesture was likely to be forthcoming, London's attention turned to the search for an alternative way of engendering Unionist confidence. In what could be seen as a third phase (October 1995 to February 1996), the British government took up the idea of a Unionist MP, Ken Maginnis, to create an international commission on decommissioning. As Mayhew stated: 'Confidence is what it's all about ... If a commission could come up with some means of generating that necessary confidence by some other means, then we would want to look at that.'[115] However, after it became clear that the so-called Mitchell commission (named after its chairman) would not come up with an alternative, but simply recommend the dropping of any decommissioning prior to inclusive negotiations, London sought to balance this proposal by pressing Mitchell for the inclusion of a reference to the idea of an elected body, which had been advanced by the new Ulster Unionist leader, David Trimble.[116] When Major singled out this idea from Mitchell's final report, Nationalists immediately accused him of erecting another obstacle on the way to inclusive negotiations. Mitchell himself, though, understood Major's intention very well:

> By proposing an alternate route to negotiations, Major signaled [sic] his willingness to move away from prior decommissioning. Although he was heavily criticized for his reaction to our report, Major's strategy proved to be workable. By focusing on elections, he provided the reassurance that the Unionists needed, and he deflected attention away from his eventual abandonment of prior decommissioning.[117]

When Major announced that it was sufficient for the Republicans 'to address' the issue of illegally held weapons (rather than actually carry out an act of decommissioning) for *Sinn Fein* to gain entry to the negotiations,[118] the IRA had already ended its ceasefire.

One factor that has been somewhat overrated in the literature is the influence of the American government.[119] Like the Irish government and the SDLP, Washington played a significant role in generating confidence amongst the Republicans. Its impact on the formulation of British government policy, however, was negligible. In late 1993, the White House had completed a review of its non-interventionist policy on Ireland, the most tangible result of which was to grant Adams a visa to visit the United States in early 1994. Given that London had just created the conditions for its indirect approach of integrating *Sinn Fein* to work, the British government perceived the American intervention as an unhelpful interference.[120] By mid-1994, though, London had managed to translate the new reality of American intervention into an asset. In the summer of 1994, Washington rejected Adams' application for another visa, thereby adding to the pressure on the IRA. In early 1995, President Bill Clinton even went on to praise Major's approach whilst lecturing Adams on the need for decommissioning, stating that 'the paramilitaries must get rid of their weapons'.[121] In November 1995, during a visit to Northern Ireland, Clinton played an important part in stabilising the IRA's ceasefire at a time when the British government was preoccupied with the search for an alternative means of generating Unionist confidence. Indeed, Mayhew now confirms that Clinton's famous handshake with Adams was stagemanaged by the NIO.[122] J. Dumbrell is therefore mistaken in arguing that Washington's positive attitude during the multiparty negotiations in 1997–98 reflected the personal chemistry between Clinton and Blair.[123] In fact, any substantial difference of approach had been resolved by the previous administration, so that any British government could have relied on the support of the White House.

Even if the period between Blair's election victory in May 1997 and the successful conclusion of the talks process in April 1998 can be seen as the climax of British policy in Northern Ireland, it involved little strategic change and will therefore be dealt with only briefly. As Mowlam herself points out, the new government's approach was almost identical to that of the previous administration,[124] except for the fact that London was now at liberty to generate the momentum which the peace process had lacked in previous years. Arguably, the 1997–98 period illustrated how Major's strategy had eventually paid off, as it not only provided an incentive for the IRA to cease its military campaign, but also the opportunity to follow it up with a viable inclusive talks process. Embracing Major's indirect approach of integrating *Sinn Fein*, the new government's first move was to announce the date for another round of constitutional talks, thus reassuring the Unionists whilst compelling the Republicans to decide in favour of another ceasefire. In what summarised British policy ever since the Brooke/Mayhew talks, Blair stated:

> My message to Sinn Fein is clear. The settlement train is leaving. I want you on that train. But it is leaving anyway, and I will not allow it to wait for you. You cannot hold the process to ransom any longer. So end the violence. Now.[125]

Considering that Dublin, Washington and the SDLP had by now become firm supporters of the British agenda for limited constitutional change, the Republicans were faced with the choice between isolation and integration yet again. In July, the IRA declared its second ceasefire, and with the controversy about prior decommissioning out of the way, it was possible to move on to inclusive negotiations without delay. Whilst the DUP chose to leave the negotiations at this point, the UUP had convinced itself that there was nothing to lose from participating in a talks process that was designed around the principle of consent.[126] It had thus turned out to be absolutely crucial that London had guarded the integrity of the process so vigorously. Put simply, the consequences of not doing so would have been disastrous: the main representatives of the majority community would have dropped out of the process, and no agreed settlement could have emerged.

Apart from the commitment to 'a new beginning' in policing and the strong emphasis on 'equality of esteem', the core provisions of the Belfast Agreement largely followed the example of previous, non-inclusive attempts at producing an agreed settlement. With a devolved Assembly, executive power-sharing and an institutionalised – albeit fairly limited – Irish dimension, the Belfast Agreement contained all the elements which London had regarded as essential ingredients of a constitutional compromise as early as 1973. In this regard, the inclusion of *Sinn Fein* made no tangible difference, and it is indeed remarkable that Irish Republicans have signed up to a partitionist arrangement that is based on the principle of consent. Whilst, from an institutional perspective, the Belfast Agreement therefore vindicated the British approach, it is nevertheless questionable whether the overall logic of the accord provides the foundation on which the long-term aims of stability and containment can be realised. Repeating the previous government's mistake, the Labour government attempted to sideline the issue of illegally held weapons. According to Mowlam, it was 'essential' to keep Adams in place,[127] and to press for a clear commitment on decommissioning was believed to destabilise the 'politicos' within the Republican leadership. As Alf Dubs, an NIO minister in 1997–99, explained:

> The rather weak wording on decommissioning was probably the best that one could get. My feeling is that *Sinn Fein* said that they would do the best to get decommissioning, but it depended on the difficult situation in their own movement, that is, they were trying to avoid defections ... Adams needed a high level of support before he could feel confident about the next move.[128]

In contrast to 1994, however, the Labour government now also removed the principal lever with which the Republicans could be enticed to make their commitment to exclusively peaceful politics permanent. There is no direct linkage between the two; and whereas prisoner releases have now been completed, the removal of illegally held weapons has not. Regardless of what Adams' intentions are, the Belfast Agreement has therefore created a situation in which the Republicans have no reason to make any further moves in the direction of constitutional politics, except when there are additional concessions on offer. In that sense, the Belfast Agreement encourages the Republicans to keep their arsenal as long as possible, and continue to employ it alongside the electoral mandate as an additional instrument with which to obtain political advantage, thus undermining the 'moderate' SDLP as an effective representative of Nationalist interests whilst reinforcing the suspicion of the majority community that the peace process is in fact a 'sell out' with nothing to offer from a Unionist perspective. As long as this asymmetry remains the predominant rationale of post-agreement politics in Northern Ireland, the fringes rather than the centre of the political spectrum are bound to benefit, and long-term stability is unlikely to emerge.

Peace through prosperity? The creation of the 'peace dividend'

Like London's political strategy, the 1989–98 period saw significant changes in the use of the economic instrument. For the first time, there was a consistent effort to make economic and social policy responsive to the objective of British government strategy. Contrary to Westminster's approach in previous periods, when the instrument of economic policy was related to the aims of London's overall strategy only in the most general sense, there was now a clear linkage between strategic objective and economic response. For instance, before the IRA declared its first ceasefire, British strategy was geared towards bringing political and military pressure upon the Republican movement, so that the IRA would eventually abandon its military campaign and resort to exclusively peaceful means. Accordingly, the purpose of economic and social policy was to complement this pressure by demonstrating how the IRA's activities destroyed jobs and damaged the prospects for economic growth, announcing precisely what parts of Northern Ireland's social and commercial infrastructure each of the IRA's attacks had destroyed, and how much money needed to be cut from social programmes in order to pay for the damage.[129] As Needham put it, the aim was 'to go on the offensive against *Sinn Fein* and the IRA, and to ask everytime they blew something up: Mr Adams, why do you do this?'[130]

When the IRA called its first ceasefire, in August 1994, it was obvious that the instrument of economic policy needed to be employed in a different manner. Apart from the symbolic reduction of the British military presence, economic policy played a key role in creating the 'feelgood factor' that was meant to make it impossible for the IRA to return to war (see above). Accordingly, London announced that savings in security would now be spent on social programmes, housing, education, and so on. Moreover, in October, Major referred to the province's 'special needs' which made it necessary to continue the high levels of public expenditure even when political life in Northern Ireland returned to normal.[131] This so-called 'peace dividend' translated into an additional investment subsidy of £73 m from the British Exchequer, a £230 m aid programme from the European Union as well as significant contributions from Commonwealth countries and the United States.[132]

In accordance with the framework outlined above, the breakdown of the IRA's ceasefire saw the return to the approach that had been implemented before the announcement of the cessation. Although money from foreign sources continued to be available, London emphasised that additional spending on security needed to be funded from other areas of Northern Ireland expenditure. According to Ancram: 'When security requirements are reintroduced as a result of changes in the secuity situation, everyone must share the pain.'[133] Likewise, the declaration of the second IRA ceasefire was followed by a similar reaction to that in 1994, even if the Labour government was slightly more cautious than Major, stressing that 'the real peace dividend for Northern Ireland...is peace itself'.[134] Yet, whilst Ingram warned that 'extremely high levels of public spending have produced a subsidy culture which cannot last',[135] a whole series of new measures and additional funds were announced during the 1998 referendum campaign, offering – in Chancellor Gordon Brown's own words – 'the chance to build peace with prosperity'.[136] Likewise, Mowlam was a strong believer in the idea of the peace dividend, stating that 'people would need to see some [economic] progress...if they were to have a belief that any peace process would work'.[137] There can be no doubt, therefore, that economic policy continued to be seen as an instrument with which to complement the overall political objective.

Regarding the issue of relative deprivation, there was an equally significant change. Contrary to the reluctant and 'discreet' approach in previous periods, the issue became a priority of London's economic and social policy. In fact, Brooke now openly declared the material inequalities between Catholics and Protestants to be 'the most fundamental structural issue facing any government'.[138] Likewise, Mayhew stated that London was 'unequivocally committed to eradicating inequality of opportunity and relative disadvantage...wherever they exist in Northern Ireland'.[139]

There is little evidence as to what caused London's enthusiasm for an issue which it had found convenient to ignore for most of the Troubles. Possibly, it was a response to the heightened awareness of economic differentials amongst Nationalist leaders and the Irish government, both of which had become passionate supporters of strong fair employment regulations only when the US-sponsored MacBride campaign had gained overwhelming momentum (see Chapter 6). On the other hand, one may argue that there was a genuine change in London's view of how material factors related to the reality of conflict and division. Whilst, in previous periods, absolute poverty was believed to be the sole economic 'cause' of the conflict (and economic parity with the rest of the United Kingdom the solution), British ministers now argued that community differentials were equally significant as 'provokers of terrorism'.[140] In addition to the Fair Employment Act, which became law in January 1990, the British government therefore launched an initiative – 'Targeting Social

Need' – that was meant to alleviate poverty in the worst affected areas. Westminster emphasised that the definition of areas followed objective criteria, and that disadvantages were to be tackled 'wherever they are to be found',[141] but it was understood that the minority community would benefit disproportionately simply because more of its members were likely to be affected by poverty. Whilst ministers were reluctant to admit that this had been the purpose of the programme, one of London's submissions to the multi-party talks made it clear that 'it is expected that over time Targeting Social Need should have the effect of reducing differentials between the two communities'.[142]

As a cynic, however, one may equally contend that London's surprising interest in the question of relative deprivation resulted from the fact that the issue had finally started to work in the government's favour, and that it was in Westminster's interest to highlight its contribution. In the first half of the 1990s, several reports by the Fair Employment Commission (FEC) showed that the 'sectarian gap' between the two communities was narrowing, and that Catholic representation in managerial jobs had significantly increased since the mid-1980s.[143] In 1997, the SACHR noted that the number of Catholics in employment had risen by 15.5 per cent in the years 1990–96, whereas the equivalent increase for Protestants was only 0.2 per cent.[144] Even if the explanations for this trend are manifold (for instance, different demographics, uneven patterns of emigration, increased overall prosperity, etc.), London was keen to claim the development as a result of its own efforts. As Mayhew declared: 'We have a better story to tell than was the case even a few years ago, and in America, in particular, we are telling it with advantage'.[145]

Conclusion

The successful conclusion of the Belfast Agreement represents the greatest achievement of British policy in Northern Ireland. The British government not only realised its traditional objective of devolution and power-sharing, but it also managed to provide for the inclusion of *Sinn Fein* into the political process, thus triggering an indefinite cessation of the IRA's military campaign.

At the outset of the 1989–98 period, the British government returned to its traditional objective of promoting an agreed cross-community settlement. Recognising the perception of political and military stalemate amongst Republicans, the British government believed that the inclusion of *Sinn Fein* into an agreed settlement could only succeed if the integrity of the political process was preserved. As Mayhew put it: 'Peace – not peace at whatever price, but peace properly attained – and an agreed political settlement are the government's twin objectives in Northern Ireland.'[146] As a consequence, the strategic instrument was rearranged as follows:

- The constitutional instrument: to facilitate agreement on devolution and a limited Irish dimension.
- The military instrument: to use the security forces as a tool with which to support the political process whilst maintaining the Republican perception of military stalemate.
- The political instrument: to launch negotiations for an agreed settlement based on the principle of consent, thus preserving the integrity of the political process whilst paving the way for the inclusion of *Sinn Fein.*
- The economic instrument: to reinforce the need for a balanced settlement through economic incentives.

Until 1993, London's strategy was consistently at odds with Dublin's urge to include *Sinn Fein* into the political process. In this regard, the JDP represented a tactical masterstroke, as it not only united the whole spectrum of constitutional Nationalism as well as the UUP behind the British agenda for limited constitutional change based on the principle of consent, but also provided a tool with which London's indirect approach of integrating *Sinn Fein* into the political process could be made effective. The successful conclusion of multi-party talks in 1997–98 must therefore be traced back to the JDP, which created the platform from which a viable and agreed peace process could be constructed.

Despite this remarkable achievement, which vindicates London's role as a facilitator, one may nevertheless contend that the integration of *Sinn Fein* into the political process has extracted a potentially high price. In the course of the 1989–98 period, the British government crucially failed to secure any commitment that would have made the Republicans' reliance on exclusively peaceful means irreversible. Before the 1994 ceasefire, the British government missed the opportunity to address the question of decommissioning, so that the first ceasefire period needed to be devoted entirely to what Thomas called the 'progressive adjustment of expectations'[147] *vis-à-vis* this particular question. Repeating the mistake, London again failed to extract any definite commitment in 1998. In contrast to 1994, however, the British government now gave away the only incentive that could have enticed the Republicans to make their adherence to peaceful means permanent.

With the early release of paramilitary prisoners and the consequent abandonment of the principle of Criminalisation, there is now no reason for *Sinn Fein* to proceed with the decommissioning of arms, except under international pressure or because of electoral considerations. On the contrary, the maintenance of a military option ensures that the Republicans are given attention far beyond what could be justified on the basis of their electoral mandate. As long as this remains the case, there is a potentially fatal asymmetry in the peace process, which benefits the fringes rather than the moderate centre, and which may well continue to endanger the achievement of the twin aims of stability and containment that London has pursued throughout the Troubles in Northern Ireland.

8
Conclusion

The preceding chapters of this study have outlined some of the dominant themes in British government policy and followed them through various periods of British involvement. As a result, it is now possible to address some of the questions that were outlined in the first chapter of this work.

Early transformation

The evolution of British strategy after 1972 cannot be explained without understanding the failure of London's approach in the previous period. When the British government first intervened in the Northern Ireland conflict, in August 1969, it was guided by two seemingly paradoxical assumptions. On the one hand, London aimed at keeping its involvement to a minimum, thus ensuring that it would not get drawn into an antagonism that appeared both insoluble and incomprehensible. On the other hand, the British government believed that the existing system of Unionist majority rule could be easily reformed in order to accommodate Catholic discontent, and that further British intervention was therefore not necessary. As a result, the objective of maintaining and stabilising the Home Rule structures at Stormont appeared feasible.

London's disregard for the sectarian dynamics of politics in the province turned out to be highly counterproductive. The demand for political reform heightened Protestant insecurity, which – in turn – strengthened Unionist hardliners whilst undermining the Unionist Party's 'moderate' leadership. The resulting inability to deliver the promised changes shattered Catholic hopes for a more equitable society, and it provided fertile soil in which the national question could re-emerge. Against this background, the IRA was at liberty to exploit

Catholic disillusionment by provoking a purely military response, which furthered the perception that the British Army represented the 'long arm' of the Unionist regime. Indeed, with no political alternative on offer, the British government increasingly relied on the military instrument to achieve its objective. With incidents like internment and Bloody Sunday, the outcome of London's approach was wholly negative in that it galvanised Nationalist opposition, leading to the withdrawal of the constitutional Nationalists from Stormont and the intensification of the IRA's campaign.

Realising that the 1969 strategy had in fact worsened its overall position by contributing to the escalation rather than the containment of the conflict, London decided to reformulate its approach. For the first time, the British government acknowledged that political stability and containment could only be achieved if the government of the province reflected the sectarian dynamics of politics in Northern Ireland, that is, if both sides were guaranteed permanent access to political power. This assumption translated into the objective of creating a devolved system of government that was acceptable to Unionists as well as Nationalists. As a consequence, the political representatives of the two communities were effectively given a veto, and the British government was left with the role of a neutral arbiter.

Throughout the following decades, the imperative of facilitating agreement remained the most important factor in conditioning London's strategy. Regarding the use of the military instrument, for example, the counterinsurgency effort had to be carried out in a way that made it possible for the political representatives of the Nationalist community to deal with London without losing the support of their constituency (the demand for 'acceptability'). Also, it needed to reflect the assumption that 'normal' law enforcement was conducive to political compromise across sectarian divisions (the demand for 'normality'). In other words, whilst the constitutional imperative of protecting life and property against any existing or anticipated use of force continued to be paramount – thus imposing a threshold below which the level of force could not fall – the new objective had imposed additional limits beyond which the security forces were not allowed to go in responding to the 'level of threat'. This strategic environment meant that the military instrument was of limited use as a means of 'vicious' bargaining. More importantly, though, it reinforced London's conviction that there could be no 'military solution', and that it was the security forces' task to 'buy time' for a political settlement in achieving an 'acceptable level of violence' (see Chapter 3). In that sense, it was the British government rather than the IRA, which had first embarked on a 'long war'.

Implementation

By upholding a mutual veto, London had provided both sides with a tool with which to prevent the British government from achieving its objective, thus making the realisation of London's aim more difficult than originally anticipated. In 1973, Westminster successfully facilitated agreement between the SDLP and Faulkner's Unionists, yet the ensuing Executive was brought down by Unionist opposition less than six months after taking office. At the 1975 Constitutional Convention, the British government adopted a lower profile, but still failed to overcome the Unionists' unwillingness to share power with the Nationalists. At the 1980 Conference, neither the Ulster Unionists nor the SDLP were prepared to become part of an accommodation on the basis of London's original proposals. In 1982, the 'rolling devolution' Assembly turned out as a 'lame duck' (see Chapter 5) once the SDLP had decided to boycott it. At the Brooke/Mayhew talks in 1991 and 1992, it was again the Nationalist side that prevented the successful emergence of a political settlement. Only with the Belfast Agreement in 1998 could both sides be persuaded to agree on how the province should be governed.

Although there can be no doubt that London's efforts to mediate a compromise were numerous, its effectiveness as a facilitator was inhibited by the various elements of its strategic tradition. Constitutionally, for example, the main difficulty was that the British government's self-declared neutrality furthered the impression of constitutional insecurity, which isolated the majority community and encouraged a 'siege mentality' among Unionists. London's unwillingness to uphold Northern Ireland's membership of the United Kingdom for any other reason than the threat of a civil war meant that any Unionist move towards a compromise was bound to be interpreted as 'lack of determination'. From a Unionist perspective, it thus weakened the pretext under which the British government was prepared to defend the Britishness of the province. In turn, Unionists regarded every British policy change with suspicion, fearing that it was a possible prelude to withdrawal. London never understood these dynamics, and its insensitivity towards the constitutional concerns of the majority community added to the perception that the British government could not be trusted as a guardian of Unionist interests, regardless of how often it repeated the consent principle.

The British government's military approach suffered from two inherent weaknesses, both of which tended to undermine its capability to maintain its own 'long war'. First, in an effort to sustain the military campaign, but also in order to 'normalise' the security effort, London decided to return the thrust of law enforcement to the UDR and – mainly – the RUC. Aware that the local security forces had lost much credibility amongst the minority community, the British government committed itself to their professionalisation, particularly from the mid-1970s when 'police primacy' attained the status of a policy. From a sectarian perspective, however, Westminster had simply transferred law enforcement from the Army back to 'Ulster Protestants in uniform'.[1] There was little understanding amongst British ministers that, in a deeply divided society, the acceptance of law enforcement was bound to be perceived in sectarian terms, and that impartiality was determined by the local security forces' communal composition as much as by their objective professionalism. In this regard, London's ignorance made it more difficult for the majority of constitutional Nationalists to embrace the security forces' campaign.

Moreover, the principle of Criminalisation was an ineffective tool with which to establish the legitimacy of London's involvement. On the one hand, the idea of drawing a firm moral line between the tactics of the insurgents and one's own side was a promising concept. It was a coherent response to the loss of credibility in the wake of internment and Bloody Sunday, yet it also suited the traditional British government instinct, which saw the IRA's campaign as a challenge to parliamentary democracy. On the other hand, the principle was rendered meaningless by the inconsistent way in which it was implemented. After prisoners had been granted Special Category status in 1972, and since they were convicted under legislation that defined terrorism as 'the use of violence for political ends', the Hunger Strikers of 1980 and 1981 could be forgiven for thinking that they were indeed 'political prisoners'. With the controversy surrounding the 1981 Hunger Strike, and the consequent rise of *Sinn Fein*, the British government paid a significant political price in order to preserve the integrity of Criminalisation. Yet, in the following decade, it chose to abandon the principle altogether. Hoping that a lasting settlement could be gained from doing so, Westminster consciously turned the issue into a bargaining chip, and eventually gave it away without having achieved any substantial concession at all. Instead of securing the 'moral high ground', London's stance on Criminalisation thus represents an incentive for political and paramilitary groups to challenge whatever principles the British government claims to be non-negotiable in the future.

Regarding the instrument of economic and social policy, it took considerable time for the British government to recognise its strategic value. Throughout the Troubles, the British government believed that there was a causal relationship between the lack of prosperity and the inclination to commit violence, which meant that the prospects of a peaceful resolution could be enhanced if general material conditions improved. However, the principle of 'peace through prosperity' was implemented rather simplistically in the 1970s, when a seemingly unlimited amount of money was made available to attract inward investment, improve housing conditions and expand the public sector. Still, with adverse economic conditions, the British government's 'wild orgy of senseless spending'[2] produced only limited results. Changing attitudes towards public spending across the Irish Sea meant that there was increasing pressure on Northern Ireland ministers to ensure 'value for money', and whilst the canons of monetarism applied to the province only in a fairly restricted sense, economic Thatcherism nevertheless prompted London to think about how the instrument of economic and social policy could be employed in a more targeted way. As a result, the focus on economic parity with the rest of the United Kingdom lessened, and the idea of the peace dividend emerged.

Equally, the importance of addressing the issue of relative inequality between the two communities was recognised relatively late. Throughout the 1970s, Westminster found it convenient to ignore what was a persistent grievance of the minority, hoping that its efforts to achieve economic parity with the rest of the United Kingdom would eventually pay off and eradicate any tangible differences in material status between the two communities. Like its approach to the communal composition of the security forces, there was little awareness that issues of economic opportunity were perceived in sectarian terms, and that the perception of unfairness could only be removed if the government was seen to pursue an approach that went beyond the creation of legal safeguards against individual discrimination. In the 1980s, Westminster's reluctance was overcome by external pressures, particularly from the United States and the Republic of Ireland. It was, however, only in the 1990s when the British government truly embraced the issue of relative inequality, partly as a result of its more targeted approach towards economic policy, but also because the narrowing economic gap between the two communities demonstrated that the issue had finally started to work in its favour.

Sidelining the mutual veto

London's lack of success in facilitating a political compromise between the two communities resulted in two attempts to sideline the political parties, both of which were meant to overcome their veto and achieve the British government's aim of containment without having to obtain local consent. First, in a plausible aberration from its constitutional tradition, London decided not to pursue any form of constitutional change in the years 1976–79. After the failure of two initiatives in the previous years, the British government believed that constitutional stability had to be achieved before any agreed political accommodation could emerge, and undiminished Direct Rule (supported by financial generosity and a hawkish attitude on security) seemed to provide an appropriate framework within which to realise this end. However, in assuming that undiminished Direct Rule was equally acceptable to both communities, and that it could be imposed as a semi-permanent system of government, the British government had committed a significant error of judgement. Neither the Irish government nor the political representatives of the minority in Northern Ireland were prepared to acquiesce in this strategy, and the resulting pressures compelled London to abandon its approach.

The intention to refrain from any more attempts to bring about an agreed form of devolution, combined with the Labour–Unionist parliamentary pact in the House of Commons, severely undermined Westminster's credibility as an honest broker. The period of undiminished Direct Rule resulted in a more intransigent attitude by the SDLP, which now insisted that the Irish government had to be given a say in how to rule the province in order to set the balance of power straight. With the Unionists strongly opposed to any form of Irish dimension, agreement on what was called an 'internal settlement' had thus become almost impossible. In this regard, the period of undiminished Direct Rule had made London's task as a political facilitator even more difficult: instead of overcoming the mutual veto on a political settlement, it had strengthened it; and rather than 'taking the constitutional question out of Northern Ireland politics', it had demonstrated that the need for an institutionalised Irish dimension was not only a natural British instinct but in fact a political necessity.

One may therefore argue that the formal recognition of the Irish dimension in the Anglo-Irish Agreement was but the official reflection of what had become a firm political imperative several years before. In that sense, the AIA needs to be seen as a response to the Nationalist pressures which had arisen from the period of undiminished Direct Rule. In fact, instead of deliberately worsening the constitutional status quo for the majority, the evidence presented in this book suggests that London simply intended the agreement to be a tool with which to accommodate the Irish government and ease the operation of Direct Rule.

Its insensitivity towards the constitutional concerns of the majority community meant that the British government had failed to see how the AIA was overbalanced towards the Nationalist position. Indeed, British ministers were genuinely surprised by the strong Unionist rejection, as they believed that the agreement had not only preserved Northern Ireland's status as part of the United Kingdom but in fact strengthened it. Given London's original intentions, the AIA had thus been a failure: instead of easing Direct Rule, it resulted in a period of sustained political stalemate and instability, which brought Westminster into direct confrontation with the Unionist majority whilst being of limited value *vis-à-vis* the goal of re-engaging the minority, or even ending the 'megaphone diplomacy' between London and Dublin.

Even so, the accord produced a series of unexpected outcomes, which turned out to be highly significant in the following decade. After years of political withdrawal, the perception that the 'centre of gravity' had shifted towards an all-Ireland setting provided an incentive for Unionists to re-engage with the other parties. On the Republican side, the fact that the British government had agreed to an accord that so obviously disadvantaged the majority community, combined with London's seemingly newfound determination to 'take on the Unionists', contributed to the impression that there was now a political and military stalemate on the British side, which – in turn – contributed to the Republicans' own perception of political and military marginalisation. Ironically, and contrary to London's expectations, the treaty had thus provided the political foundation on which the British government's traditional objective of facilitating political agreement between the two communities could be realised.

Success

Some authors have argued that the AIA resolved the principal contradiction of British strategy, as it allowed the British government to, side with Unionist interests whilst leaving Nationalist concerns to the Irish government.[3] This hypothesis remains open to challenge. Whilst there can be no doubt that the AIA generated enormous confidence amongst

Nationalists, little had changed from a British perspective. To be an even-handed mediator between the conflicting national aspirations continued to be seen as a necessity, if not a governmental duty. Paul Murphy, Mowlam's deputy in the years 1997–99, put this point across very strongly:

> It is often said that the Irish government looks after the Nationalists, and the British government looks after the Unionists. We couldn't do it like that, because – whatever you think about it – the British government actually governs both communities. That's the difference. As it happens, Nationalists and Unionists in Northern Ireland both live under the British state. There's a responsibility on behalf of British statesmen to look after everybody in that part of the United Kingdom. The Irish government don't govern Northern Ireland – we do. We have a special responsibility to look after everybody's interest, and especially to bring them together and work out a compromise.[4]

In the 1989–98 period, London returned to its traditional role as an honest broker and facilitator for agreement. In contrast to previous periods, however, it did so with great skill. Even if the Frameworks document of 1995 was a significant error of judgement (displaying Westminster's innocence with regard to Unionist sensitivities once more), the British government was largely successful in gearing its strategy towards the facilitation of political agreement. Indeed, given the huge strain imposed by the Nationalist demand for the inclusion of *Sinn Fein*, the Joint Declaration for Peace was possibly the most remarkable political achievement of the entire 1969–98 period. It united the whole spectrum of constitutional Nationalism and the largest Unionist party behind the British agenda for an agreed settlement based on the principle of consent, limited constitutional change and Nationalist–Unionist co-operation in a devolved system of government. Most significantly, in doing so, it compelled the IRA to declare an indefinite cessation of violence without having obtained any privileges, assurances or concessions.

From London's perspective, the inclusion of *Sinn Fein* into the political process had never represented an insurmountable ideological problem. As this author has shown throughout this study, the British government always believed that any group could become part of the 'moderate centre' as long as it rejected violence as a means of political expression. It is therefore mistaken to argue that London's position somehow shifted from 'moderation' towards 'inclusion of paramilitaries', as Cunningham suggests.[5] In fact, Westminster's position has been far more consistent than that of any other actor in the conflict. As early as 1972, representatives of the British government were trying to woo the Republicans into the political process. After the failure of the 1974 Executive, the idea that 'extremists' needed to be turned into 'doves' became even more of a political imperative, as the fate of the first power-sharing experiment seemed to illustrate that any 'coalition' needed to be 'broadly based'. From the middle of the 1970s, the Republican movement's 'Armalite and ballot box' strategy suggested that there was no genuine interest in either ceasing violence or engaging with constitutional parties, so that London's approach towards *Sinn Fein* appeared to become more hostile, yet even during Thatcher's term in office, the British government kept to its traditional position, stating that the Republicans were excluded not because of the nature of their political aims but because they used violence in order to achieve them, and that once they had abandoned violence, the possibilities were almost limitless. As Major put it in 1993: 'Let me make explicit what has always been implicit. Those who decline to renounce violence can never have a place at the conference table in our democracy, but if the IRA end violence for good then ... Sinn Fein can enter the political arena as a democratic party'.[6]

Rather than an ideological problem, the inclusion of *Sinn Fein* was a practical one. As the self-declared guardian of the process, London was concerned about how to construct a viable political process, and it was almost alone in recognising that there was little point in including *Sinn Fein* into the political process if in doing so, it would trigger the Unionists' exit. The difference between the Irish and the British governments in the early 1990s was therefore one of procedure. Whilst London would have preferred to launch the political process without *Sinn Fein* in order to create a dynamic that attracted the Republicans into constitutional politics, the Nationalists had decided that the political process needed to be halted until the Republicans found its conditions acceptable. The fact that the largest Unionist party was eventually prepared to sit down at the same negotiating table as *Sinn Fein* resulted from Westminster's effort to construct a political process that was attractive enough for Nationalists whilst generating sufficient confidence amongst Unionists in order to make a negotiated and inclusive settlement between the representatives of both communities possible.

Failure?

At first glance, the Belfast Agreement vindicates London's approach. The British government has eventually realised its objective, and by participating in the devolved institutions, it could be argued that even Sinn Fein now subscribes to the ideas and principles which have been advocated by the British government ever since the abolition of Stormont in 1972.

Even so, in its eagerness to capitalise on the unique opportunity to integrate the Republican movement into the political process, London potentially compromised the achievement of its aim, namely, to contain the conflict. For more than five years, Westminster has now failed to extract any tangible commitment from the Republican movement that its commitment to exclusively peaceful means is absolute. Anxious not to destabilise the Republican leadership, the issue had been sidelined, hoping that the conclusion of a settlement would allow for a 'deal' involving the release of prisoners in return for the decommissioning of illegally held weapons. In the final hours of negotiation, however, the principle of Criminalisation was bargained away without having obtained any concession on decommissioning.

By removing any incentive for the Republican movement to make its commitment to peaceful means absolute, the British government has institutionalised an asymmetry between fully constitutional parties and those with links to paramilitaries. As long as the Republicans are allowed to employ the threat of violence *in addition* to their electoral mandate, they are bound to be more effective at securing concessions for their constituency than the parties who rely on the ballot box alone. As a consequence, the peace process in its current form has furthered extremists at the expense of genuine 'moderates'. In doing so, it continues to represent a source of instability, and prevents London from achieving the aim of reducing its political, physical and financial commitment to the province. Britain's long war, it seems, is not quite over yet.

Appendices

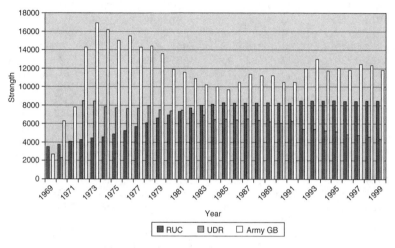

Figure A1 Security forces: manpower, 1969–99

Source: see Table A.1.

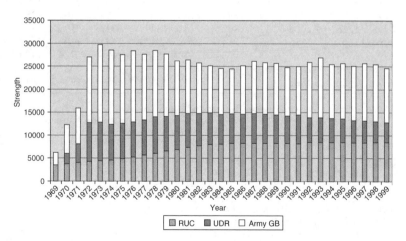

Figure A2 Overall security presence, 1969–99

Source: see Table A.1.

Table A1   Security forces' strength, 1969–99

Year	Army total	GB Reg	UDR total	UDR FT	UDR PT	RUC total	RUC Reg	RUC Res FT	RUC Res PT
1969	2700	2700	—	—	—	3500	3500	—	—
1970	8592	6300	2292	49	2243	3750	3100	50*	600*
1971	11844	7800	4044	226	3818	4083	2564	150*	1369
1972	22766	14300	8476	595	7881	4273	2139	300*	1834
1973	25343	16900	8443	866	7577	4421	1021	400*	3000
1974	24015	16200	7815	864	6951	4563	703	510	3350
1975	22692	15000	7692	1406	6286	4902	83	661	4158
1976	23145	15500	7645	1528	6117	5253	556	870	3827
1977	21951	14300	7651	1707	5944	5692	1006	1002	3684
1978	22370	14400	7970	2314	5656	6110	1505	1188	3417
1979	21118	13600	7518	2495	5023	6614	2100	1305	3209
1980	19276	11900	7376	2610	4766	6935	2183	1685	3067
1981	19070	11600	7470	2723	4747	7334	2464	2060	2810
1982	18011	10900	7111	2793	4318	7717	2878	2173	2666
1983	17125	10200	6925	2690	4235	8003	3510	2295	2198
1984	16468	10000	6468	2689	3779	8127	3687	2533	1907
1985	16194	9700	6494	2755	3739	8259	3751	2755	1753
1986	16908	10500	6408	2672	3736	8234	3821	2753	1660
1987	17931	11400	6531	2785	3746	8236	3590	2987	1659
1988	17593	11200	6393	2858	3535	8231	3577	2993	1661
1989	17430	11200	6230	2947	3283	8259	3635	3018	1606
1990	16543	10500*	6043	2955	3088	8243	3697	2990	1556
1991	16776	10500*	6276	3277	2999	8222	3663	3042	1517
1992	17417	12000	5417	2797	2620	8483	3891	3160	1432
1993	18412	13000	5412	2902	2510	8470	3896	3185	1389
1994	17000	11759	5241	2956	2285	8469	3897	3184	1388
1995	17189	12019	5170	3036	2134	8499	3812	3199	1488
1996	16670	11815	4855	2847	2008	8424	3741	3101	1582
1997	17234	12477	4757	2754	2003	8430	4028	2929	1473
1998	16934	12346	4598	2627	1961	8495	4190	2982	1323
1999	16200	11823	4377	2536	1841	8465	4294	2936	1235

* Numbers are estimates based on publicly available information.
Abbreviations: FT, Full Time; GB Reg, Army regiments based in Great Britain; PT, Part Time; Reg, Regulars; Res, Reserve; RUC, Royal Ulster Constabulary; UDR, Ulster Defence Regiment (including Royal Irish Regiment, Home Service).

Sources
- HC, Vol. 826, *cc*.1513–15w, 25 November 1971
- HC, Vol. 836, *c*.577w, 4 May 1972
- HC, Vol. 836, *cc*.467–8w, 12 May 1972
- HL, Vol. 335, *c*.1404, 22 September 1972
- HC, Vol. 843, *cc*.382–3w, 26 October 1972
- HC, Vol. 846, *c*.187w, 16 November 1972
- HC, Vol. 849, *c*.415w, 31 January 1973
- HC, Vol. 868, *c*.89w, 29 January 1974

- HC, Vol. 945, *c*.1590, 9 March 1978
- HC, Vol. 983, *c*.558w, 30 April1980
- HC, Vol. 9, *c*.304w, 27 July 1981
- HC, Vol. 217, *cc*.661–8w, 26 January 1993
- HC, Vol. 219, *c*.890, 24 February 1993
- HC, Vol. 247, *cc*.343–6w, 20 July 1994
- HC, Vol. 259, *c*.548w, 11 May 1995
- HC, Vol. 300, *c*.323w, 6 November 1997
- HC, Vol. 359, *c*.217w, 15 December 1999
- HL, Vol. 633, *c*.29w, 25 March 2002
- If unavailable from official sources, numbers were obtained from the Conflict Archive on the Internet; http://cain.ulst.ac.uk/ni/ security.htm

Table A2   British government office holders, 1969–99

Year	Prime Minister	Secretary of State	Minister of State	Parl. Under-Secretary
8/69	Harold Wilson	James Callaghan*		
6/70	Edward Heath	Reginald Maudling*		
3/72		William Whitelaw	Lord Windlesham (–6/73), Paul Channon (–11/72)	David Howell (-11/72)
11/72			Howell, William van Straubenzee	Peter Mills
6/73				Lord Belstead
12/73		Francis Pym	Howell, Straubenzee	Belstead, Mills
3/74	Wilson	Merlyn Rees	Stanley Orme	Lord Donaldson
6/74			Roland Moyle	Don Concannon
4/76	Callaghan		Concannon, Moyle	James Dunn, Raymond Carter
9/76		Roy Mason	Concannon, Lord Melchett	Dunn, Carter
11/78				Tom Pendry
5/79	Margaret Thatcher	Humphrey Atkins	Michael Alison, Hugh Rossi (–1/81) Adam Butler	Lord Elton, Philip Goodhart (–1/81), Giles Shaw (–1/81) David Mitchell, John Patten
9/81		James Prior	Butler, Lord Gowrie (–6/83)	Mitchell (–6/83), Patten (–6/83), Nicholas Scott
6/83				
4/84			Lord Mansfield (–4/84)	Chris Patten Lord Lyell
9/84		Douglas Hurd	Rhodes Boysonn	Patten, Scott, Lyell
9/85		Tom King	Boyson (-9/86),	Lyell, Richard Needham, Scott (–9/86)
1/86				Brian Mawhinney

Table A2 (*Contd.*)

Year	Prime Minister	Secretary of State	Minister of State	Parl. Under-Secretary
9/86			Scott (–6/87)	Pete Viggers
6/87			John Stanley (–7/88)	
7/88			Ian Stewart	
7/89		Peter Brooke	John Cope	Peter Bottomley (–7/90), Mawhinney, Needham, Lord Skelmesdale
11/90	John Major		Mawhinney	Lord Belstead, Jeremy Hanley, Needham
4/92		Patrick Mayhew	Robert Atkins (–1/94), Michael Mates (–6/93)	Lord Arran (–1/94)
6/93			John Wheeler	Michael Ancram (–1/94)
1/94			Ancram	Baroness Denton, Tim Smith (–10/94)
10/94				Malcolm Moss
5/97	Tony Blair	Marjorie Mowlam	Adam Ingram, Paul Murphy (–7/99)	Tony Worthington (–7/98), Lord Dubs
7/98				John McFall
7/99				George Howarth
10/99		Peter Mandelson	Ingram	Dubs (–12/99), McFall (–12/99), Howarth

Unless otherwise stated, a minister remained in his post until the following change of Prime Minister and/or Secretary of State.

* The office of Northern Ireland Secretary was introduced in March 1972. Previously, the province had been the responsibility of the Home Secretary.

Notes

1 Introduction

1 W.S. Churchill, *The World Crisis. The Aftermath* (London 1929), p. 319.
2 M.L.R. Smith, 'Peace in Ulster? A Warning from History', *Jane's Intelligence Review*, July 1998, p. 14.
3 See A.P. Schmid, 'The Response Problem as a Definition Problem' in A.P. Schmid and R.D. Crelinsten (eds), *Western Responses to Terrorism* (London 1993), p. 8.
4 T.R. Mockaitis, *British Counterinsurgency, 1919–60* (London 1990), p. 3.
5 C. von Clausewitz, *On War*, M. Howard and P. Paret (trans. and ed.), (Princeton 1984), p. 128.
6 M. Howard, *The Causes of Wars* (London 1983), p. 36.
7 B.H. Liddell Hart, *Strategy: the Indirect Approach* (London 1967), p. 335.
8 T.C. Schelling, *Choice and Consequence* (London 1984), p. 200.
9 M.L.R. Smith, *The Role of the Military Instrument in Irish Republican Thinking. An Evolutionary Analysis*, PhD (University of London, 1991), p. 11.
10 M.L.R. Smith, 'Holding Fire: Strategic Theory and the Missing Military Dimension in the Academic Study of Northern Ireland' in A. O'Day (ed.), *Terrorism's Laboratory: The Case of Northern Ireland* (Aldershot 1995), p. 231.
11 S.M. Lynn-Jones, 'Realism and Security Studies' in C.A. Snyder (ed.), *Contemporary Security and Strategy* (London 1999), p. 54.
12 E.H. Carr, *The Twenty Years Crisis: 1919–39* (London 1946), p. 85.
13 See K. Waltz, 'The Emerging Structure of International Politics', *International Security*, 18: 2 (1993), pp. 44–79.
14 J. Garnett, 'Strategic Studies and Its Assumptions' in J. Baylis *et al.* (eds), *Contemporary Strategy I* (Hertfordshire 1987), p. 12.
15 Clausewitz, p. 69.
16 Ibid., p. 605.
17 Ibid., p. 75.
18 T.C. Schelling, *Arms and Influence* (New Haven 1966), p. 2.
19 Clausewitz, p. 77.
20 Schelling, *Choice and Consequence*, p. 198.
21 F. Lopez-Alves, 'Political Crises, Strategic Choices, and Terrorism: The Rise and Fall of the Uruguayan Tuparmaros', *Terrorism and Political Violence*, 1:2 (1989), p. 204.
22 K. Waltz, 'Anarchic Orders and Balances of Power', in R.O. Keohane (ed.), *Neorealism and Its Critics* (New York 1986), p. 118.
23 J. Garnett, 'Strategic Studies', p. 19.
24 Clausewitz, p. 86.
25 See G.D. Boyce, A. O'Day, 'Introduction. Revisionism and the Revisionist Controversy' in G.D. Boyce, A. O'Day (eds), *The Making of Modern Irish History. Revisionism and the Revisionist Controversy* (London 1996), pp. 1–14.

26   R. Kee, *The Green Flag Volume 1. The Most Distressful Country* (London 1989), p. 9.
27   Ibid., p. 10.
28   P. Adelman, *Great Britain and the Irish Question, 1800–1922* (Abingdon 1996), p. 3.
29   S. McMahon, *A Short History of Ireland* (Dublin 1996), p. 76.
30   R. Douglas, L. Harte, J. O'Hara, *Ireland since 1690* (Belfast 1999), p. 13.
31   S.J. Connolly, 'Eighteenth-Century Ireland. Colony or Ancien Régime?' in Boyce, *The Making*, p. 26.
32   The term 'Protestant Ascendancy' is misleading, as it was in fact only the landowning Anglican minority of the Protestant population that controlled land as well as parliament.; see J.C. Beckett, *Geschichte Irlands* (Stuttgart 1997), p. 133.
33   Connolly, p. 23.
34   Lord Cornwallis, quoted in G.M. Trevelyan, *British History in the Nineteenth Century and After, 1782–1919* (London 1965), p. 113.
35   O. MacDonagh, *Ireland* (Englewood Cliffs 1968), pp. 2–3.
36   L. Kennedy, D.S. Johnson, 'The Union of Ireland and Britain, 1801–1921' in Boyce, *The Making*, p. 64.
37   R.F. Foster, *Modern Ireland, 1600–1972* (London 1989), p. 301.
38   Ibid., pp. 309–11.
39   The latter was not regarded as in any way special to the Irish case: 'The idea that food produced in the country should not be exported was not adopted anywhere [in Europe], and would have been considered an economic irrelevance'; see Foster, p. 325.
40   'Modern Ireland', *Ulster Magazine*, 1:1 (1860), quoted in P. Bew, 'The National Question, Land, and "Revisionism"' in Boyce, *The Making*, p. 93.
41   Foster, p. 320.
42   C. Townshend, 'British Policy in Ireland, 1906–1921' in D.G. Boyce (ed.), *The Revolution in Ireland, 1879–1923* (London 1988), p. 175.
43   G. Costigan, *A History of Modern Ireland* (New York 1969), p. 205.
44   D.G. Boyce, *The Irish Question and British Politics, 1868–1996* (London 1996), p. 7.
45   See J. Smith, *Britain and Ireland: From Home Rule to Independence* (Harlow 2000), pp. 35–43.
46   Ibid., p. 47.
47   N. Mansergh, *The Irish Question, 1840–1921* (London 1965), p. 288.
48   Asquith, quoted in Townshend, 'British Policy', p. 181.
49   D. Reed, *Ireland: The Key to the British Revolution* (London 1984), p. 56.
50   Townshend, 'British Policy', p. 187.
51   I. Budge, C. O'Leary, *Belfast: Approach to Crisis – A Study of Belfast Politics, 1613–1970* (London 1973); see also W.D. Birrell, 'The Stormont–Westminster Relationship', *Parliamentary Affairs*, 26:4 (1973), pp. 471–4.
52   Boyce, *The Irish Question*, p. 96.
53   See J.H. Whyte, 'How much discrimination was there under the Unionist regime?' in T. Gallagher, J. O'Connell (eds), *Contemporary Irish Studies* (Manchester 1983), pp. 1–35.
54   See P. Rose, 'Labour, Northern Ireland and the Decision to Send in the Troops' in P. Catterall, S. McDougall (eds), *The Northern Ireland Question in British Politics* (London 1996), pp. 88–101.

55   J.J. Lee, *Ireland: Politics and Society 1912–1985* (Cambridge 1989), pp. 411–29.
56   P. Bew, P. Gibbon, H. Patterson, *Northern Ireland, 1921–1996: Political Forces and Social Classes* (London 1996), p. 159.
57   See P. Rose, *How the Troubles Came to Northern Ireland* (London 2000), pp. 11–30.
58   R. Crossman, *The Diaries of a Cabinet Minister, Volume Three* (London 1977), p. 381.
59   M. Cunningham, *British Government Policy in Northern Ireland, 1969–89* (Manchester 1991), p. 19.
60   J. Callaghan, *A House Divided: The Dilemma of Northern Ireland* (London 1973), p. 15.

2   The Strategic Tradition of the British Government in Northern Ireland

1   M. Burke, *Divide and Rule. Britain's Strategy in Ireland* (Dublin 1993), pp. 13–14.
2   Reed, *Ireland*, p. 384.
3   See R. Faligot, *Britain's Military Strategy in Ireland. The Kitson Experiment* (London 1983).
4   See J. McGarry, B. O'Leary, *Explaining Northern Ireland* (Oxford 1995), pp. 80–1.
5   T.O. Lloyd, *The British Empire, 1558–1995* (Oxford 1996), p. 339.
6   N. Owen, 'Decolonisation and Postwar Consensus' in H. Jones, M. Kandiah (eds), *The Myth of Consensus. New Views on British History, 1945–64* (London 1996), p. 169.
7   Hugh Rossi, letter to author, 5 July 2001.
8   See, for example, E. Powell, 'Dirty tricks that link Dublin and Westland', *The Guardian*, 20 January 1986.
9   S. Orme, 'The View From Dublin', *New Statesman*, 28 July 1972, p. 113. Apparently, this view was shared by Prime Minister Edward Heath; see 'Excerpts from Interview with Prime Minister Heath', *New York Times*, 27 February 1972.
10   See P. Gillespie, 'From Anglo-Irish to British–Irish relations' in M. Cox, A. Guelke, F. Stephen (eds), *A Farewell to Arms? From 'Long War' to Long Peace in Northern Ireland* (Manchester 2000), pp. 189–92.
11   See J. Prior, *A Balance of Power* (London 1986), p. 220.
12   Public Record Office (PRO), CAB, 128/47/1, 23 June 1970.
13   'A switch in line saves time', *The Economist*, 18 June 1977.
14   Roland Moyle, interview with author, 7 March 2001.
15   Thatcher, quoted in F. Mount, 'Experiences of an Irish PM', *The Spectator*, 14 November 1981.
16   Wilson, quoted in D. Anderson, *14 May Days. The Inside Story of the Loyalist Strike of 1974* (Dublin 1994), p. 135.
17   M. Thatcher, *The Downing Street Years* (London 1993), p. 385.
18   Gowrie, quoted in P. Bew, G. Gillespie, *Northern Ireland. A Chronology of the Troubles, 1968–1993* (Dublin 1993), p. 163.
19   R. Maudling, *Memoirs* (London 1978), p. 180.
20   Thatcher, p. 385.

21   Rees, quoted in T. Benn, *Against the Tide. Diaries, 1973–6* (London 1989), p. 457.
22   H. Wilson, *Final Term. The Labour Government, 1974–1976* (London 1979), p. 67.
23   Lord Carrington, Heath's Defence Secretary; P.A.R. Carrington, *Reflect on Things Past* (London 1988), p. 247.
24   See Gillepsie, 'From Anglo-Irish', pp. 189–90.
25   Wilson, *Final Term*, p. 67.
26   Callaghan, quoted in G. Fitzgerald, *All in a Life* (London 1991), p. 271.
27   HC, Vol. 230, *c*.490, 22 October 1993.
28   Concannon, quoted in P. O'Malley, *The Uncivil Wars* (Belfast 1983), p. 219.
29   J. Ruane, J. Todd, *The Dynamics of Conflict in Northern Ireland* (Cambridge 1996), p. 227.
30   HC, Vol. 979, *c*.1616, 29 November 1979.
31   Lord Gowrie, interview with author, 13 December 2001.
32   The author's operationalisation of the term 'level of force' follows the British government's own definition of the security effort in Northern Ireland; see 'Liaison Sub-Committee on Confidence Building Measures: Security Issues – Paper by HMG', *Multi-Party Talks*, 23 March 1998.
33   Mockaitis, *British Counterinsurgency*, p. 27.
34   Callaghan, quoted in C. Warman, T. Jones, 'Callaghan warning to Ulster agitators', *The Times*, 9 October 1969.
35   HC, Vol. 63, *c*.27, 2 July 1984.
36   PRO, CAB 128/49/16, 22 March 1971.
37   Wilson, quoted in T. Benn, *Office Without Power: Diaries 1968–72* (London 1988), p. 197.
38   An MoD briefing paper stated that '[f]or the most part, terrorist activity has tended to be concentrated in nationalist areas. This has inevitably meant that the operations of all the security forces … have had a greater impact on the normal life of the minority community'; quoted in C. Ryder, *The Ulster Defence Regiment – an Instrument of Peace?* (London 1991), p. 212.
39   J. Major, *John Major. The Autobiography* (London 1999), p. 492.
40   Wilson, *The Labour Government*, p. 872.
41   PRO, CAB 128/49/9, 9 February 1971.
42   For a collection of opinion polls, see McGarry, *Explaining*, pp. 115–19.
43   R. Rose, I. McAllister, P. Mair, *Is There a Concurring Majority about Northern Ireland?* (Glasgow 1978), p. 25.
44   G. Brock, 'For Prior's heir, an even harder task', *The Times*, 23 August 1984.
45   'This great city …', *Daily Mirror*, 26 April 1993.
46   Northern Ireland Secretary Francis Pym; HC, Vol. 866, *c*.670, 13 December 1973.
47   Maudling, quoted in J. Chartres, 'Home Secretary says IRA may never be totally eliminated', *The Times*, 16 December 1971.
48   Lord Cope, interview with author, 5 March 2002.
49   See, for example, P. Johnson, 'Ending fear of the IRA', The Spectator, 2 April 1988.
50   HC, Vol. 181, c.24, 19 November 1990.
51   D. Kavanagh, Political Culture (London 1972), p. 10.
52   P. Norton, The British Polity (London 1984), p. 49.

53   D. Dutton, British Politics Since 1945. The Rise and Fall of Consensus (Oxford 1991), pp. 6–7.
54   Lord Balfour (Arthur Balfour), quoted in D. Kavanagh, P. Morris, Consensus Politics. From Attlee to Major (Oxford 1989), p. 16.
55   'One Nation', The Spectator, 9 December 2000.
56   Thatcher, quoted in 'Thatcher speech in Ulster', The Times, 29 May 1981.
57   E. Heath, The Course of My Life (London 1998), p. 420.
58   HC, Vol. 799, c.321, 7 April 1970.
59   Maudling; HC, Vol. 827, c.41, 29 November 1971.
60   Lord Prior (James Prior), interview with author, 27 November 2001.
61   Peter Mandelson, who became Northern Ireland Secretary in 1999, believed that 'we have to make [the distinction] between those terrorists who have political objectives and are prepared to negotiate those objectives ... I don't call them terrorists when they reach that stage. They are resisters. They are freedom-fighters ... And it's what stage of development they're at, what attitude they have to politics, whether they're prepared to engage'; Mandelson, quoted in 'The Year the World Changed', Channel 4, 29 December 2001.
62   See P. Neumann, 'Freedom-fighters, not quitters', Fortnight, February 2002.
63   Heath, p. 438.
64   Wilson, quoted in R. Fisk, 'New security steps discussed', The Times, 19 April 1974.
65   Mayhew; HC, Vol. 230, c.587, 25 October 1993.
66   A. Aughey, Under Siege. Ulster Unionism and the Anglo-Irish Agreement (London 1989), pp. 39–40.
67   Northern Ireland Secretary Douglas Hurd; HC, Vol. 81, cc.970–1, 26 June 1985.
68   Orme; HC, Vol. 874, c.1182, 4 June 1974.
69   P. Rose, Northern Ireland. A Time of Choice (London 1976), pp. 107–10, 167–72.
70   See McGarry, Explaining, p. 134.
71   A. Lijphart, Democracy in Plural Societies. A Comparative Exploration (New Haven 1977), pp. 134–41.
72   D. Gladstone, The Twentieth-Century Welfare State (London 1999), pp. 40–2.
73   Beveridge, quoted in Kavanagh, Consensus, p. 36.
74   B. Coxall, L. Robins, British Politics since the War (London 1998), p. 53.
75   Kavanagh, Consensus, p. 80.
76   S. Pollard, The Development of the British Economy, 3rd edition (London 1983), p. 271.
77   A. Sked, Britain's Decline. Problems and Perspectives (Oxford 1987), p. 76.
78   PRO, CAB 128/44/42, 4 September 1969.
79   HC, Vol. 230, c.483, 22 October 1993.
80   Lord Prior, interview with author, 27 November 2001.
81   Peter Viggers, interview with author, 28 November 2001.
82   See M. Melaugh, 'Majority–Minority Differentials: Unemployment, Housing and Health' in S. Dunn (ed.), Facets of the Conflict in Northern Ireland (London 1995), pp. 131–48.
83   See D. Smith and G. Chambers, Inequality in Northern Ireland (Oxford 1991); P.A. Compton, 'Employment Differentials in Northern Ireland and Job Discrimination: A Critique' in P.J. Roche, B. Barton, The Northern Ireland Question: Myth and Reality (Aldershot 1991), pp. 40–76.

84 See D. Smith, G. Chambers, *Equality and Inequality in Northern Ireland: Perceptions and Views* (London 1987).
85 HC, Vol. 788, *c*.59, 13 October 1969.
86 HC, Vol. 841, *c*.1329, 24 July 1972.
87 See, for example, P. Teague, 'Multinational Companies in the Northern Ireland Economy: An Outmoded Model of Industrial Development?' in P. Teague (ed.), *Beyond the Rhetoric. Politics, the Economy and Social Policy in Northern Ireland* (London 1987), pp. 160–82.
88 See J. Edwards, *Affirmative Action in a Sectarian Society: Fair Employment Policy in Northern Ireland* (Aldershot 1995), pp. 18–26.
89 Compton, p. 71.
90 M. Rees, *Northern Ireland. A Personal Perspective* (London 1985), p. 221.
91 O'Malley, *The Uncivil*, p. 254.

3   Avoiding Responsibility? London on the Defensive, 1969–72

1   See Callaghan, *A House*, p. 105.
2   PRO, CAB 128/44/41, 19 August 1969.
3   Ibid.
4   Callaghan, *A House*, p. 117.
5   Healey, quoted in Crossmann, p. 478.
6   Wilson, *The Labour Government*, p. 876.
7   'Dublin's voice – and some dangers', *The Times*, 15 August 1969.
8   Benn, *Office Without Power*, p. 196.
9   Crossmann, p. 622.
10 Benn, *Office Without Power*, p. 198.
11 'Text of a Communiqué and Declaration issued after a meeting held at 10 Downing Street on 19 August 1969', Cmd. 4154 (London 1969), p. 3.
12 Ibid.
13 See H. Roberts, *Northern Ireland and the Algerian Analogy* (Belfast 1986), p. 11.
14 'Ulster finds her Husak', *The Spectator*, 23 August 1969.
15 K.O. Morgan, *Callaghan. A Life* (Oxford 1997), p. 349.
16 B. Faulkner, *Memoirs of a Statesman* (London 1978), p. 92.
17 Lord Callaghan of Cardiff (James Callaghan), letter to author, 26 July 2000.
18 'Ulster direct rule hint by Maudling', *The Times*, 11 August 1970.
19 PRO, CAB 128/49/40, 22 July 1971.
20 Ibid.
21 PRO, CAB 129/158/24, 30 September 1971.
22 Heath, p. 430.
23 PRO, CAB 129/49/47, 21 September 1971.
24 Ibid.
25 Heath, pp. 430, 432.
26 PRO, CAB 128/49/9, 9 February 1971.
27 See J. Peck, *Dublin from Downing Street* (London 1978), pp. 124–39.
28 PRO, CAB 128/49/44, 16 August 1971.
29 Lynch, quoted in Peck, p. 135.
30 Heath, p. 432.

31 Heath, quoted in HC, Vol. 826, *c*.1586, 17 November 1971.
32 HC, Vol. 827, *c*.38, 29 November 1971.
33 Ibid., *cc*.40–1.
34 PRO, CAB 129/162/1, 3 March 1972.
35 Ibid.
36 Ibid.
37 Ibid.
38 PRO, CAB 128/48/3, 7 March 1972.
39 PRO, CAB 128/48/3, 9 March 1972.
40 PRO, CAB 128/48/3, 23 March 1972.
41 Wilson, *The Labour Government*, p. 872.
42 PRO, CAB, 128/44/41, 19 August 1969.
43 PRO, CAB, 128/44/42, 4 September 1969.
44 Wilson, *The Labour Government*, p. 877.
45 'Peter', quoted in J. Lindsay (ed.), *Brits Speak Out. British Soldiers' Impressions of the Northern Ireland Conflict* (Londonderry 1998), p. 25.
46 Young, quoted in 'Military police take over in Bogside', *The Times*, 13 October 1969.
47 Callaghan, *A House*, p. 131.
48 HC, Vol. 795, c.125w, 4 February 1970.
49 R. Mansbach (ed.), *Northern Ireland. Half a Century of Partition* (New York 1973), p. 75.
50 M.L.R. Smith, *Fighting for Ireland? The Military Strategy of the Irish Republican Movement* (London 1995), pp. 91–2.
51 T.C. Schelling, *The Strategy of Conflict* (Cambridge 1980), p. 90.
52 Ruairi O'Bradaigh, quoted in C.C. O'Brien, *States of Ireland* (London 1972), p. 229.
53 D. Wilsworth, 'A "tangible and obvious" threat', *The Times*, 5 August 1970.
54 HC, Vol. 799, *c*.321, 7 April 1970.
55 Ibid.
56 'Army "now facing terrorist threat"', *Irish News*, 3 Novermber 1970.
57 PRO, DEFE 4/253/2, 5 January 1971.
58 PRO, CAB 128/49/9, 9 February 1971.
59 PRO, CAB, 128/47/2, 29 June 1970.
60 M. O'Doherty, *The Trouble with Guns: Republican Strategy and the Provisional IRA* (Belfast 1998), pp. 69–70.
61 Maudling, quoted in 'Holding the Cat's Cradle', *The Times*, 2 March 1971.
62 HC, Vol. 815, *c*.368, 6 April 1971.
63 Maudling, quoted in 'Progress in Ulster top Maudling priority', *The Times*, 3 April 1971.
64 'More than a name', *The Economist*, 6 December 1969.
65 HC, Vol. 807, *c*.601, 26 November 1971.
66 HC, Vol. 815, *cc*.263–4, 6 April 1971.
67 Maudling, quoted in 'Search and arrest in Ulster', *The Times*, 20 January 1971.
68 See 'Instructions by the Director of Operations for Opening Fire', *The Times*, 1 February 1972.
69 'Army statement', 1 November 1971, quoted in R. Deutsch, V. Magowan, *Northern Ireland 1968–72. A Chronology of Events. Vol. 1, 1968–71* (Belfast 1973), p. 80.

70   Sunday Times Insight Team, *Ulster* (London 1972), pp. 236–45.
71   Carrington, quoted in P. Evans, 'Westminster adamant over role of troops', *The Times*, 20 March 1971.
72   PRO, CAB 128/49/40, 22 July 1971.
73   Maudling, quoted in HC, Vol. 815, *c*.268, 6 April 1971.
74   PRO, CAB 128/49/40, 22 July 1971.
75   Sunday Times, pp. 263–8.
76   PRO, CAB 128/49/44, 16 August 1971.
77   HC, Vol. 832, *cc*.378–9, 6 March 1972.
78   See HC, Vol. 828, *c*.313, 16 December 1971.
79   See 'Report of the enquiry into allegations against the security forces of physical brutality in Northern Ireland arising out of events on the 9th August, 1971', Cmnd. 4832 (London 1971).
80   See PRO, CAB 130/522, 10 August 1971.
81   HC, Vol. 826, *c*.235, 16 November 1971.
82   HC, Vol. 822, *c*. 160w, 29 July 1971.
83   P. Taylor, *Brits: The War Against the IRA* (London 2001), p. 226.
84   Tuzo, quoted in J. Kelly, *The Genesis of Revolution* (Dublin 1976), p. 16.
85   Maudling, quoted in J. Chartres, 'Home Secretary says IRA may never be totally eliminated', *The Times*, 16 December 1971.
86   Ibid.
87   See Benn, *Office Without Power*, pp. 196–8.
88   PRO, CAB, 128/44/41, 19 August 1969.
89   Crossman, p. 622.
90   Callaghan, *A House*, p. 71.
91   Callaghan; HC, Vol. 788, *c*.49, 13 October 1969.
92   Crossmann, p. 864.
93   Callaghan, *A House*, p. 54.
94   Benn, *Office Without Power*, p. 198.
95   See S. Elliott, W.D. Flackes, *Northern Ireland. A Political Directory, 1968–1999* (Belfast 1999), p. 198.
96   See 'Disturbances in Northern Ireland: report of the commission appointed by the Governor of Northern Ireland' (Cameron Report), Cmd. 532 (Belfast 1969).
97   'Text of a Communiqué and Declaration', pp. 3–4.
98   See 'Report of the Advisory Committee on Police in Northern Ireland' (Hunt Report), Cmd. 535 (Belfast 1969).
99   See 'Text of a Communiqué issued on 29 August 1969 at the conclusion of the visit of the Secretary of State for the Home Department to Northern Ireland', Cmd. 4158 (London 1969); 'Text of a Communiqué issued following discussions between the Secretary of State for the Home Department and the Northern Ireland Government in Belfast on 9th and 10th October 1969', Cmd. 4178 (London 1969).
100 P. Walsh, *From Civil Rights to National War* (Belfast 1989), pp. 51–2.
101 HC, Vol. 788, *c*.64, 13 October 1969.
102 C. Warman, T. Jones, 'Callaghan warning to Ulster agitators', *The Times*, 9 October 1969.
103 PRO, CAB, 128/45/21, 7 May 1970.
104 HC, Vol. 798, *c*.298, 7 April 1970.

105 Callaghan, quoted in Crossmann, p. 636.
106 C. Warman, T. Jones, 'Callaghan warning to Ulster agitators', *The Times*, 9 October 1969.
107 HC, Vol. 811, *cc*.1319–21, 15 February 1971.
108 Ibid.
109 See SDLP statement, 16 July 1971, quoted in H. Kelly, *How Stormont Fell* (Dublin 1972), pp. 52–5.
110 Ibid., p. 54.
111 Even before the introduction of internment, the GOC, Lieutenant General Tuzo, had acknowledged that 'half the Catholic population sympathises with the IRA, and up to a quarter – that is, about 120,000 people – is ready to give the organisation active support'; see Tuzo, quoted in 'A fateful decision', *The Economist*, 7 August 1971.
112 HC, Vol. 823, *cc*.14–15, 22 September 1971.
113 PRO, CAB 128/49/44, 16 August 1971.
114 PRO, CAB 128/49/45, 2 September 1971.
115 PRO, CAB 128/49/46, 9 September 1971.
116 Ibid.
117 Sir Kenneth Bloomfield, interview with author, 10 August 2000.
118 Faulkner, pp. 127–31.
119 PRO, CAB 129/162/1, 7 March 1972.
120 PRO, CAB 128/48/3, 7 March 1972.
121 Crossman, p. 187.
122 See Wilson, *The Labour Government*, p. 845; Callaghan, *A House*, p. 10.
123 HC, Vol. 788, *c*.59, 13 October 1969.
124 'A faint sense of community', *The Economist*, 29 May 1971.
125 PRO, CAB, 128/44/42, 4 September 1969.
126 Callaghan, *A House*, p. 137.
127 HC, Vol. 788, *c*.59, 13 October 1969.
128 See 'Northern Ireland Development Plan', Cmd. 547 (Belfast 1970).
129 See J.P. Mackintosh, 'The Report of the Review Body on Local Government in Northern Ireland 1970: The Macrory Report', *Public Administration*, 49:1 (1971), pp. 13–24.
130 HC, Vol. 823, *c*.12, 22 September 1971.
131 PRO, CAB 129/162/1, 2 March 1972.
132 L. O'Dowd, 'Regional Policy' in L. O'Dowd, B. Rolston, M. Tomlinson (eds), *Northern Ireland: Between Civil Rights and Civil War* (London 1980), p. 41.
133 PRO, CAB 128/48/3, 14 March 1972.
134 R. Fanning, 'Britain's greatest initiative', *The Spectator*, 1 April 1972.

4   No Quick Fix: Execution and Failure of British Strategy, 1972–75

1 'The responsibility comes home', *The Times*, 25 March 1972.
2 PRO, CAB 129/162/24, 12 May 1972.
3 Whitelaw; HC, Vol. 838, *c*.1072, 12 June 1972.
4 Heath; HC, Vol. 853, *c*.1321, 28 March 1973.
5 Lord Howell, interview with author, 6 March 2001.

6   Indeed, the 'Border Poll' had been Maudling's idea; see PRO, CAB 129/162/1, 3 March 1972.
7   Northern Ireland Office, *The Future of Northern Ireland. A Paper for Discussion* (London 1972), p. 33.
8   Lord Howell, interview with author, 6 March 2001.
9   See M. Holland, 'Second Thoughts on Sunningdale', *New Statesman*, 14 December 1973.
10   HC, Vol. 866, *c*.38, 13 December 1973.
11   Ibid.
12   Faulkner, pp. 229, 237.
13   See Heath; HC, Vol. 866, *c*.32, 13 December 1973.
14   W. Whitelaw, *The Whitelaw Memoirs* (London 1987), p. 122.
15   Heath, quoted in 'Ulster: No integration', *The Spectator*, 29 September 1973.
16   'The Future of Northern Ireland – A Survey of Public Opinion', *The Listener*, 9 May 1974, pp. 590–4.
17   Hume, quoted in 'Political integration with UK possible "only if all else fails" ', *The Times*, 19 September 1973.
18   'So who does rule?', *The Economist*, 1 June 1974.
19   See, for example, Benn, *Against*, pp. 137–8.
20   Rees, pp. 99–100, 206, 210.
21   HC, Vol. 903, *c*.51, 12 January 1976; see J. Langdon, 'Labour "thought of Ulster pull-out" ', *The Guardian*, 19 July 1983; P. Webster, 'Disclosure by Rees angers Dublin', *The Times*, 20 July 1983.
22   C. Walker, 'UDI talk disloyal', *The Times*, 3 June 1975.
23   Lord Merlyn-Rees, interview with author, 6 March 2001.
24   Rees, p. 93.
25   HC, Vol. 882, *c*.1956, 5 December 1974.
26   HC, Vol. 888, *c*.786, 15 March 1975.
27   P. Devlin, *Straight Left. An Autobiography* (Belfast 1993), pp. 256–7.
28   FitzGerald, p. 244.
29   Arlow, quoted in C. Walker, 'Storm over forecast of Ulster withdrawal', *The Times*, 26 May 1975.
30   Orme; HC, Vol. 896, *cc*.2483–4, 1 August 1975.
31   Rees, p. 210.
32   Ibid., p. 277.
33   Ibid., p. 277.
34   Lord Windlesham, 'Ulster beyond the breaking point', *The Guardian*, 5 December 1972.
35   M. Dewar, *The British Army in Northern Ireland* (London 1996), p. 64.
36   Whitelaw, p. 92.
37   R. Deutsch, V. Magowan, *Northern Ireland 1972–73. A Chronology of Events. Vol. 2, 1972–73* (Belfast 1974), p. 263.
38   V. Hanna, 'Internment: What are the facts?', *The Listener*, 19 December 1974.
39   Whitelaw, quoted in Faulkner, pp. 212, 223.
40   PRO, CAB 128/48/3, 13 April 1972.
41   HC, Vol. 838, *c*.1077, 12 June 1972.
42   Despite the limitations of the procedure, it is notable that the Commissioners decided in favour of the internee in more than one in three cases; see V. Hanna, 'Internment: What are the facts?', *The Listener*, 19 December 1974, pp. 790–1.

43 The court system was named after Lord Diplock who chaired the commission which recommended its introduction; see 'Report of the Commission to consider legal procedures to deal with terrorist activities in Northern Ireland' (Diplock Report), Cmd. 5185 (London 1972).

44 PRO, CAB 128/49/48, 29 September 1971.

45 Lord Howell, interview with author, 6 April 2001.

46 Whitelaw, quoted in J. Chartres, 'Whitelaw sees "modest success" in peace moves', *The Times*, 13 May 1972.

47 PRO, CAB 128/48/3, 13 July 1972.

48 PRO, CAB 128/48/3, 27 July 1972.

49 Ibid.

50 Ibid.

51 Simon Winchester, '4,000 More Troops Move in for Ulster Offensive', *The Guardian*, 28 July 1972.

52 PRO, CAB 128/48/3, 27 July 1972.

53 C. De Baróid, *Ballymurphy and the Irish War*, 2nd edition(London 2000), p. 137.

54 Smith, *Fighting for Ireland?*, p. 110.

55 For a concise exploration of Motorman's political impact, see R. Fanning, 'After the military', *The Spectator*, 5 August 1972.

56 Anderson, *14 May Days*, p. 43.

57 Wilson, *Final Term*, p. 78.

58 Lord Merlyn-Rees, interview with author, 6 March 2001.

59 Lord Orme (Stanley Orme), interview with author, 6 March 2001.

60 Wilson had warned the House of Commons about the so-called 'Scorched Earth' plan which the security forces had discovered in an IRA hideout; see HC, Vol. 873, cc.891–2, 13 May 1974.

61 The decision to take over some petrol stations on 27 May was a token gesture which was meant to protect Westminster from accusations of inaction; see Rees, p. 82.

62 See R. Fisk, *The Point of No Return* (London 1975), p. 154.

63 Sir Edward Heath, letter to author, 22 February 2001.

64 Rees, quoted in P. Taylor, *Provos. The IRA and Sinn Fein* (London1997), p. 165.

65 See Rees; HC, Vol. 892, c.644, 15 May 1975.

66 Similar conclusions were reached by the so-called Gardiner Committee which was set up in 1974; see 'Report of a Committee to consider, in the context of civil liberties and human rights, measures to deal with terrorism in Northern Ireland' (Gardiner Report), Cmd. 5847 (London 1975).

67 HC, Vol. 876, c.1281, 9 July 1974.

68 HC, Vol. 854, c.590, 5 April 1973.

69 Rees, quoted in 'How all can help – Rees', *Belfast Telegraph*, 4 September 1974.

70 Moyle, interview with author.

71 Ibid.

72 See, for example, McGarry, *Explaining*, p. 86; for an exploration of this issue, see P.R. Neumann, 'The Myth of Ulsterisation in British Security Policy in Northern Ireland', *Studies in Conflict & Terrorism*, 26:5 (2003), pp. 365–74.

73 Rees, p. 180.

74 See, for example, the case of IRA leader Seamus Twomey; C. Walker, 'Mr Rees accused of misleading Commons over IRA leader', *The Times*, 30 August 1975.

75   HC, Vol. 894, *c*.649, 26 June 1975.
76   D. Howell, 'The policies which prepared the ground for trust in Ulster', *The Times*, 10 February 1975.
77   Lord Windlesham, 'Ulster beyond the breaking point', *The Guardian*, 5 December 1972.
78   PRO, CAB 129/163/9, 13 June 1972.
79   PRO, CAB 128/48/3, 3 March 1972.
80   PRO, CAB 128/48/3, 13 April 1972.
81   See M. McGuire, *To Take Arms. A Year in the Provisional IRA* (London 1973).
82   M. Holland, 'Miss McGuire and Mr Whitelaw', *New Statesman*, 8 September 1972, p. 307.
83   PRO, CAB 128/48/3, 22 June 1972.
84   Whitelaw, p. 101.
85   Whitelaw, quoted in PRO, CAB 128/48/3, 15 June 1972.
86   Heath, quoted in 'Heath supports Sinn Fein talks', *The Guardian*, 19 July 1993.
87   See Smith, *Fighting for Ireland?*, p. 106.
88   P. Bew, H. Patterson, *The British State and the Ulster Crisis* (London 1986), p. 51.
89   'Worried about Willie', *The Economist*, 15 July 1972.
90   Whitelaw, quoted in R. Fanning, 'After the military', *The Spectator*, 5 August 1972.
91   See Maudling's reasons for withdrawing Stormont's law and order powers: PRO, CAB 129/162/1, 2 March 1972.
92   'Northern Ireland Constitutional Proposals' (White Paper), Cmd. 5259 (London 1973), pp. 15–16.
93   H. Patterson, 'Trimble disarmed', *The Guardian*, 27 October 2001.
94   For Heath's ideas on police reform, see 'Mr Heath warns Ulster leaders', *The Times*, 30 August 1973.
95   See 'Ulster: the troops go in, and Jack lends a helping hand', *The Economist*, 5 August 1972.
96   'The Facts: A Reasonable Deal For Ulster', NIO leaflet, March 1973.
97   H. Patterson, 'British Governments and the "Protestant Backlash", 1969–74', in Y. Alexander, A. O'Day (eds), *Ireland's Terrorist Dilemma* (Dordrecht 1986), pp. 243–5.
98   For an exploration of the different hypotheses, see P. Dixon, *Northern Ireland. The Politics of War and Peace* (Houndsmills 2001), pp. 154–6; B. O'Duffy, 'The Price of Containment: Deaths and Debate on Northern Ireland in the House of Commons 1968–94' in Catterall, *The Northern*, pp. 109–10.
99   Lord Merlyn-Rees, interview with author, 6 March 2001.
100 Rees, p. 110.
101 Ibid, p. 174.
102 'The Northern Ireland Constitution', Cmd. 5675 (London 1974), p. 19.
103 Ibid.
104 HC, Vol. 874, *c*.1182, 4 June 1974.
105 FitzGerald, p. 247.
106 Meeting on 5 March 1975; see Taylor, p. 187.

107 Brendan O'Brien, *The Long War: the IRA and Sinn Fein* (Dublin: O'Brien Press, 1993), p. 112.
108 Rees, quoted in FitzGerald, p. 278.
109 Lord Howell, interview with author, 6 March 2001.
110 B. Rowthorn, N. Wayne, *The Political Economy of Northern Ireland* (Cambridge 1988), pp. 85–7.
111 HC, Vol. 874, *c*.1047, 4 June 1974.
112 Heath, quoted in R. Fisk, 'Threat to stop £200 m aid if UK tie is cut', *The Times*, 17 November 1972.
113 See Northern Ireland Office, *Northern Ireland. Finance and the economy* (London 1974).
114 Lord Merlyn-Rees, interview with author, 6 March 2001.
115 Wilson, *Final Term*, p. 77.
116 Orme; HC, Vol. 894, *c*.2475, 1 August 1975; for the pre-1974 figures, see HC, Vol. 930, *c*.57, 19 April 1977.
117 NIO minister Paul Channon; HC, Vol. 836, *c*.178, 4 May 1972.
118 Orme; HC, Vol. 894, *c*.2481, 1 August 1975.
119 Rowthorn, p. 84.
120 Faulkner, pp. 206, 214.
121 FitzGerald, p. 201.
122 Lord Howell, interview with author, 6 March 2001.
123 FitzGerald, p. 203.
124 Whitelaw, quoted in Faulkner, p. 212.
125 See 'Report and Recommendations of the Working Party on Discrimination in the Private Sector of Employment' (Van Straubenzee Report), (Belfast 1973).
126 Orme, quoted in Rees, p. 288.
127 HC, Vol. 848, *c*.601, 14 December 1972.
128 HC, Vol. 853, *c*.1441, 29 March 1973.

5 Going it Alone? Direct Rule under Pressure, 1976–82

1 F. Emery, 'Taking a new turn in the Irish maze', *The Times*, 13 December 1980.
2 Boyce, *The Irish Question*, p. 123.
3 R. Mason, *Paying the Price* (London 1999), p. 218.
4 Ibid., p. 161.
5 Mason, quoted in 'Mr Mason cites benefits of direct rule in province', *The Times*, 14 September 1977.
6 FitzGerald, p. 247.
7 Irish Prime Minister Charles Haughey, quoted in M. Holland, 'A man who will not be patronised', *New Statesman*, 14 December 1979.
8 'Lynch lunges out', *The Economist*, 14 January 1978.
9 F. Emery, 'Taking a new turn in the Irish maze', *The Times*, 13 December 1980.
10 PRO, CAB 128/48/3, 13 April 1972.
11 J. Callaghan, *Time and Chance* (London 1987), p. 499.
12 Thatcher, p. 385.

13   See C. Walker, 'Dublin contempt for British allegations', *The Times*, 10 March 1978.
14   Raymond Carter, interview with author, 30 July 2001.
15   Thatcher, p. 385.
16   According to Haughey, it was 'better to try to unite Irish-American opinion behind the policy of the Irish government than to excommunicate those who sympathised in varying degrees with armed struggle in the North'; Haughey, quoted in M. Mansergh, 'The background to the Irish peace process' in Cox, *A Farewell*, p. 15.
17   See 'Candid friends', *The Economist*, 24 March 1979.
18   'A leaking kettle may not boil', *The Economist*, 27 August 1977.
19   A. Guelke, *Northern Ireland: the International Perspective* (Dublin 1988), p. 137.
20   'US "is neutral on Ulster"', *Daily Telegraph*, 6 September 1979.
21   FitzGerald, p. 372.
22   See J. Dumbrell, ' "Hope and history": the US and peace in Northern Ireland' in Cox, *A Farewell*, p. 215.
23   A.J. Wilson, *Irish America and the Ulster Conflict, 1968–95* (Belfast 1995), pp. 162–4.
24   Lord Orme, interview with author, 21 August 2001.
25   Atkins; HC, Vol. 972, *c*.618, 25 October 1979.
26   Thatcher, p. 384.
27   HC, Vol. 935, *c*.1829, 21 July 1977.
28   Mason, quoted in C. Walker, 'Mr Mason rules out devolution in Ulster', *The Times*, 14 September 1977.
29   HC, Vol. 939, *c*.1726, 24 November 1977; for the full text of the letter, see HC, Vol. 941, *cc*.1839–40, 12 January 1978.
30   Callaghan, *Time*, p. 499.
31   HC, Vol. 967, *c*.1205, 24 May 1979.
32   Thatcher, p. 58.
33   Ibid., p. 57.
34   J. Wightman, 'What Mr Lynch says and what Mr Lynch does', *Daily Telegraph*, 4 September 1979.
35   See, for example, G. Clark, 'Reassurance on talks with Mr Haughey', *The Times*, 6 March 1981.
36   Haughey, quoted in J. Joyce, P. Murtagh, *The Boss: Charles J. Haughey in Government* (Dublin 1983), p. 150.
37   D. Hamill, *Pig in the Middle. The Army in Northern Ireland, 1969–84* (London 1985), p. 199.
38   HC, Vol. 926, *c*.1502, 23 February 1977.
39   Ibid., *cc*.1506–7.
40   HC, Vol. 922, *c*.1938, 17 December 1976.
41   Mason, p. 224.
42   Ibid., pp. 171–2.
43   See Home Office, 'Statistics on the Operation of the Prevention of Terrorism Legislation' in *Home Office Statistical Bulletin*, 4 February 1988; Northern Ireland Office, 'Annual Statistics on the Operation of the Northern Ireland (Emergency Provisions) Act 1996' in *Northern Ireland Research & Statistical Bulletin*, 1999 (Table 7a).

44   Rees, quoted in M. Urban, *Big Boys' Rules. The SAS and the Secret Struggle against the IRA* (London 1992), p. 9.
45   See, for instance, the case of Sean McKenna who claims that he was abducted from his home in the Republic of Ireland; J. Adams, A. Bambridge, R. Morgan, *Ambush. The War between the SAS and the IRA* (London 1998), p. 77.
46   HC, Vol. 918, *c*.686, 28 October 1976.
47   Mason, quoted in Hamill, p. 220.
48   'No happy new year', *The Economist*, 1 January 1977.
49   See, for example, the RUC advertisement 'In 3 months', *Belfast Telegraph*, 4 April 1977.
50   L. Curtis, *Ireland. The Propaganda War* (London 1984), pp. 188–9.
51   J. Holland, 'RUC calling the shots', *Hibernia*, 18 March 1977.
52   Smith, *Fighting for Ireland?*, pp. 152–61.
53   The report is reproduced in Faligot, pp. 223–42.
54   Bew, *The British*, p. 57.
55   HC, Vol. 892, *c*.634, 15 May 1975.
56   K. Boyle and T. Hadden, *Northern Ireland: A Positive Proposal* (London 1985), p. 70.
57   R.J. Weitzer, *Policing under Fire* (New York 1995), pp. 75–9.
58   See P. Taylor, *Beating the Terrorists? Interrogation in Omagh, Gough and Castlereagh* (Harmondsworth 1980); Amnesty International, *Report of an Amnesty International Mission to Northern Ireland* (London 1978).
59   Thatcher, quoted in 'Mrs Thatcher pledges no sellout on Ulster', *The Times*, 6 March 1981.
60   Thatcher, quoted in J. Dana, 'The 1981 Hungerstrike', http://larkspirit.com/hungerstrikes/1981.html
61   Tom McElwee, quoted ibid.
62   See HC, Vol. 882, *c*.635, 28 November 1974.
63   M. von Tangen Page, *Peace Prisoners and Terrorism* (London 1998), pp. 63–4.
64   Rees, quoted in Benn, *Against*, p. 526.
65   Rees, quoted in R. Fox, 'Ulster: exit Mr. Softly Softly', *The Listener*, 16 September 1976.
66   'Roy Mason on the economic prospects in Northern Ireland', *The Listener*, 24 February 1977.
67   C. Walker, 'Action man Mr Roy Mason has made his mark in Ulster', *The Times*, 27 January 1977.
68   Rees, p. 290.
69   Enoch Powell, who became an Ulster Unionist MP in 1974, was the most prominent advocate of full integration; see E. Powell, 'The test of Britain's will to be a nation', in The Guardian (ed.), *Ulster '80. Year of Decision?* (London 1980), p. 2.
70   Callaghan, *Time*, p. 455.
71   Contrary to his successors, who described the Unionist demand as 'unreasonable', Maudling – when contemplating the introduction of Direct Rule in 1972 – believed that Northern Ireland was 'entitled to a substantially increased representation at Westminster and this I think it would be only fair to accord to them'; see PRO, CAB 129/162/1, 2 March 1972.
72   M. Holland, 'Jim Callaghan's other allies', *New Statesman*, 14 October 1977.

73 Rees, quoted in P. Dixon, ' "The usual English doubletalk": the British political parties and the Ulster Unionists, 1974–94', *Irish Political Studies*, 9:1 (1994), p. 29.
74 For a comprehensive account of the 1977 Loyalist strike, see Bew, *Northern Ireland. A Chronology*, pp. 118–21.
75 Ibid., p. 28.
76 HC, Vol. 941, *c*.1840, 12 January 1978.
77 HC, Vol. 953, *c*.1713, 13 July 1978.
78 HC, Vol. 952, *c*.1830, 30 June 1978.
79 'Blue and Orange?', *The Economist*, 24 June 1978, p. 19.
80 Sir Philipp Goodhart, interview with author, 10 July 2001.
81 'Towards a New Ireland – Policy Review' (SDLP policy document).
82 'The Government of Northern Ireland – a Working Paper for a Conference', Cmd. 7763 (London 1979), p. 3. For a comprehensive account of the origins of 'rolling devolution', see C. O'Leary, S. Elliott, R.A. Wilford, *The Northern Ireland Assembly* (London 1988), pp. 67–80.
83 HC, Vol. 941, *c*.1836, 12 January 1978.
84 'The Government', Cmd. 7763, pp. 9–11.
85 See 'Northern Ireland: A Framework for Devolution', Cmd. 8541 (London 1982).
86 HC, Vol. 46, *c*.555, 21 July 1983.
87 'Back to go', *The Economist*, 21 January 1978.
88 See B. Hadfield, 'Northern Ireland affairs at Westminster' in P. Roche, B. Barton (eds), *The Northern Ireland Question: Myth and Reality* (Aldershot 1991), pp. 143–6.
89 Prior, p. 192.
90 Lord Prior (James Prior), interview with author, 27 November 2001.
91 See P. Bishop, E. Mallie, *The Provisional IRA* (London 1987), p. 362.
92 Sir Philip Goodhart, interview with author, 21 July 2001.
93 Corrigan, quoted in O'Malley, *The Uncivil*, p. 268.
94 Bew, *The British*, p. 92.
95 B. O'Leary, J. McGarry, *The Politics of Antagonism. Understanding Northern Ireland*, 2nd edition, (London 1996), p. 218.
96 Raymond Carter, interview with author, 30 July 2001.
97 Rowthorn, pp. 82–3.
98 HC, Vol. 918, *c*.679, 28 October 1976.
99 Report by Review Team, *Economic and Industrial Strategy for Northern Ireland* (Belfast 1976), pp. 66–7.
100 Ibid.
101 See B. Rolston, M. Tomlinson, *Unemployment in West Belfast. The Obair Report* (Belfast 1988), p. 82.
102 I. Fallon, J. Srodes, *DeLorean. The Rise and Fall of a Dream-Maker* (London 1983), p. 127.
103 Mason, p. 221.
104 See NIO minister Adam Butler; HC, Vol. 2, *c*.1104, April 1981.
105 Prior, p. 209.
106 Report, *Economic and*, p. 67.
107 C. Walker, 'It still pays to be Protestant', *The Times*, 12 January 1978.
108 Report, *Economic and*, p. 66.

109 V. McCormack, *Enduring Inequality: Religious Discrimination in Employment in Northern Ireland* (London 1990), p. 33.
110 HC, Vol. 957, *c*.1177, 9 November 1978.
111 HC, Vol. 978, *c*.721, 7 February 1980.
112 Rowthorn, p. 87.
113 HC, Vol. 10, *c*.979, 29 October 1981.
114 Prior, p. 210.
115 'Investment incentives', *The Times*, 30 April 1980.
116 HC, Vol. 1, *cc*.332–4, 18 March 1981.
117 Rowthorn, p. 86.
118 F. Gaffikin, M. Morissey, *Northern Ireland. The Thatcher Years* (London 1990), p. 84.
119 Mason, quoted in C. Walker, 'Mr Mason rules out devolution in Ulster', *The Times*, 14 September 1977.

6   Sharing the Burden: the Refinement of British Strategy, 1982–88

1   D. McKittrick, 'Unionists see only sinister cloud with no silver linings', *The Listener*, 21 November 1985.
2   Thatcher, p. 398.
3   Sir Robert Andrew, interview with author, 21 November 2001.
4   Sir Christopher Mallaby, interview with author, 15 November 2001.
5   FitzGerald, quoted in J. Havilland, 'Thatcher welcomes Dublin offer to tackle terrorism', *The Times*, 24 December 1983.
6   FitzGerald, p. 502.
7   Sir Christopher Mallaby, interview with author, 15 November 2001.
8   Ibid.
9   Thatchter, quoted in P. Webster, 'Irish summit again soon after "realistic" talks', *The Times*, 20 November 1984.
10 Lord Hurd (Douglas Hurd), interview with author, 4 December 2001.
11 Thatcher, p. 401.
12 Lord Hurd, interview with author, 4 December 2001.
13 For a comprehensive review of the different interpretations, see O'Leary, *The Politics*, pp. 220–41.
14 See 'Agreement between United Kingdom and Republic of Ireland on matters relating to Northern Ireland (Hillsborough, 15 November 1985)', Cmnd. 9690 (London 1985).
15 HC, Vol. 87, *cc*.19–20, 18 November 1985.
16 For the full text of the Final Act, see http://www.house.gov/csce/finalact.htm
17 To avoid conflict with the territorial claim in the Irish Constitution, the Irish government's copy of the AIA referred to the UK simply as 'United Kingdom' rather than 'United Kingdom of Great Britain and Northern Ireland'.
18 Lord Hurd, interview with author, 4 December 2001.
19 E. Haslett, *The Anglo-Irish Agreement. Northern Ireland Perspectives* (Belfast n.d.), p. 15.

20   Hume, quoted in P. O'Malley, *Northern Ireland. Questions of Nuance* (Belfast 1990), p. 59.
21   Lord Howe, interview with author, 27 November 2001.
22   HC, Vol. 985, *c.*250, 20 May 1980.
23   HC, Vol. 81, *c.*972, 26 June 1985.
24   See Molyneaux, quoted in 'Endgame in Ireland? Part 1', *BBC2*, 25 June 2001.
25   Lord Prior, interview with author, 27 November 2001.
26   Lord Hurd, interview with author, 4 December 2001.
27   Thatcher, p. 384.
28   See, for example, her speech at the 1988 Conservative party conference in Brighton, where she claimed that 'this Government will never surrender to the IRA'; quoted in R. Harris, *The Collected Speeches of Margaret Thatcher* (London 1997), pp. 342–3.
29   Thatcher, p. 408.
30   Ibid.
31   Ibid., p. 412.
32   T. Gifford, *Supergrasses. The Use of Accomplice Evidence in Northern Ireland* (London 1984), p. 11.
33   Hurd; HC, Vol. 70, *c.*583, 20 December 1984.
34   E. Moloney, 'Will Supergrass sow a bitter harvest?', *The Times*, 13 September 1983.
35   See M. Holland, 'Using tainted evidence', *New Statesman*, 23 September 1983.
36   M. Cunningham, *British Government Policy in Northern Ireland, 1969–2000* (Manchester 2001), p. 58.
37   HC, Vol. 50, *c.*518, 8 December 1983.
38   Lord Prior, interview with author, 27 November 2001.
39   Lord Gowrie, interview with author, 13 December 2001.
40   Lord Hurd, interview with author, 4 December 2001.
41   Sir Richard Needham, interview with author, 14 November 2001.
42   Prior; HC, Vol. 50, *c.*519, 8 December 1983.
43   Prior, quoted in Urban, p. 166.
44   Ibid., pp. 164–5.
45   For example, the killing of eight IRA members who were about to attack an RUC station in Loughgall, Co. Armagh, in May 1987; the shooting dead of three IRA operatives on a mission in Gibraltar in March 1988; the killing of three IRA near Drumnakilly, Co. Tyrone, in August 1988.
46   Sir John Wheeler, interview with author, 18 February 2002.
47   See Smith, *Fighting for Ireland?*, p. 215.
48   Thatcher, p. 398.
49   HC, Vol. 87, *c.*749, 26 November 1985.
50   For an evaluation of Anglo-Irish security co-operation, see 'After Enniskillen', *The Economist*, 14 November 1987.
51   FitzGerald, quoted in 'Courting trouble', *The Economist*, 3 October 1987, p. 33; for London's justification of the Diplock court system, see HC, Vol. 107, *cc.*1082–3, 16 December 1986; for a summary of the extradition issue, see T. Hadden, K. Boyle, *The Anglo-Irish Agreement. Commentary, Text and Official Review* (London 1989), pp. 59–64.
52   King, quoted in R. Ford, 'King says Garda needs help to tackle terrorism', *The Times*, 4 September 1986.

53 King; HC, Vol. 119, *c*.198, 7 July 1987.
54 Sir Robert Andrew, interview with author, 21 November 2001.
55 See FitzGerald, p. 516.
56 Ibid., p. 552.
57 See Neumann, 'The Myth'.
58 Ryder, *The Ulster*, pp. 213–15.
59 See Ruane, *The dynamics*, pp. 132–5.
60 Thatcher; HC, Vol. 86, *c*.681, 14 November 1985.
61 Lord Hurd, interview with author, 4 December 2001.
62 Sir Richard Needham, interview with author, 14 November 2001.
63 See, for example, T.E. Utley, 'The torments of a bad treaty', *The Times*, 1 March 1988.
64 Thatcher, p. 413.
65 Lord Howe, interview with author, 27 November 2001.
66 O'Duffy, 'The Price', pp. 120–1.
67 P. Brooke, 'Ango-Irish Agreement gives Catholics equality of esteem', *New Statesman*, 10 October 1986, p. 8.
68 FitzGerald, p. 529.
69 Ibid., p. 520.
70 See D. Goodall, 'Actually it's all working out almost exactly to plan', *Parliamentary Brief*, 5:6 (1998), p. 54.
71 Sir Robert Andrew, interview with author, 21 November 2001.
72 Lord Prior, interview with author, 27 November 2001.
73 Lord Hurd, interview with author, 4 December 2001.
74 Sir Christopher Mallaby, interview with author, 15 November 2001.
75 Prior, p. 243.
76 Hurd's diaries, quoted in M. Stuart, *Douglas Hurd. The Public Servant* (London 1998), p. 138.
77 ' "Parroting" critics are attacked by King', *The Times*, 18 November 1985.
78 Lord Lyell, interview with author, 8 November 2001.
79 King; HC, Vol. 93, *c*.156, 4 March 1986.
80 O'Leary and McGarry are correct in asserting that Thatcher's comment was misleading as, within the terms of the agreement, devolved government could reduce the scope of the IGC, but not replace it completely; see O'Leary, *The Politics*, p. 234.
81 A. Bevins, 'Breakthrough on Ulster deadlock', *The Times*, 26 February 1986.
82 Lord Hurd, interview with author, 4 December 2001.
83 See 'Whose oxygen', *The Economist*, 22 October 1988, p. 41.
84 HC, Vol. 46, *c*.551, 21 July 1983.
85 HC, Vol. 34, *c*.1059, 23 December 1982.
86 Lord Gowrie, interview with author, 13 December 2001.
87 Scott; HC, Vol. 81, *c*.1025, 26 June 1985.
88 M. Holland, 'Closing ranks for a united Ireland', *The Times*, 16 March 1983.
89 See Adams, quoted in R. Ford, 'Us versus the rest, Sinn Fein says', *The Times*, 27 May 1983.
90 Adams, quoted in Mallie, *The Fight*, p. 59.
91 Sinn Fein, *Hillsborough – The Balance Sheet, 1985–88* (Dublin 1989), p. 12.
92 Sir Robert Andrew, interview with author, 19 November 2001; Sir Alan Goodison, interview with author, 21 November 2001.

93   Lord King (Tom King), interview with author, 27 November 2001.
94   HC, Vol. 87, *c*.824, 26 November 1985.
95   'Dependence or bust', *The Economist*, 2 June 1984.
96   R. Needham, *Battling for Peace* (Belfast 1998), p. 136.
97   Ibid., p. 196.
98   Sinn Fein, *Hillsborough*, p. 10.
99   DeBaroid, pp. 286–7.
100 Viggers; HC, Vol. 136, *c*.698, 1 July 1988.
101 Needham, pp. 202–3, 204.
102 For the 1986 (revised) version of the MacBride Principles, see McCormack, pp. 42–3.
103 NIO spokesman, quoted in M. Farrell, 'Does Ulster need "reverse discrimination" on jobs?', *The Listener*, 24 September 1987.
104 'The Colour Green', *The Economist*, 3 May 1986.
105 J. Cooney, 'Jobs: can King win over America?', *The Times*, 19 September 1987.
106 See NIO, *Developments*, p. 3.
107 Lord King, interview with author, 27 November 2001; Peter Viggers, interview with author, 28 November 2001.
108 HC, Vol. 136, *c*.636, 1 July 1988.
109 Viggers; HC, Vol. 636, *c*.697, 1 July 1988.
110 See McCormack, pp. 66–7.
111 Ibid., *c*.639.

7   The war is over? Success and failure of British strategy, 1989–98

1   Seamus Mallon, quoted in J. Tonge, *Northern Ireland. Conflict and Change*, 2nd edition (Harlow 2000), p. 185; for some differences between 1974 and 1998, see P.R. Neumann, 'Why 1974 was different', *Belfast Telegraph*, 23 April 2001.
2   Accordingly, Mayhew rejected a motion at the 1994 Conservative Party conference which called for the British government to assume the role of 'persuader for the Union', stating that 'we are persuaders for the future of Northern Ireland to be decided by the people of Northern Ireland without external impediment'; see P. Wintour, 'Union persuader role is rejected', *The Guardian*, 14 October 1994.
3   HC, Vol. 253, *c*.1098, 1 February 1995.
4   Tony Worthington, interview with author, 19 March 2002.
5   Lord Brooke (Peter Brooke), interview with author, 14 March 2002.
6   HC, Vol. 172, *cc*.1143–4, 5 July 1990.
7   Lord Brooke, interview with author, 14 March 2002.
8   Brooke; HC, Vol. 172, *c*.1141, 5 July 1990.
9   Bew, *Northern Ireland: A Chronology*, pp. 276–8.
10 Lord Mayhew (Patrick Mayhew), interview with author, 7 March 2002.
11 The various drafts as well as the document that was presented to the British government in June 1993 are reproduced in Mallie, *The Fight*, pp. 411–20.
12 Major, p. 447.

13 'Prime Minister: Joint Declaration issued by Prime Minister Rt Hon John Major MP and Taoiseach Albert Reynolds TD', Cmnd. 2442 (London 1994).

14 HC, Vol. 248, *c*.1026, 27 October 1994.

15 'A New Framework of Agreement' is the second of the so-called Frameworks documents, contained in 'Frameworks for the Future', Cmnd. 2964 (London 1995), pp. 15–24.

16 This is presumably the reason why *Sinn Fein* welcomed it; see ' "Peace deal first, then weapons" ', *The Independent*, 27 February 1995.

17 Dixon, *Northern Ireland*, p. 252.

18 'British minister', quoted in 'Unionists out on a limb', *The Guardian*, 23 February 1995.

19 Michael Ancram, interview with author, 1 May 2002.

20 'Strand 2 Discussions', *Multi-Party Talks*, January 1998.

21 For a reproduction of the document, see Cox, *A Farewell*, pp. 344–5.

22 G. Mitchell, *Making Peace* (London 1999), p. 134.

23 T. Hennessy, *The Northern Ireland Peace Process: Ending the Troubles?* (London 2000), p. 163.

24 Paul Murphy, interview with author, 20 March 2002.

25 'The Belfast Agreement: agreement reached in multi-party negotiations', Cmnd. 3883 (London 1998), pp. 11–16, 25, 29.

26 D. McKittrick, C. Brown, 'Brooke hints at talks with Sinn Fein', *The Independent*, 4 November 1989.

27 ' "IRA defeated" says security minister', *The Independent*, 26 August 1993.

28 See Brooke; HC, Vol. 170, *c*.132, 12 March 1990.

29 Sir John Wheeler, interview with author, 18 February 2002.

30 Brooke, quoted in Hennessy, p. 68.

31 Major, quoted in O. Boycott, M. White, 'Major says troops strengths are not negotiable', *The Guardian*, 22 November 1993.

32 See Smith, *Fighting for Ireland?*, pp. 6–9.

33 See, for example, P. Whelan, 'Nationalist unity against Britain's military agenda', *An Phoblacht/Republican News*, 4 December 1997.

34 Adam Ingram, interview with author, 4 March 2002.

35 Sir John Wheeler, interview with author, 18 February 2002.

36 This is what *Sinn Fein*'s own records show; see Sinn Fein, *Setting the Record Straight* (Dublin 1994), p. 30.

37 Sir John Wheeler, interview with author, 18 February 2002; HC, Vol. 202, *c*.21, 20 January 1992.

38 Sir John Wheeler, interview with author, 18 February 2002.

39 'Security Service could have finished the IRA', *BBC News*, 26 August 1997; http://www.bbc.co.uk/politics97/news/08/0826/secret.shtml

40 Major, p. 433.

41 HC, Vol. 227, *c*.469, 24 June 1993; O. Boycott, 'RUC may call supergrass scheme back', *The Guardian*, 9 September 1993.

42 See D. Sharrock, 'RUC chief confident IRA on road to peace', *The Guardian*, 25 May 1995.

43 HC, Vol. 248, *c*.1021, 27 October 1994.

44 Major, p. 459.

45 D. Sharrock, 'Army reduced RUC support', *The Guardian*, 18 October 1994.

46   See, for example, J. Hibbs, T. Harnden, R. Savill, 'Bomb fury isolates Sinn Fein', *Daily Telegraph*, 17 June 1996.

47   M. Mowlam, *Momentum* (London 2002), p. 157.

48   Adam Ingram, interview with author, 4 March 2002.

49   Dixon, *Northern Ireland*, p. 263.

50   Annesley outlined his assessment of the situation on 14 July 1996 in an interview on BBC Radio 4. It is reproduced in C. Ryder, V. Kearney, *Drumcree. The Organge Order's Last Stand* (London 2001), pp. 172–4.

51   For a description of the precise circumstances, see Mowlam, pp. 90–7.

52   Adam Ingram, interview with author, 4 March 2002.

53   HC, Vol. 172, *c*.1927, 15 May 1990.

54   In addition to several IRA informers within the Irish Garda, the case of Eamon Collins (who was a member of the IRA whilst working for Her Majesty's Customs and Excise) shows that, even for Republicans, it was possible to abuse official positions within the British civil service; see E. Collins with M. McGovern, *Killing Rage* (London 1997).

55   Lord Cope (Sir John Cope), interview with author, 5 March 2002.

56   O. Boycott, 'Emergency call-up for UDR troops', *The Guardian*, 20 July 1991.

57   Peter Bottomley, interview with author, 14 February 2002.

58   See 'Foundations for Policing', Cmnd. 3249 (London 1996).

59   For a summary of the reforms, see G. Jones, D. Sharrock, 'RUC is stripped of royal title', *Daily Telegraph*, 20 January 2000.

60   HC, Vol. 310, *cc*.493–5, 20 April 1998.

61   See, for example, Mowlam, pp. 227–8.

62   HC, Vol. 209, *c*.414, 10 June 1992.

63   HC, Vol. 233, *c*.794, 29 November 1993.

64   Sir Quentin Thomas, interview with author, 20 February 2002.

65   Michael Mates, interview with author, 21 March 2002.

66   Mowlam, pp. 220–1, 227.

67   Sir Quentin Thomas, interview with author, 20 February 2001.

68   Major, pp. 441–2.

69   Sir Quentin Thomas, interview with author, 20 February 2002.

70   This is the argument advanced by E. Mallie and D. McKittrick; see, for example, Mallie, *The Fight*, pp. 92–112.

71   Ruane, p. 321.

72   D. McKittrick, C. Brown, 'Brooke hints at talks with Sinn Fein', *The Independent*, 4 November 1989.

73   Brooke, quoted in Hennessy, p. 69.

74   Mayhew, quoted in ibid., p. 72.

75   See, for example, R. MacGinty, J. Darby, *Guns and Government: the Management of the Northern Ireland Peace Process* (Houndmills 2001), pp. 26–7.

76   Lord King, interview with author, 27 November 2001.

77   Lord Brooke, interview with author, 14 March 2002.

78   Brooke, quoted in Mallie, *The Fight*, p. 244.

79   HC, Vol. 233, *c*.785, 29 November 1993.

80   A possible explanation is that the Derry-City priest, who had acted as a go-between, failed to make clear that the written summary of his conversation with the Republican leadership did not reflect the participants' actual choice of words; confidential interview with Belfast journalist, 9 August 2000.

81 This is what Mayhew told the Labour MP Clive Soley in 1994; Soley's diaries are quoted in J. Langdon, *Mo Mowlam* (London 2000), p. 273.

82 London's version of events, starting with the message in February 1993, can be found in HC, Vol. 233, *cc*.785–7, 29 November 1993. The Republicans' account was published by *Sinn Fein*, see Sinn Fein, *Setting the Record Straight* (Dublin 1994).

83 E. Delaney, *An Accidental Diplomat: My Years in the Irish Foreign Service, 1987–1995* (Dublin 2001), pp. 320–2.

84 See Mansergh, 'The background', pp. 16–17.

85 Reynolds, quoted in Mallie, *The Fight*, p. 158.

86 Reynolds, quoted in S. Duignan, *One Spin on the Merry-Go-Round* (Dublin 1995), p. 119.

87 Dixon, *Northern Ireland*, pp. 218–19.

88 Lord Mayhew, interview with author, 7 March 2002.

89 Lord Butler (Sir Robin Butler), interview with author, 6 March 2002.

90 Delaney, p. 344.

91 G. McMichael, *An Ulster Voice. In Search of Common Ground in Northern Ireland* (Boulder 1999), p. 49.

92 For a description of the events which preceded the announcement of the declaration, see Mallie, *The Fight*, pp. 185–220, 258–72.

93 'Downing Street Declaration – a dead duck', *Ulster Unionist Information Institute*, March 1994, pp. 4–5.

94 Adams, quoted in Hennessy, p. 84.

95 See Major, pp. 462–3.

96 Reynolds, quoted in Duignan, p. 144.

97 Mallie, *The Fight*, p. 228.

98 See M. White, 'London shifts ground on terms of Anglo-Irish deal', *The Guardian*, 17 May 1994.

99 Mowlam, p. 32.

100 See D. Sharrock, 'PM "broke word on Ulster talks"', *The Guardian*, 21 June 1995.

101 P. Bew, G. Gillespie, *The Northern Ireland Peace Process, 1993–1996: A Chronology* (London 1996), p. 35.

102 For the full text of the statement, see O. Boycott, 'Sinn Fein told no further playing for time', *The Guardian*, 20 May 1994.

103 Adams, quoted in Bew, *The Northern Ireland*, p. 41.

104 See K.E. Schulze, M.L.R. Smith, *Dilemmas of Decommissioning* (London 1999), pp. 17–35.

105 Butler states Dublin and London were 'at one in this respect at the time of the [JDP]'; see Lord Butler, interview with author, 6 March 2002.

106 See HC, Vol. 287, *cc*.22–6, 9 December 1996.

107 Major, p. 445.

108 Sir Quentin Thomas, interview with author, 20 February 2002.

109 See 'A joyful time, for some', *The Economist*, 10 September 1994, p. 25.

110 HC, Vol. 267, *c*.1201, 29 November 1995.

111 P. Wintour, 'Major makes surrender of Semtex "crucial" test of IRA ceasefire in run-up to talks with Sinn Fein', *The Guardian*, 19 October 1994.

112 M. Walker, D. Sharrock, 'IRA arms surrender need only be "token"', *The Guardian*, 8 March 1995.

113   D. Sharrock, P. Wintour, 'Arms climbdown clears way for Sinn Fein talks', *The Guardian*, 25 April 1995.
114   Michael Ancram, interview with author, 1 May 2002.
115   Mayhew, quoted in D. Sharrock, 'Mayhew tempers gun surrender call', *The Guardian*, 18 October 1995.
116   Mitchell, *Making Peace*, p. 34.
117   Ibid., p. 40.
118   HC, Vol. 272, *c*.900, 28 February 1996.
119   See, for example, O'Leary, *The Politics*, p. 330.
120   The US ambassador in London provides a brief account of the events surrounding the decision to grant the visa; see R. Seitz, *Over Here* (London 1998), pp. 288–92.
121   S. Bates, 'Clinton boosts Major's standing', *The Guardian*, 5 April 1995.
122   Lord Mayhew, interview with author, 7 March 2002.
123   Dumbrell, 'Hope and history', p. 218.
124   Marjorie Mowlam, letter to author, 6 March 2002.
125   'Speech by the Prime Minister at the Royal Ulster Agricultural Show Belfast', speech by Prime Minister Tony Blair, 16 May 1997; http://www2.nio.gov.uk/speeches.htm
126   See Hennessy, p. 110.
127   Mowlam, p. 164.
128   Lord Dubs (Alf Dubs), interview with author, 7 March 2002.
129   See, for example, Bew, *Northern Ireland: A Chronology*, p. 243.
130   Sir Richard Needham, interview with author, 14 November 2001.
131   HC, Vol. 248, *c*.1101, 27 October 1994.
132   Ibid.
133   HC, Vol. 291, *c*.412, 27 February 1997.
134   Ingram, quoted in G. Gudgin, 'A tougher life ahead for the economy', *Parliamentary Brief*, 5:6 (1998), p. 44.
135   Ibid.
136   'Northern Ireland: Towards a Prosperous Future', speech by Chancellor Gordon Brown, 12 May 1998; http://www2.nio. gov.uk/speeches.htm
137   Mowlam, p. 6.
138   HC, Vol. 205, *c*.498, 5 March 1992.
139   HC, Vol. 209, *cc*.1056–7, 18 June 1992.
140   Tony Worthington, interview with author, 19 March 2002.
141   Mayhew; HC, Vol. 227, *c*.472, 24 June 1993.
142   'Liaison Sub-Committee on Confidence Building Measures: Economic and social development: further paper by the British government', *Multi-party talks*, 13 January 1998.
143   See, for example, O. Boycott, 'Sectarian job gap closing in Ulster', *The Guardian*, 26 June 1993.
144   T. Harnden, 'Ulster Catholics getting more jobs', *Daily Telegraph*, 28 June 1997.
145   HC, Vol. 230, *c*.486, 22 October 1993.
146   HC, Vol. 216, *c*.1177, 24 January 1993.
147   Sir Quentin Thomas, interview with author, 20 February 2002.

8 Conclusion

1 McGarry, *Explaining*, p. 85.
2 Butler; HC, Vol. 1, *c*.335, 18 March 1981.
3 See, for example, H. Cox, 'From Hillsborough to Downing Street – and After' in Catterall, *The Northern Ireland*, p. 196; Dixon, *The Northern Ireland*, pp. 218–19.
4 Paul Murphy, interview with author, 20 March 2002.
5 Cunningham, *British Government Policy, 1969–2000*, p. 154.
6 Major, quoted in M. White, O. Boycott, 'Major bars Unionist peace vote', *The Guardian*, 16 November 1993.

Select Bibliography

Structured interviews

Michael Ancram MP, 1993–94 Parliamentary Under Secretary of State, 1994–97 Minister of State, NIO, London, 29 April 2002.

Sir Robert Andrew, 1984–88 Permanent Under Secretary of State, NIO, London, 21 November 2001.

Sir Kenneth Bloomfield, 1969–72 Deputy Secretary Northern Ireland Cabinet; 1984–91 Head of Northern Ireland Civil Service, Holywood (Co. Down), 10 August 2000.

Peter Bottomley MP, 1989–90 Parliamentary Under Secretary of State, NIO, London, 18 February 2002.

Lord Brooke of Sutton Maudeville (Peter Brooke), 1989–92 Secretary of State, NIO, London, 14 March 2002.

Lord Butler of Brockwell (Sir Robin Butler), 1988–98 Cabinet Secretary, Oxford, 6 March 2002.

Raymond Carter, 1976–79 Parliamentary Under Secretary of State, NIO, London, 30 July 2001.

Lord Cope of Berkeley (Sir John Cope), 1989–90 Minister of State, NIO, London, 5 March 2002.

Lord Dubs (Alf Dubs), 1997–99 Minister of State, NIO, London, 7 March 2002.

Sir Philip Goodhart, 1979–81 Parliamentary Under Secretary of State, NIO, London, 10 July 2001.

Sir Alan Goodison, 1983–86 British Ambassador in Dublin, London, 19 November 2001.

Lord Gowrie, 1981–83 Minister of State, NIO, London, 13 December 2001.

Lord Howe of Aberavon (Geoffrey Howe), 1983–89 Foreign Secretary, London, 27 November 2001.

Lord Howell of Guildford (David Howell), 1972–73 Minister of State, NIO, London, 6 March 2001.

Lord Hurd (Douglas Hurd), 1984–85 Secretary of State, NIO, London, 4 December 2001.

Adam Ingram MP, 1997–2001 Minister of State, NIO, London, 4 March 2002.

Lord King (Tom King), 1985–89 Secretary of State, NIO, London, 21 November 2001.

Lord Lyell, 1984–89 Parliamentary Under Secretary of State, NIO, London, 2 November 2001.

Sir Christopher Mallaby, 1985–88 Deputy Permanent Secretary, Cabinet Office, London, 15 November 2001.

Michael Mates MP, 1992–93 Minister of State, NIO, London, 19 March 2002.

Lord Mayhew (Sir Patrick Mayhew), 1992–97 Secretary of State, NIO, London, 7 March 2002.

Roland Moyle, 1974–76 Minister of State, NIO, London, 7 March 2001.

Paul Murphy MP, 1997–99 Minister of State, NIO, London, 20 March 2002.

Sir Richard Needham, 1985–92 Parliamentary Under Secretary of State, NIO, London, 14 November 2001.
Lord Orme (Stanley Orme), 1974–76 Minister of State, NIO, London, 6 March 2001, 21 August 2001.
Lord Prior (James Prior), 1981–84 Secretary of State, NIO, London, 27 November 2001.
Lord Merlyn-Rees (Merlyn Rees), 1974–76 Secretary of State, NIO, London, 6 March 2001.
Sir Quentin Thomas, 1991–98 Deputy Permanent Secretary and Political Director, NIO, London, 20 February 2002.
Peter Viggers MP, 1986–89 Parliamentary Under Secretary of State, NIO, London, 28 November 2001.
Sir John Wheeler, 1993–97 Minister of State, NIO, London, 18 February 2002.
Tony Worthington MP, 1997–98 Parliamentary Under Secretary of State, NIO, London, 19 March 2002.

Correspondence with author

Lord Callaghan of Cardiff (James Callaghan), 1967–70 Home Secretary, 1974–76 Foreign Secretary, 1976–79 Prime Minister, 26 July 2000.
Sir Edward Heath, 1970–74 Prime Minister, 22 February 2001.
Marjorie Mowlam, 1997–99 Secretary of State, NIO, 6 March 2002.
Sir Hugh Rossi, 1979–81 Minister of State, NIO, 5 July 2001.

Unpublished documents

Multi-party talks minutes, 1997–98 (various).
Cabinet minutes, 1969–72 (128–29 series).
MoD papers, 1969–72 (various).

Parliamentary resources

Hansard, House of Commons Debates, 1969–99.
Hansard, House of Lords Debates, 1969–99.

Published documents (HMSO)

'Agreement between United Kingdom and Republic of Ireland on matters relating to Northern Ireland (Hillsborough, 15 November 1985)', Cmnd. 9690 (London 1985).
'Anglo-Irish Intergovernmental Council: Communique of the Anglo-Irish Summit on 7 November 1983 and related documents', Cmnd. 9094 (London 1983).
'Anglo-Irish Joint Studies. Joint Report', Cmnd. 8414 (London 1981).
'Disturbances in Northern Ireland' (Cameron Report), Cmd. 532 (Belfast 1969).
'Fair Employment in Northern Ireland', Cmnd. 380 (London 1988).
'Formation of the Ulster Defence Regiment', Cmd. 4188 (London 1969).

'Foundations for Policing', Cmnd. 3249 (London 1996).

'Frameworks for the Future', Cmnd. 2964 (London 1995).

'Northern Ireland Constitutional Proposals' (White Paper), Cmd. 5259 (London 1973).

'Northern Ireland Development Programme, 1970–75', Cmd. 547 (Belfast 1970).

Northern Ireland Office, *Northern Ireland Discussion Paper 3 – Government of Northern Ireland* (London 1975).

Northern Ireland Office, *Northern Ireland Discussion Paper – Finance and the Economy* (London 1974).

Northern Ireland Office, *The Future of Northern Ireland. A Paper for Discussion* (London 1972).

'Northern Ireland: A Framework for Devolution', Cmd. 8541 (London 1982).

'Northern Ireland: Ground Rules for Substantive All-Party Negotiations', Cmnd. 3232 (London 1996).

'Prime Minister: Joint Declaration issued by Prime Minister Rt Hon John Major MP and Taoiseach Albert Reynolds TD', Cmnd. 2442 (London 1994).

'Report and Recommendations of the Working Party on Discrimination in the Private Sector of Employment' (Van Straubenzee Report), (Belfast 1973).

Report by Review Team, *Economic and Industrial Strategy for Northern Ireland* (Belfast 1976).

'Report of a Committee to consider, in the context of civil liberties and human rights, measures to deal with terrorism in Northern Ireland' (Gardiner Report), Cmd. 5847 (London 1975).

'Report of the Advisory Committee on Police in Northern Ireland' (Hunt Report), Cmd. 535 (Belfast 1969).

'Report of the Commission to consider legal procedures to deal with terrorist activities in Northern Ireland' (Diplock Report), Cmd. 5185 (London 1972).

'Report of the Committee of Privy Counsellors appointed to consider authorised procedures for the interrogation of persons suspected of terrorism' (Parker Report), Cmd. 4901 (London 1971).

'Report of the Inquiry into Allegations against the Security Forces of Physical Brutality in Northern Ireland, arising out of events on the 9th August, 1971' (Compton Report), Cmd. 4832 (London 1971).

'Report of the Law Enforcement Commission', Cmd. 5627, London 1974 'Report of the Review Body on Local Government in Northern Ireland' (Macrory Report), Cmd. 546 (Belfast 1970).

'Review of the Northern Ireland (Emergency Provisions) Act 1991', Cmnd. 2706 (London 1995).

'Review of the Northern Ireland (Emergency Provisions) Acts 1978 and 1987. By Viscount Colville of Culross', Cmnd. 1115 (London 1990).

'Text of a Communique and Declaration issued after a meeting held at Downing St. on 19/8/69' (Downing Street Declaration 1969), Cmd. 4154 (London 1969).

'Text of a Communique issued on 29 August 1969 at the conclusion of the visit of the Secretary of State for the Home Department to Northern Ireland', Cmd. 4158 (London 1969).

'Text of a Communique issued on 29 August 1969 at the conclusion of the visit of the Secretary of State for the Home Department and the Northern Ireland Government in Belfast on 9th and 10th October 1969', Cmd. 4178 (London 1969).

'The Belfast Agreement: agreement reached in multi-party negotiations', Cmnd. 3883 (London 1998).
'The Government of Northern Ireland – A Working Paper for a Conference', Cmnd. 7763 (London 1979).
'The Government of Northern Ireland – Proposals for Further Discussion', Cmnd. 7950 (London 1980).
'The Northern Ireland Constitution', Cmnd. 5675 (London 1974).
'The Northern Ireland Constitutional Convention: Text of a letter from the Secretary of State for Northern Ireland to the Chairman of the Convention', Cmnd. 6387 (London 1976).
'Violence and Civil Disturbances in Northern Ireland in 1969' (Scarman Report), Cmnd. 566 (Belfast 1972).

Newspapers and magazines

The Belfast Telegraph (various)
The Daily Telegraph
The Economist
The Guardian
The Independent
The Irish News (various)
The Irish Times (various)
The Listener
New Statesman
The Observer (various)
The Spectator
The Times

Diaries, memoirs and collections of speeches

T. Benn, *Against the Tide: Diaries* 1973–76 (London 1989)
T. Benn, *Conflicts of Interest. Diaries,* 1977–80 (London 1990)
T. Benn, *Office Without Power: Diaries* 1968–72 (London 1988)
K. Bloomfield, *Stormont in Crisis* (Belfast 1994)
R. Boyson, *Speaking My Mind* (London 1995)
J. Callaghan, *A House Divided* (London 1973)
J. Callaghan, *Time and Chance* (London 1987)
P.A.R. Carrington, *Reflect on Things Past* (London 1988)
B. Castle, *The Castle Diaries,* 1974–76 (London 1980)
B. Devlin, *The Price of My Soul* (London 1969)
W.S. Churchill, *The World Crisis. The Aftermath* (London, 1929)
E. Collins (with M. McGovern), *Killing Rage* (London 1997)
R. Crossmann, *Diaries of a Cabinet Minister, Volume Three* (London 1977)
E. Delaney, *An Accidental Diploma: My years in the Irish Foreign Service,* 1987–1995 (Dublin 2001)
P. Devlin, *Straight Left. An Autobiography* (Belfast 1993)
B. Donoghue, *The Conduct of Policy under Harold Wilson and James Callaghan* (London 1987)
S. Duignan, *One Spin on the Merry-Go-Round* (Dublin 1995)

B. Faulkner, *Memoirs of a Statesman* (London 1978)

G. FitzGerald, *All in a Life. An Autobiography* (London 1991)

R. Harris, *The Collected Speeches of Margaret Thatcher* (London 1997)

M. Hayes, *Minority Verdict. Experiences of a Catholic Public Servant* (Belfast 1995)

E. Heath, *The Course of My Life* (London 1998)

G. Howe, *Conflict of Loyalty* (London 1994)

J. Hume, *Personal Views. Politics, Peace and Reconciliation in Ireland* (Dublin 1996)

M. McGuire, *To Take Arms: A Year in the Provisional IRA* (London 1973)

G. McMichael, *An Ulster Voice: In Search of Common Ground in Northern Ireland* (Boulder 1999)

S. MacStiofain, *Memoirs of a Revolutionary* (Edinburgh 1975)

J. Major, *John Major: The Autobiography* (London 1999)

R. Mason, *Paying the Price* (London 1999)

R. Maudling, *Memoirs* (London 1978)

B. Mawhinney, *In the Firing Line: Politics, Faith, Power and Forgiveness* (London 1999)

G. Mitchell, *Making Peace* (London 1999)

M. Mowlam, *Momentum* (London 2002)

R. Needham, *Battling for Peace* (Belfast 1998)

C.C. O'Brien, *States of Ireland* (London 1972)

J.A. Oliver, *Working at Stormont* (London 1978)

J. Peck, *Dublin from Downing Street* (London 1978)

J. Prior, *A Balance of Power* (London 1986)

M. Rees, *Northern Ireland: A Personal Perspective* (London 1985)

R. Seitz, *Over Here* (London 1998)

M. Stuart, *Douglas Hurd: The Public Servant* (London 1998) (contains excerpts from Hurd's diaries)

M. Thatcher, *The Downing Street Years* (London 1993)

W. Whitelaw, *The Whitelaw Memoirs* (London 1989)

H. Wilson, *Final Term. The Labour Government, 1974–76* (London 1979)

H. Wilson, *The Labour Government, 1964–70* (London 1971)

Select reading list

P. Arthur, *Special Relationships: Britain, Ireland and the Northern Ireland Problem* (Belfast 2000)

A. Aughey, *Under Siege: Ulster Unionism and the Anglo-Irish Agreement* (Belfast 1989)

D. Barzilay, *The British Army in Ulster, Vols. 1, 2, 3, and 4* (Belfast 1973–81)

J. Baylis, K. Booth, J. Garnett, P. Williams (eds), *Contemporary Strategy: Theories and Concepts* (London 1987)

P. Bew, P. Gibbon, H. Patterson, *Northern Ireland, 1921–2001: Political Forces and Social Classes* (London 2002)

P. Bew and H. Patterson, *The British State and the Ulster Crisis* (London 1985)

W.D. Birrell, 'The Stormont–Westminster Relationship', *Parliamentary Affairs*, 26:4 (1973), pp. 471–91

D. Bloomfield, *Developing Dialogue in Northern Ireland: The Mayhew Talks 1992* (Basingstoke 2001)

D. Bloomfield, *Political Dialogue in Northern Ireland: The Brooke Initiative, 1989–92* (London 1989)

D.G. Boyce and A. O'Day (eds), *The Making of Modern Irish History: Revisionism and the Revisionist Controversy* (London 1996)

D.G. Boyce, *The Irish Question and British Politics, 1868–1996*, 2nd edition (London 1996)

P. Catterall and S. McDougall (eds), *The Northern Ireland Question in British Politics* (London 1996)

C. von Clausewitz, *On War*, translated by Michael Howard and Peter Paret (Princeton 1984)

M. Cox, A. Guelke, F. Stephen (eds), *A Farewell to Arms? From 'Long War' to Long Peace in Northern Ireland* (Manchester 2000)

M. Cunningham, *British Government Policy in Northern Ireland, 1969–89* (Manchester 1991)

M. Cunningham, *British Government Policy in Northern Ireland, 1969–2000* (Manchester 2001)

M. Dewar, *The British Army in Northern Ireland* (London 1996)

P. Dixon, *Northern Ireland: The Politics of War and Peace* (Basingstoke 2001)

P. Dixon, ' "The Usual English Doubletalk": the British Political Parties and the Ulster Unionists, 1974–94', *Irish Political Studies*, 9:1 (1995), pp. 25–40

L.K. Donohue, *Counter-terrorist Law and Emergency Powers in the United Kingdom, 1922–2000* (London 2000)

M. Elliott, *The Long Road to Peace in Northern Ireland* (Liverpool 2002)

R. Evelegh, *Peace Keeping in a Democratic Society: The Lessons of Northern Ireland* (London 1978)

R. Faligot, *Britain's Military Strategy in Ireland: The Kitson Experiment* (London 1983)

M. Farrell, *Northern Ireland: The Orange State* (London 1980)

W.D. Flackes and S. Elliott, *Northern Ireland – A Political Directory* (Belfast 2000)

F. Gaffikin and M. Morrissey, *Northern Ireland: The Thatcher Years* (London 1990)

T. Geraghty, *The Irish War: The Military History of a Domestic Conflict* (London 1998)

M. Gove, *The Price of Peace: An Analysis of British Policy in Northern Ireland* (London 2000)

A. Guelke, *Northern Ireland: The International Perspective* (Dublin 1988)

T. Hadden and K. Boyle, *The Anglo-Irish Agreement: Commentary, Text and Official Review* (London 1989), pp. 59–64

D. Hamill, *Pig in the Middle: The Army in Northern Ireland, 1969–84* (London 1985)

T. Hennessey, *The Northern Ireland Peace Process: Ending the Troubles?* (London 2000)

V. McCormack, *Enduring Inequality: Religious Discrimination in Employment in Northern Ireland* (London 1990)

R. MacGinty and J. Darby, *Guns and Government: The Management of the Northern Ireland Peace Process* (Basingstoke 2002)

A. McIntyre, 'Modern Irish Republicanism: The Product of British State Strategies', *Irish Political Studies*, 10:1 (1995), pp. 94–118

E. Mallie and D. McKittrick, *The Fight for Peace: The Inside Story of the Irish Peace Process* (London 1997)

T.R. Mockaitis, *British Counterinsurgency, 1919–60* (London 1990)

P.R. Neumann, 'The Myth of Ulsterisation in British Security Policy in Northern Ireland', *Studies in Conflict & Terrorism*, 26:5 (2003), pp. 365–74

M. O'Doherty, *The Trouble with Guns: Republican Strategy and the Provisional IRA* (Belfast 1998)

B. O'Leary and J. McGarry, *The Politics of Antagonism: Understanding Northern Ireland* (London 1996)

B. O'Leary, 'The Belfast Agreement and the Labour Government' in A. Seldon (ed.), *The Blair Effect: The Blair Government, 1997–2001* (London 2001), pp. 449–88

L. O'Dowd, B. Rolston, M. Tomlinson (eds), *Northern Ireland Between Civil Rights and Civil War* (London 1980)

P. O'Malley, *The Uncivil Wars* (Belfast 1983)

H. Patterson, 'From Insulation to Appeasement: the Major and Blair Governments Reconsidered' in R. Wilford (ed.), *Aspects of the Belfast Agreement* (Oxford 2001), pp. 166–83

D. Reed, *Ireland: The Key to the British Revolution* (London 1984)

P. Rose, *How the Troubles Came to Northern Ireland* (London 2000)

T.C. Schelling, *Arms and Influence* (London 1967)

T.C. Schelling, *Choice and Consequence* (Cambridge 1984)

T.C. Schelling, *The Strategy of Conflict*, 2nd edition (Cambridge 1980)

M.L.R. Smith, *Fighting for Ireland? The Military Strategy of the Irish Republican Movement* (London 1995)

M. von Tangen Page, *Peace, Prisoners and Terrorism* (London 1998)

P. Taylor, *Brits: The War Against the IRA* (London 2001)

M. Tomlinson, 'Walking Backwards into the Sunset: British Policy and the Insecurity of Northern Ireland' in D. Miller (ed.), *Rethinking Northern Ireland* (London 1998), pp. 96–124

C. Townshend, *Britain's Civil Wars: Counterinsurgency in the Twentieth Century* (London 1986)

T.E. Utley, *Lessons of Ulster* (London 1975)

M. Wallace, *British Government in Northern Ireland* (London 1982)

Index